Storymaking and Drama

Storymaking and Drama

An Approach to Teaching Language and Literature
At the Secondary and Postsecondary Levels

Nancy King

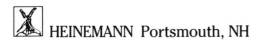 HEINEMANN Portsmouth, NH

HEINEMANN
A division of Reed Publishing (USA) Inc.
361 Hanover Street
Portsmouth, NH 03801-3912
Offices and agents throughout the world

The author and the publisher would like to thank the following for permission to reprint material from copyrighted works:

Pages 104, 108, 112, 115: "Human Boy Found in Indian Jungle Among Wolf Pack," "Woman Picked Up by UFO, Flown into Black Hole," "Meteoroid Falls in Farmer's Back Yard," "Beauty Queen Has Monster Child" by Jeanne Murray Walker. From *Coming Into History,* Cleveland State University Poetry Center, Cleveland, Ohio. Reprinted by permission of the author and the publisher.
Page 128: Katharina M. and Christopher C. Wilson: "Homecoming," by Árpád Göncz, in *Árpád Göncz: Plays and Other Writings.* Garland Publishing, Inc., 1990.
Pages 131–34: "The Woman from America" by Bessie Head. Copyright © The Bessie Head Estate 1989. From *Tales of Tenderness and Power* first published by Heinemann International in the African Writers Series in 1990. Reprinted by permission.
Pages 164–172: Excerpts reprinted by permission of the Putnam Publishing Group from *The Joy Luck Club* by Amy Tan. Copyright © 1989 by Amy Tan.
Pages 176–77: From *When the Legends Die* by Hal Borland. Reprinted by permission of HarperCollins Publishers.

Every effort has been made to contact the copyright holders for permission to reprint borrowed material. We regret any oversights that may have occurred and would be happy to rectify them in future printings of this work.

Library of Congress Cataloging-in-Publication Data
King, Nancy, 1936–
    Storymaking and drama : an approach to language and literature at the secondary and postsecondary levels / by Nancy King.
        p.   cm.
    Includes bibliographical references and index.
    ISBN 0-435-08625-1
    1. Storytelling.   2. Drama in education.   3. Language arts (Secondary)   4. Literature—Study and teaching (Secondary)
    I. Title.
LB1042.K52   1993
808.543—dc20   93-29079
                                                                          CIP

Front cover art by Kyra Teis.
Cover design by Catherine Hawkes.
Text design by Jenny Jensen Greenleaf.
Printed on acid-free paper in the United States of America.
97 96 95 94 93   1 2 3 4 5 6

This book is dedicated to

Stig Starrsjö

A man of imagination and possibility

Contents

Acknowledgments

I wish to thank Joan Bennett, Robert Brown, Judy Greene, Sara Horowitz, Glover Jones, Barbara Lou Morrison, David Pody, and Jeanne Walker for their advice, support, and encouragement. I am lucky to have them as colleagues and friends.

I also wish to thank Anita Grünbaum, Karin Gustafsson, Fiddeli Persson, and Stig Starrsjö of Sweden; Grethe Eller of Denmark; and Marianne Nikolov of Hungary for making it possible for me to work with them in their countries. I value highly their contribution to this book and to my life.

I appreciate the support, advice, and knowledge of Lisa A. Barnett, my editor at Heinemann. Working with her has been pure pleasure.

....

Introduction

To tell a story is to create community. Whether the story is told by moving, acting, painting, or telling, essentially, the teller requires consent of the told. Storymaking, storytelling, and the making of drama are integrative activities requiring the storymaker/teller/dramatist to unite disparate bits of information into a whole (story) that sustains the viewer's/listener's interest. Yet uncovering our stories is not a simple process. We forget, repress, block, or don't know the stories we might otherwise wish to know or share. Part of our creative research is to discover our inner knowing, the stories of our lives that help to make us who we are and who we may wish to become. In this book, we will discover ways to reconnect inner knowing with outer expression through a variety of experiences, many based on imagemaking processes such as finger painting, sculpting, word collages, and word play. When we make an image using paint or clay or by doodling, we express a whole concept that can then be explored through oral and written activity. Einstein wrote of the process he used:

> The words or the language, as they are written or spoken, do not seem to play any role in my mechanism of thought. The psychical entities which seem to serve as elements in thought are certain signs and more or less clear images which can be "voluntarily" reproduced and combined.
> There is, of course, a certain connection between those elements and relevant logical concepts. It is also clear that the desire to arrive finally at logically connected concepts is the emotional basis of this rather vague play with the above mentioned elements. . . . This combinatory play seems to be an essential feature in productive thought—before there is any connection with logical construction in words or other kinds of signs which can be communicated to others. (Ghiselin, p. 43)

Stories, evoked through the use of such imagemaking processes, help students to overcome writer's block and improve their ability to organize thoughts and approaches to writing papers. Through storymaking and drama, those who make, tell, and perform stories—whether the storymaker is a member of a tribe who has no written language or a student struggling to read—learn something about who they are, develop a sense of their own authentic voice, and begin to appreciate, in a new way, their value as human beings. Stories and drama cannot be made in isolation; each teller/maker of drama conceives her or his story in the context of a complex of others' stories, some very like one's own stories and some differing. We do not have to work with our own stories exclusively; we can also use tales told from around the world that broaden our horizons, cultivate empathy for those thought to be different from ourselves, and provide the possibility for connections across time, culture, and experience. Sharing world stories enriches our capacity to integrate disparate inner and outer fragments, clarifying and enlarging our sense of identity and our place in our community and the world.

Many old stories (myths, legends, fairy tales, and folk tales) are short and are useful in the classroom in that they can be quickly told to a class to provide a communal experience through which students respond uniquely to shared tasks. Teachers might use stories in their classes in several ways. For example, a story can serve as the basis for dramatic dialogue as part of the process for studying a piece of literature. It can provide the context for a writing exercise—a short story about one of the characters. A story from a developing country can be used to create a setting for exploring issues facing a particular culture in the midst of monumental change. Other instructional uses of stories can be devised if we give our imagination free rein to discover them. My own teaching experience has shown that sharing stories and making drama help to make the abstract more concrete, diverse facts more understandable, and arouse interest in learning as students become engrossed, not only in the story itself, but in the cultural or social context in which it is told. For example, many students in the United States know virtually nothing about Native American peoples beyond the stereotypes portrayed in film, literature, and on television. After working with a Cherokee creation myth, "How the Sun Came," one student shook his head and smiled, "The Indians didn't really write that story."

Shocked, I tried to hide my concern by saying, "No, not in the beginning when stories were told, not written."

"That's not what I meant," he insisted. "I just can't believe they could make up such a good story."

"Why not?"

"Well . . . they were savages. We all know that savages don't tell stories." Subsequent class experience and discussion pushed him to admit that his view of Native Americans came from television and film, not necessarily reliable sources for discovering the truth about people whose history has been told by the "winning" side. The work with stories helped all of the students to gain a deeper appreciation for the power and beauty of civilizations that many early settlers chose to destroy in order to build their own settlements and society.

Myths, tales, and legends from around the world, old stories, those retold rather than authored, can be found in libraries and in children's book collections. Students can use these old stories to develop resources that are tapped when they share books from their childhoods and tell stories told to them by grandparents, relatives, and old family friends, thereby providing themselves and classmates with the opportunity to reconnect to their own heritage.

For many years, I have been sharing old and new stories, novels, films, and autobiographies with my students and with the students of colleagues to stimulate discussion, cultivate deeper multicultural awareness, promote access to personal imagination and creativity, and foster critical thinking and writing in a collaborative learning environment. Some of the courses I have taught in which I have used storymaking and drama are: "Imagination, Creativity, and Expression"; "Giving Form to Expression"; "Interiors and Edges: The Text, The Self, The World"; "Myth and Expression"; "Playing with Stories"; "Creating Theatre from Myth"; "Theatre Process and Performance"; "Film and Fantasy"; and "To Walk in Someone's Shoes: Stories of the Self." I never cease to be astonished at the power literature has to stimulate students to think deeply about issues in their lives as they create drama, make new stories, and develop questions that have been evoked by their experiences with storymaking and drama. Given the rapid rate of change in cultures throughout the world, storymaking and drama contribute to the development of new attitudes, ideas, and resources.

There is much talk in the United States today about how our present educational systems fail to stimulate and encourage students to read, write, think, and solve problems. Recent studies report findings that suggest that throughout students' education, from elementary school through the college lecture hall, teachers are seldom given the necessary time to allow students to develop the skill of thinking for themselves, to pose personally meaningful questions, or to draw on their own unique perspectives. For example:

> A recent report from the National Assessment of Educational Progress found that, among other things, American school-children possess the capacity to absorb information but falter when it comes to using that information to reason effectively. (Stone, p. 48)

Based on my experience in the classroom, I believe that the creative use of stories and the making of drama can help teachers at all levels to overcome this deficiency.

U.S. educator Neil Postman concurs that students need stories to provide both moral and intellectual frameworks. Because stories and drama help us to understand what things mean, they assist us to make selections and understand more about what we need to know and encourage us to ask ourselves, "How do I know what I know? How do I know that I know it? In what context did I learn it? Is this learning still important? If so, why?" Stories provide necessary structures for our perceptions; only through stories do facts assume appropriate meaning for our lives.

> Children everywhere ask, as soon as they have the command of language to do so, "Where did I come from?" and, shortly after, "What will happen when I die?" They require a story to give meaning to their existence. Without air, our cells die. Without a story, our selves die. . . . A story gives us direction by providing a kind of theory about how the world works—and how it needs to work if we are to survive. Without such a theory, such a tale, people have no idea what to do with information. They cannot even tell what is information and what is not. (Postman, pp. 119–124)

To this I would add that without telling and sharing stories through storymaking and drama, our communities die. Many of us already feel a sense of isolation, a lack of real community. We live very separate lives, often at great distance from family and childhood homes. We learn to keep our thoughts and feelings to ourselves. Many teachers have told me that they wish their students would be more forthcoming in class discussion. Sharing stories and making drama are excellent ways to build community within the classroom, to create a communal space where students feel safe to express opinions not yet fully formed or clearly understood and to discover the stories of their lives and of their society. People around the world know the importance of storymaking and drama. The San people of South Africa say, "Without a story of your own to live, you haven't got a life of your own" (Van der Post). We, as teachers, must help students to understand that they have much more at stake in their learning than merely a grade on an exam or at the end of a course.

I realize there are many problems to be faced: large classes; short teaching/learning periods; insufficient planning time; unsympathetic administrations; students who are unable to read, focus, or concentrate; unyielding required curricula; and lack of creative expertise. And yet, there is the human spirit, which thrives on imagery and expression. In this book I share ideas with teachers to establish a network of educators who create classrooms where real learning can take place.

Imagemaking, Storymaking, and Making Drama in the Classroom

Creating stories and making drama may appear to be unusual activity for many students, particularly in classrooms where there are time constraints and academic standards to be met. However, imagemaking is a productive means of evoking stories and drama, all of which improve student understanding of a text. To encourage teachers to consider this way of working with language and literature, particularly when students are experiencing difficulties with a text, I include three examples to illustrate how working with storymaking and drama benefits students.

Example 1: Discovering connections: Bringing out there in here

Students in a course "Philosophical and Religious Themes in Modern Literature" found *The Plague* by Camus a rather difficult novel in which to involve themselves. Although they were aware of parallels between the plague in the novel and AIDS, the story itself left most of them cold. To help them make connections between themselves and characters in the novel, we asked the students to select some passages that seemed important, powerful, disturbing, or otherwise memorable. They were then asked to select one passage and to finger paint an image that came to mind when they read their chosen passage. After painting, they briefly wrote about why the passage mattered to them. The images, passages, and writings were shared.

Students reflected on the issues raised and on questions evoked by the commentary.

Following this discussion, students were asked to pick one character in the novel and to answer the following questions:

- Why am I choosing this character?
- What information do I want to obtain?
- Why do I want to know this? Why does this matter to me?
- What questions will I ask my selected character?
- If I were working as a writer, where would my material be published? (Describe nature and purpose of newspaper, journal, book.)
- If I were creating a drama, where would I choose to have it be seen? As a play in a theatre? On television? As a full-length feature film? What affects my choice?

To facilitate the questioning, students were asked to paint an image of themselves and their character in relationship, describing the meeting with words or phrases that came spontaneously to mind. Although we did not have time to hear everyone's questions and answers, there was such great interest in the process that students chose to discuss their work with each other after class and to continue sharing during the next class.

We ended the session with a bit of role playing. Each student selected a character and agreed to answer all questions as this character. One student who chose to interview the narrator of the novel asked, "How do you keep going?" All of the students who picked this character answered the question, giving different perspectives and answers, yet all responses were plausible and within the context of the novel. By the time the class ended, discussion about issues raised by the novel was heated and intense. *The Plague* was no longer "out there," it was "in here."

Example 2: From Despair to Empowerment

Students studying Milton's *Samson Agonistes* were polite but not involved with the text. I asked them to consider the question, "How did Samson get from impotent despair to his courage to act?" Because Milton doesn't tell us, the students were asked to think about this untold story and to consider what might have helped Samson move from despair to empowerment. The first activity involved students finger painting an image of Samson as they imagined him, at the height of his power and glory. They wrote down phrases or a passage from the text to describe him as they thought he was before the beginning of the text. The second image they painted portrayed Samson at the beginning of the text at any point up to the entrance of Dalila. Students selected a passage or phrases from the text to describe how Samson thinks and feels about himself in his present circumstances. The third image they painted focused on Samson as revealed by the passage that begins:

> Be of good courage; I begin to feel
> Some rousing motions in me, which dispose
> To something extraordinary my thoughts.

The students then wrote the story between the stories, what they thought happened to Samson between his hopelessness at the time of the second image and his energy to act by the third image. As part of their writing they were asked to use a passage or phrases from Milton's text to shape their language and enhance their sense of Milton's style. Before writing their story, students were asked to decide who they were (Samson, Manoa, Chorus, Chronicler, Dalila) and why they were writing this narrative. Before sharing their work, students were asked to create an epitaph for Samson and to design his tombstone or memorial. Two samples illustrate the range and power of the student responses. Milton's words are in quotes.

1. "My trust is in the living God who gave me at my Nativity this strength." It is not possible to think that One so powerful will abandon me. I understand and accept all that I have incurred upon myself, but I am beginning to see more of the true nature of God, to see that God makes each person with more than one gift, and I will be valued at the time of judgement with respect to the insight and understanding I have gained. I feel no fear or anxiety at this time of change, because all I can do is trust.

2. O, I will tell thee how I rose from
   My dark, undefined and entrapped chamber
   Which disclosed to all how bound
   Were my truths and passions.
   But, I have, in that time
   Discovered the great blackness
   And devised through light of my mind's third eye
   All the colors of my once confused passions.
   Yea! And I will tell you how
   So further suffering in human kind

May be appreciated in its experienced form
For I have learned.
True God may be perceived from the eye
But only understood, experienced, achieved
And lived in the soul.
Now I will rise to save my people
And I tell you this so all of mankind
Might save themselves individually
Through study of inward courage
Not of outward sight.
A simple lesson my brother,
"Not so much to see Truth
But to feel truth and hold Truth."

After each text was read, students showed their epitaph and memo-rial. As we reflected on the writings, epitaphs, and symbolic designs, students said that having to make images based on the text forced them to consider how they personally thought and felt about the text. Writing the story enabled them to consider what the meaning of the piece was for them and how they derived this insight. The ensuing exchange was lively and provocative with students asking questions of each other rather than waiting for the instructor to initiate the dis-cussion. As I was leaving class, I overheard some students arguing about how Samson reconnected with his inner resources. I stopped and asked them if they were willing to act as if they were their version of Samson and to tell what he wanted the others to know. We went back into the classroom. The ensuing monologues were amazingly powerful and various. One student reflected, after hearing all the versions, "I didn't know we knew so much about Samson." Another volunteered, "I didn't know I cared what happened to him." A third admitted, "I didn't know his life could matter to me." Although this text may be too difficult for many high school students, I include this response to *Samson Agonistes* because my experiences suggest that storymaking and drama help to make texts that may initially appear to be too complex, more accessible to many students.

Third Example: What's in a Story?

A student in the course "Giving Form to Expression" was asked to explore a myth and to uncover the meaning the myth had for her. She chose an Eastern European tale, "The Fern Girl," about an old woman who plants a fern that transforms into a beautiful girl. The old woman rescues the girl and assists the young woman to marry the man of her choice. The student wrote at great length about the loneliness of the old woman, the misery of the girl forced to marry a man she cannot trust, and the man who chose to hunt rather than accompany his bride to their new home. While discussing the paper with the student, I asked her how she knew the old woman was lonely, the girl miserable, the man uncaring. She said, "It's in the story." I returned the story to her and asked her to find passages to support her conclusions. After several minutes she looked up and said, astonished, "I can't find them. But I'm sure I saw them when I read the story. How is this possible?"

We talked about how the story resonated within her, the images evoked by the story, the issues uncovered by the narrative. She admitted she was very lonely, that her first year of college had been very difficult, and that she was unable to meet all of her academic responsibilities. We looked at the information provided by the story and the material she imposed on it as a way of understanding what her issues were and how her life experiences colored her reading of the text. Not only was she able to write a new paper that differentiated her experience from the characters in the story, she also understood why she was receiving poor grades in the literature class she was taking. She learned strategies to improve her critical analysis without losing sight of what the text meant to her.

When teachers use storymaking and drama in their classrooms, some students view the experience as childish, others refuse to accept that they can learn anything from making images, playing with stories, or creating drama. At the same time, many are faced with powerful issues of identity and meaning and often feel discouraged and uncertain about making their way in the world. Yet in every course in which I use imagemaking, storymaking, and drama as part of normal classroom activity, I learn that students who previously could find no connection to the literary works they were forced to read now feel as if working with stories and drama has virtually saved their lives, although they are not always able to articulate why this is so. Their enthusiastic, thoughtful responses encourage me to accept any initially discouraging student reactions because when students derive insight from an experience, they are newly empowered to direct further self exploration. Sharing stories and creating drama with my students also comforts me as I remember that many of my favorite stories are thousands of years old. I am merely doing my part to keep our human heritage vital.

This book is composed of four sections designed to help teachers to use storymaking and drama in their classrooms. In "Groundwork" teachers will find background information that supports and frames the ideas in the section dealing with activities. "Sourcework" provides readers with poems, stories (myths, legends, folk tales, and modern short stories), novels, and autobiographies and discusses ways to prepare and focus ideas from a text, create imagery as a way of knowing, develop oral and written expression, evolve ideas for the exploration of language and literature, and use reflection as part of each lesson. "Evaluation" examines the relationship of criticism, evaluation, and reflection to learning, processes that can deepen, extend, enlarge, and enhance student work. "Storymaking and Drama in the Teaching of English as a Second Language" contains techniques to stimulate oral and written language designed to effect and improve language development when teaching English as a foreign or second language. "Drama in Performance" includes suggestions and ideas for extending work beyond the classroom. The Bibliography lists books of interest to teachers working with storymaking and drama.

I hope the material described in this book will enable teachers who think they do not have enough expertise in storymaking and creating drama to begin, to feel the power that comes from sharing, "Once upon a time . . ."

1

The Importance of "Making"

All of the methodology in this book is predicated on the premise that active participation in our educational process facilitates and stimulates our capacity to learn meaningfully. I believe this is particularly important in a culture that encourages passivity—watching rather than doing, being a spectator rather than a participant. This is because part of how we know who we are is knowing what we are able to do. This knowledge affects our self-confidence and, ultimately, our ability to learn. When planning lessons and projects for their students, good teachers take into account the differences in their students, those who motivate themselves, those who follow the lead of others, and those whose self-esteem is so low that just thinking about trying something new becomes traumatic. Our inability or ability to learn affects our entire being—in and out of the classroom. Any experience that enhances our self-esteem, confidence, ability, and courage is worth noticing and promoting. What I have discovered in all my years of teaching is that the more we invest in learning, the more profoundly we learn. This is why the process of "making" is so important in the classroom.

Making—whether we write a poem or a story, paint an image, create a drama, or compose music—is the process whereby we take experience from our inner world, give it form, and make it accessible to those in our outer world. Developing our authentic voice enables us to make a unique statement about who we are and what and how we think and feel. We establish our place in our world. This active engagement enhances our ability to question, reflect, explore alternatives, and make new choices based on our own experience.

Nowhere is this more true than in the classroom where students have learned to be passive and teachers have learned to be the sole source of wisdom. Based on my classroom experience in high schools, colleges, elementary schools, preschools, prisons, and mental hospitals, when students engage in the process of making, everything changes. I had to learn how to deal with the noise, chaos, and excitement of student exploration: sharing, arguing, discussing, designing, trying out, acting out. Creation is usually untidy, unpredictable, frustrating, exhausting, and exhilarating. Yet the ends justify the means when students transform from bored, unhappy, discouraged class members into active participants willing to enter into meaningful dialogue. Helping students to become empowered, to come into their own, is what makes teaching worth doing.

In my own life, the process of making is what enables me to deal with my anger, joy, fury, curiosity, rage, frustration—all of the feelings and issues that are part of what it means to be human. After reading an article about why students don't learn I wrote a small poem that captured my rage.

The Cant of Can't

You there, the one who's just been told you
Can't dance.
Can't write.
Can't think.
Can't talk.
Can't draw.
Can't do.
You there, the one who thinks and feels, "I can't."
You come to me.
I'll show you that you can.
Always.

Teachers who do not think of themselves as creative or talented, or those with little experience as makers, are often afraid to risk exploring the connection between making and learning. And although there are very understandable reasons for these fears, the rewards greatly outweigh the difficulties. The Cherokee story about how Grandmother Spider brings light to the world gives courage to those of us who feel too small, too weak, too old, or too unimportant to even try to make a difference.

How Light Came to the Dark World

The people were stumbling about in the cold and the dark as they gathered together to hold a meeting. Someone said, "I heard there are people on the other side who have light. Maybe they will give us some."

"No, they want to keep it to themselves."

"Well then, if they will not give it to us, we will take it."

There was a lot of talk about who would go, but, in the end, the biggest and strongest bird flew off to the other side. The people of the light were watching, and when the biggest and the strongest bird came, they were prepared. They forced the intruder to return home empty-handed.

The next bird, almost as big and strong as the first bird, flew off determined to succeed, but he too came home without any light. A third bird, equally resolute though not quite as big and strong as the first two, flew to the people with the light. He also failed.

Disheartened, the people held another meeting. No one knew what to do. They sat in discouraged silence.

Then someone with a tiny, fragile voice spoke, "The biggest and the strongest of our warriors have tried and failed. Perhaps it is time for someone like myself who is old and weak to try." People laughed.

"Who is making such a joke?" asked someone.

"I am not joking," retorted Grandmother Spider.

"How can you hope to succeed? You have no strength to fly such a distance. You have no feathers to hide the light you steal. Why do you waste our time?"

"Let me try. If I do not return you will have only lost an unimportant old woman." In the end, reluctantly, they agreed.

Very early the next morning Grandmother Spider fashioned a tiny clay bowl that she secured around her body as she spun a long, delicate strand. The people of the light were alert, looking for a big, strong bird, so they never noticed the fragile thread on which Grandmother Spider made her way. They did not see Grandmother Spider put a tiny piece of light into her little clay bowl. By the time they discovered a tiny bit of light was missing, Grandmother Spider was already home, sharing the light with her people. Grateful, the people honored Grandmother Spider for her daring, her courage, and her skill.

SUGGESTIONS FOR EXPLORATION

Think about a piece of clothing you would like to own. Consider its style, color, flow, use, fabric, and weight. Use crayons, paints, colored pencil, or pastels to design the garment of your dreams. Give yourself no more than five minutes to complete your design. Observe your own process. What, if anything, keeps you from beginning?   **1**

What "voices" speak to you as you explore? Are these voices helpful? Unhelpful? Whose voices are they? What, if anything, hinders your capacity to have fun while playing with ideas? What would it take for you to share your ideas with someone? What is at stake?

2 Think of a book you have read that has left a strong impression on you. Pick one moment in the book that seems important to you. Using paint, clay, crayon, or any material of your choice, fashion an image of this telling moment. Give yourself no more than two minutes to complete the image. Now think about this image in relationship to the whole book. Take one moment to write down any and all ideas that come to mind without censoring or judging. When you look at your work what is your first impulse? To judge? To enjoy? To reflect? To compare? What would it take for you to make an image without censoring or judging? What role does enjoyment have in your ability to consider alternatives and play with ideas?

3 Think of a newspaper story, television program, film, or book you have read or seen. Select one person or character who intrigues you. Create a one-minute monologue to tell this character what you think and how you feel about an issue he or she raises. How do you choose your words? How do you connect your feelings and thoughts in your presentation? Create a one-minute monologue for the person or character you have chosen to talk back to you. What helps or hinders you from saying what you genuinely think and feel? What helps or hinders you to think and feel from the viewpoint of the other person or character? What would it take to share this material with someone else who has read or seen the same material? How does the process of creating drama capture the essence of an experience? Would this process be different if you wrote a poem? A short story? If so, how?

Suggestions for Making

- Begin slowly. Establish clear parameters regarding time available and scope of activity. Don't ask yourself to write a play or even a scene. Instead, focus on one page or one minute of dialogue.
- Be very kind to yourself. Empowering yourself to make takes energy and courage. Don't underestimate the difficulty of beginning.
- Be very careful when you decide to share your work. Choose someone who understands and/or is interested in what you are trying to do and why you are exploring new ways. Avoid anyone who has a tendency to put you down, judge, or censor. Instead, look for people who ask you helpful questions, who help you find a way to accomplish your goals, and those who have no agenda other than sharing ideas and feelings.
- Value your own struggles. Creating and discovering is hard work.
- Take care of your process. No one creates without becoming vulnerable and open to one's ideas. Respect your feelings and honor your attempts.
- If you become grumpy when you can't find the word you want or the idea that eludes you, this will pass. No feeling lasts forever.

Groundwork

The Gift of Imagination

All discovery, in science as well as art, requires the ability to be imaginative, to see what could be as well as what is. The capacity to imagine is part of our genetic makeup, our natural heritage. Yet we often make judgments, about our students and ourselves, that we have little or no imagination so there is no use asking us to be imaginative. But imagination is affected by use. Too much television, which requires passive viewing and no imaginative effort or image-making, atrophies our imaginative capability, also depleting our ingenuity and resourcefulness. However, this loss can be remedied by turning off the television set and turning on the radio, reading a book, or using our imagination through activity such as painting, sculpting, making drama or dance, and so on. Creating something from nothing develops our imagination muscles. Continued imaginative activity ensures their strength and vitality.

My students notice that painting, sculpting, making drama, or the like requires them to play with ideas, to explore possibilities, and finally, to make choices. They also notice they have more energy afterward than they had before. Not only does this process allow them to tap into their unknown sources of energy, it also nourishes their capacity to solve problems. As one student said, "All this messing about clears my mind."

To exemplify how imagination can be nourished, I will share one of my favorite stories from Thailand and then suggest techniques to enhance imaginative response. Old stories from around the world can broaden student perspectives and provide short powerful pieces of literature with which to begin the process of connecting inner life and outer experience.

The Voice of Wisdom

Long ago, people discovered an intelligent bird who could speak with little teaching. Not only was Lorikeet able to repeat what it heard, it could also give voice to its own thoughts.

One day, a farmer working in his rice fields saw his neighbor's buffalo. He killed the buffalo, cut it up, made a fine meal for himself, then hid what he could not eat.

His neighbor came by to ask if the farmer had seen his buffalo. The farmer denied knowing anything about the missing animal.

Lorikeet flew to the neighbor and told him that the farmer had killed and eaten part of his buffalo and had hidden the remains in his fields and rice house. The neighbor looked in those places and saw the meat, just as the bird foretold. But the farmer insisted it was his own buffalo meat and that the neighbor had no proof that it was his.

Lorikeet repeated his story until the neighbor was thoroughly confused. The puzzled neighbor wondered who was speaking the truth, so he asked the magistrate to hear the case the following day.

The clever farmer covered Lorikeet's cage with a huge pot. All night he beat on the pot to make the sounds of thunder, poured water over the pot to create rain, and shook the pot to make wind.

In the morning, the farmer appeared in court with Lorikeet. The bird told its story with clarity. The judge was impressed by the bird's intelligence. But the farmer asked the judge to ask the bird to describe the weather of the night before.

The judge agreed. Lorikeet told about the ferocious storm with much thunder, heavy rains, and a strong wind. The judge dismissed the case because everyone knew there had been calm, clear weather during the night.

Lorikeet was exiled to the forest. One day it saw a new bird covered with brilliantly colored feathers and questioned its appearance. Parrot preened and told Lorikeet it had come from another country. The bird boasted how gifted it was and how well it spoke the language of men.

Lorikeet welcomed the new arrival to the forest and warned it that men were not to be trusted, that it should tell them what they wanted to hear rather than what was true. Parrot took Lorikeet's advice. Men are content.

SUGGESTIONS FOR EXPLORATION

| 1 | Select a partner: | Each person select a character. Together, script a one-page dialogue for the characters to speak to each |

Groundwork

.... 19

other. It doesn't matter if the episode occurs within the story or is totally imagined. What matters is that a one-page script for two characters emerges.

Share: Dialogues with class.

Reflect:
- What are the factors that made you choose your character?
- How did you select the part of the story to script?
- From whose point of view did you script your dialogue?
- What assumptions did you make? How would your script change if you changed your assumptions?
- What is the most powerful or meaningful part of your script for you? Why?

Reconsider: The ideas and suggestions that emerge from reading your script and reflecting on your choices.

Rewrite: Your script to reflect new understanding.

Share: Reworked scripts.

Reflect: On the process. Consider:
- What is at stake for each character?
- What strategies does each character use to convince an audience each is telling the truth?
- How do we develop a particular point of view? How does this affect subsequent choices?
- What circumstances might make us change our point of view?

Choose: Two characters from the story who interest you. ⬛2

Prepare: Each of your two characters to be interviewed by the local newspaper. Each of your characters will be asked to tell her or his story and to give the reporter a brief written account of what "really" happened. You will then have one minute of radio time to tell your "correct" version.

Select partner:	To share roles of interviewing and being interviewed.
Share:	One-minute versions with the whole class.
Reflect:	How do your feelings and ideas change when you switch from being the farmer to the judge or to Lorikeet? Knowing what you now know, how might your strategies change in order to affect the final outcome?
Collect:	The written accounts, and redistribute them letting each person select two.
Read:	Out loud each of the two accounts as if you believe each story is true and that it reflects your opinion.
Reflect:	On the process. Consider: • What are the differences, if any, between writing a story, telling a story, or being interviewed? • What do you do or say to make sure people believe you? • As you keep telling your story, does it change? If so, how? • Do your feelings change as you remember more or differently?

3

Paint:	Images of Lorikeet from the point of view of the farmer, the judge, and the neighbor.
Share:	Images.
Reflect:	On various visions. What seems to be similar? Different?
Paint:	Two images of Lorikeet as it sees itself—at the beginning and at the end of the story.
Create:	The story Lorikeet tells its grandchild about how Lorikeet first came to live in the forest.

Groundwork

.... 21

Share: Stories.

Reflect: On process. Consider:
- How do we form our view of who we are?
- How might reflection from other people about who we are or who they think we are affect our vision of ourselves?
- Might there be differences in the story Lorikeet told many years after its exile from the story it might have told soon after it arrived in the forest? If so, what might some of these differences be?

Rewrite: The story adding as much dialogue as you can.   [4]

Share: Stories.

Reflect: On process. Consider:
- How do you choose who says what?
- How do you decide what words to use?
- How do you create authentic tone, voice, and point of view so that each character speaks with a distinct voice?
- How does adding dialogue affect the story?
- What are reasons for incorporating dialogue into a story?
- What are reasons for telling/writing a story without dialogue?

The above examples are meant to show how imagination always involves playing with ideas, seeing without judgment. The more we allow ourselves to consider possibilities, without comment, the more we are able to free ourselves from traditional constraints that may not be in our best interest. A favorite question of mine, for myself and for my students, when considering a piece of work is, "How else can I think (feel) about this?" Of course there comes a time when we have to make choices, exert judgment, select the best possible word or action, but this is the end of the working, not the beginning.

I always give my students a time limit—perhaps thirty to sixty seconds to make an image, two minutes to write a paragraph, or five minutes to create a monologue. Students complain I don't give them enough time. This is true. I force them to work so quickly they become desperate and scribble words or daub paint, or smush clay, all with no preplanning and very little self-consciousness. What results from this explosion of energy is the essence of their ideas and feelings, which subsequent work allows them to explore more deeply. A funny thing happens on the way; time stretches. The thirty seconds that was totally inadequate becomes quite enough or sometimes too much time. As class members become used to working spontaneously, people lose their fear of premature judgment and focus on the task at hand.

Naturally this process doesn't happen by itself. When they ask me in agonized voices, "How long does this story have to be?" I answer, "As long as you need it to be. One sentence can contain a whole story." It takes time and good experience for students to trust themselves, the process, and me, but in the end, we emerge from working together with a powerful knowing: We have imagination. We can count on it. No one can take it away from us. As we develop deeper access to our imagination, we reconnect with our most profound source of creative energy and hope.

Suggestions to Increase Use of Imagination in the Classroom

- Allow the material to work through students rather than insist they follow the words of the text exactly. This means the students are encouraged to work with themes, ideas, or feelings evoked by the story, so the story becomes a beacon and not a prison.
- Be clear about the nature of the learning experience. Do you want to improve access to imagination? Enhance language skills? Develop dialogue? Strengthen group participation? Introduce the nature of collaborative learning?
- Focus on evoking authentic response even if it conflicts with your ideas, with what you want or expect. Make room for diverse experience.
- Set clear boundaries for participation by clearly defining the task, setting firm time limits, requiring a group to find its own ending, working with a timer, practicing signals to stop work, articulating the nature of the process (we are working on developing ideas or organizing approaches, or whatever). Act on what you establish. If you give the group three

minutes, stop them after three minutes. Explore the effectiveness of giving the group a sense of how much time they have by saying, "One more minute."

- Avoid pointed questions that have one right answer. Rather than have people guess, suggest that students share possible responses.
- Encourage class members to ask each other for help rather than making the teacher the source of all knowing.
- Be honest. If their noise is more than you can manage, tell this to the class and ask for suggestions to reduce noise levels. If their language choice discomfits you, explore alternatives without condemning their choices.
- Encourage exploration and discovery. If you do not consider yourself artistic or creative, explore your strengths and use them. Perhaps you are a good listener or have a wonderful sense of humor. What matters is the recognition that we all carry pieces of the puzzle. Helping each other enhances the development of everyone.
- Have fun! If you or the class is stuck, find ways to rest or stop rather than worry about finding an end. Consider all work as work in process.

Nonverbal Communication

Nonverbal communication affects every classroom transaction. Not being aware of its implications can leave students and teachers unable to communicate meaningfully. Neither knows what the other is thinking or feeling. Perhaps even more important, neither knows how to resolve the conflict, often covert, that inevitably arises when what is said is different from what is done or meant.

The teacher smiles, "I know you didn't mean to knock over that pile of books. Finish your work." The student returns to work feeling terrible. Why? Perhaps it was the teacher's lack of eye contact, a feeling that the smile was empty, the words hollow. Yet if the student was to confront the teacher what would each person say? The teacher's words are caring. The student's feelings are "just" feelings. Still, the student's feelings are real, and the transaction is a common occurrence. The communication transmitted by nonverbal activity must be congruent with the verbal communication, or the recipient feels lost, uncomfortable, or frustrated, often without knowing why. Although young children are particularly sensitive to that which is communicated without words, all of us count on our ability to to read situations and to make judgments based on how we sense what is happening.

I have never made a situation worse by talking about what I sense is going on. I have occasionally made things worse by not handling an incident as well as I might have. Still, talking about what is occurring makes improvement possible. Not talking about what is happening can accentuate an uncomfortable situation and can be a factor in the deterioration of the learning climate. If a teacher is uncomfortable with a particular activity, the class will notice this, in spite of ways the teacher might use to hide this feeling. If there is no opportunity or mechanism to check out what is happening, students will make a decision regarding the value of the activity with little or no attention to what the teacher is saying. Therefore it is important for teachers to structure a climate where students can express their bewilderment, unease, worry, and the like without fear of ridicule or scolding.

Creating this climate is not difficult. What is required is that people, both students and teachers, feel comfortable enough to express what is going on in terms of "I feel," or "I sense," or "I need to know." Setting up this way of talking can be included in the teacher's description of the philosophy and structure of the class. Additionally, the teacher can use the investigation of a piece of literature as part of the examination of the role of nonverbal communication in the total communication process.

For example: Consider the story of Little Red Riding Hood. Have two actors play the wolf and the little girl. As a class, suggest and explore techniques the wolf employs to convince the little girl he is her grandmother. Play with possibilities regarding what each says, the distance each keeps from the other, the tone of voice used and how these might change as each tries to outmaneuver the other. What does he need to do to convince her all is well? What are the cues and clues the little girl reads to form her judgment? What does she do to test his intentions? After many possibilities are explored, teachers can move from the particular to the universal and ask students: "How do you convince someone you are being truthful when you are actually lying? Under what circumstances might you do this? Have you ever felt someone was saying one thing and meaning another? What was your situation? How did you feel? What did you use to base your decision upon? How did you account for the discrepancy?"

As students and teachers improve their capacity to describe their internal and external realities, they will better learn to trust themselves. Concurrently, not only will the classroom become a safer

Groundwork

.... 25

place, students will look for these discrepancies when they study literature, create drama, and explore character motivation. Additionally, when the effects of gesture, tone of voice, and body tensions are understood or at least noticed, the class will become more sensitive to what people are really saying and can be more helpful to each other in the teaching/learning process.

Considerations for Nonverbal Communication in the Classroom:

- Describe what is going on in terms of "I."
- Use feelings of discomfort or tension to explore open communication.
- Consider description rather than judgment when talking about a situation.
- Welcome diverse commentary even though stories may directly conflict.
- When working with drama, explore possible character behavior in active terms, rather than merely talking about possibilities, so that students can see for themselves the effect of specific nonverbal activity on character choice and interaction. For example, a character is walking home from work. How would the character walk if he had just lost his job? If she has just been promoted? If it is dark, and the neighborhood is unfamiliar? Perhaps the person you are playing is angry. How might the expression of your anger be affected if the person you are angry at is your teacher? Your parent? Students in your class?

Knowing How and When to Begin

The Chinese have a proverb that says, "The longest journey begins with the first step." So it is with introducing new ways of teaching and learning; both teacher and students have to take a step—no one can do it for anyone else. How do you get thirty people with varying degrees of willingness to try something new, to take even the smallest of steps? How do you help students to suspend initial judgment to give new methods or ideas a fair chance?

To make beginnings easier, use simple material and ideas. Connect the known to the unknown by starting with a question such as, "If this room were a room you had never seen before, how would you decide its purpose?" You might select a common object and ask students to imagine seeing it for the first time. Some religious cultures talk about cultivating the "beginner's mind," which is a state of being where nothing is taken for granted and everything is explored with a fresh state of mind, as if for the first time.

I am a great believer in introducing new ideas through the use of old stories. The experience of telling connects me with the world tradition of storytelling and helps to create an environment that is special, apart from the usual classroom interaction. Sharing a favorite story with students whose receptivity may range from none to great is a challenge. What seems to work best for me is to tell them I'd like to share a story. Most often they're willing to give me the one to five minutes I need. The story sets the tone and the context, making all subsequent steps a little easier. Perhaps it's because most of us are starved for stories. Maybe it's more simple. Maybe listening to a story is just more pleasurable than "real work."

Let us explore some ways to begin through the use of a story I heard from a Thai woman who told me she first heard it from her Laotian mother.

A Community of Knowing

In former times, the Akha people had letters. One year, all the letters were swallowed by the water buffalo and imprinted on its skin. When the time came to make their yearly move, the people discovered the water buffalo's skin was too big and too heavy for them to move to their new location. The people were perplexed. They did not want to leave their letters, and they could not move the skin.

They went to Headman. He thought about the problem, "If we cannot move the water buffalo's skin, we must eat the water buffalo's skin. This way we will keep the letters inside us forever."

And so the water buffalo's skin was cut up into the number of people in the group. Each person swallowed a piece. Thus the letters were kept within the tribe forever.

SUGGESTIONS FOR EXPLORATION

1	**Write:**	A brief bit of information on a small piece of paper that you would like to see remembered, perhaps to be shared with people who might not know you, maybe for a time capsule. Do not sign.
	Pass:	Papers around. Each person takes one.

Share: Bits of information.

Reflect: On story and process. Consider:
- What kinds of information seem to be important?
- Is hearing all the bits different from simply writing yours in private? If so how?

Consider: People have been making quilts for years. AIDS activists and people working for peace have designed and made huge quilts from pieces designed and sewn by people from every part of the world.   **2**
- How might the impact be affected if the quilt is made by one person or by one thousand?
- What might your class consider so important that you decide as a group to work together to share your vision or ideas or point of view? How do you decide? How do you negotiate difference?

Select: A theme of interest to everyone. Make it large enough to encompass many and diverse possibilities.

Design: A class quilt from papers cut into pieces four inches square.

Create: An image using paint, crayon, or charcoal that symbolizes your theme.

Assemble: The pieces of the quilt using tape to make a whole of many parts.

String: Up a rope so that you can hang up the quilt using clothespins or string.

Reflect: On the process. Consider:
- How is your theme affected by being part of an idea quilt?
- What is the impact for you when you look at the quilt?
- How does making the quilt affect your connection to the class?

3	**Paint:**	An image of a telling moment (a part of the story you consider to be memorable, important, disturbing, or whatever).
	Title:	Your image and write it on a separate piece of paper.
	Share:	Images and titles.
	Collect:	The titles. As a class, put them into an order so they form a poem. Each person suggests at which point his or her title is most effectively added.
	Read:	Poem out loud. Negotiate any changes people think need to be made to improve the poem in terms of impact, order of titles, rhythm, or dynamics.
	Reflect:	On the process. Consider: • What themes emerge? • What happens to your ideas and feelings about your title, if anything, when all the titles are merged into one piece of work? Do new ideas about your title emerge from seeing it as part of a new and larger whole? • How does the negotiation process work for you? What techniques could facilitate this process or make it more enjoyable? • Does the poem work for you? If so, why? If not, why not? • How does it feel to create collaboratively, as a group?

Suggestions to Consider About How to Begin

• Keep initial tasks clear and simple. Give one direction at a time. If people continue to ask for clarification, remind them, "The task at hand is to paint an image or label an image or write a paragraph." Focus on how students will know when the task is completed rather than making judgments about quality.

• Avoid introducing judgment inadvertently. Don't ask for an exciting idea, ask for an idea.

- If students are hesitant, afraid, incredulous, or the like, acknowledge the feelings, and take them into active consideration when you design transitions. What is named loses some of its power to frighten or confuse. What is acknowledged can be considered and discussed.
- Have at least two or three ideas in mind as to how to begin a new activity so you can quickly shift if one idea is not well received.
- Connect what you have done previously, either in the class or in a previous class, to what you intend to do to provide a context and a framework.
- Ask class for suggestions to make difficult transitions easier.
- If you are nervous or unsure, don't pretend to be completely certain; many students will sense your lack of ease, and this may make them nervous.

Suggestions to Consider About When to Begin

- When you want to introduce a new book, topic, mode of learning, or new way of thinking, storymaking and drama can provide an exciting and dynamic beginning that may help students to explore the material in new ways.
- When students as a class seem to be in a rut, unfocused, or worried about exams, changing the nature of class activity can allow students collectively to take a breath and regain access to inner resources.
- When a project has ended, a section of work completed, or unsettling events such as weather, politics, or community events have distracted students, working with stories and drama as a group can help to energize and focus the group as well as providing a context for people to explore and express ideas only tangentially related to class and curriculum.
- If you feel you are in a downward spiral regarding your ability to reach your students, working with storymaking and drama allows for a fresh start and may improve classroom climate as the result of the activity without pointed discussion.

Arranging Space

One of my students came to class early, saw the chair desks arranged in rows and left. When several more students came in I asked them to help me rearrange the chairs to make a circle. When the first student returned with a form to drop my course, he looked puzzled. "What happened? I came—it was a rows of desks. I leave and return—the desks are in a circle."

"Why do you want to drop this course? We haven't even started."

"I can't stand small classes where we all sit in rows and stare at the teacher. It makes me feel like a trained seal. I just won't do it."

Neither will I *if I have any choice in the matter.* Chairs in rows force students to see only the backs of the necks of the people in front of them. This arrangement says, nonverbally, that the only person who matters is the teacher. This organization also makes classroom dialogue extremely difficult, especially when you want students to talk about ideas and issues of importance to them.

So what to do about fixed desks when one has no alternative, as many teachers don't? I have had students sit on their desks when they were nailed to the floor. When teaching in a theatre I have moved everyone in a circle in front of the rows of chairs. In the worst cases, I talk about my discomfort with the arrangement and ask for suggestions as I talk about the importance of face-to-face communication. Even when we cannot find a satisfactory solution, I make students aware of the problem, and this helps us devise ways to feel connected. Good classroom communication depends on people being easily able to see each other. If you want dialogue, and you're getting tired of having your own voice be the only voice in town, consider rearranging the space if and how you can.

Arranging Time

There are two primary issues of time management in class. One involves the rate at which you ask your students to work; the second has to do with the way you use the total time available. Designing tasks so that students have to work too quickly helps them to bypass their inner censor and encourages them to get out of their heads so they can work spontaneously and imaginatively. I have tried an experiment many times. At the beginning of the first class I tell students they have thirty seconds to make an image. They groan and complain that they need more time. At the end of the semester I give them thirty seconds to make an image. Most finish in ten to fifteen seconds, and many comment that they don't need so much time. What has changed? Thinking "I can't," "I don't know what to do," or "What can I do that's good?" takes a lot of time. As students accustom themselves to working quickly, with no preplanning, time appears to stretch. In fact, they do have more time because no time is wasted on useless inner censoring or worrying about judgment prematurely.

Having students work quickly underscores your interest in their exploration of a multitude of ideas, of helping them to extract the essence of their thoughts and feelings as a way of beginning. If you give students a lot of time *in class* to produce a finished piece of work, the resulting work is often less imaginative, less creative, and less enjoyable than the work that emerges from working quickly. The big issue is trust. Good students know that really fine work takes time, many drafts, much consideration. They are outraged when asked to produce an image, a story, or a bit of drama with insufficient preparation. But this confuses ends with beginnings. Spontaneity is essential when playing with ideas. Working quickly, in unfamiliar ways, encourages the formation of new ideas. Only after all the ideas are expressed in one form or another is it appropriate to consider, select, hone, shape.

Although all of us occasionally plan too much for too short a period of time, the experience usually disconcerts students, leaving them less willing to trust you in the next class. Closure is as important as content. Teachers who ignore the issue of closure in their rush to cover the material may find their students increasingly unresponsive. Therefore, I design the end of every class as carefully as I conceive the beginning and middle, whether it's a recap of what we've been doing, a reflection on the process or text, or a recognition of what we've been experiencing. This helps students to gather themselves (mind, body, and belongings) and eases the transition of leaving to go to the next class, which is usually totally different from their work with me. If the period ends before the planned class material is completed, students leave feeling discombobulated, not finished with my class, not ready to begin the next. I have discovered that because students trust my time management, they attend to their work without worrying about running out of class time.

Many teachers consider their time allotments too short, that they barely begin before the class is ending. Yet, given the reality of forty-five or fifty minutes of class time, it is still important to take the time to warn students that their time is ending, to give them a chance to organize themselves, and to allow them to leave your class with a sense of closure.

Suggestions to Consider When Arranging Space and Time

- Facilitate face-to-face contact among students. Create a circular teaching arrangement as often as possible.

- If desks are fixed and cannot be moved or the class is too large to accommodate in one circle, at least present the issue to the class to help make them aware of the difficulty of communicating in hierarchically arranged space.
- Know that when you push students to work more quickly than they feel is comfortable you must be very careful to avoid judgment of their spontaneous work. Encourage the notion of play and exploration rather than giving premature importance to work in progress.
- Plan carefully to allow time for closure at the end of class.

On Working in New Ways

The most important thing to remember when trying a new method or teaching a new subject is that beginner's vision can be enormously valuable in seeing what is happening to and with your class. In some philosophical traditions participants are taught to develop a beginner's mind, and to use the freshness of vision that can accompany lack of assumption as a way to see the world with increased clarity. As we assume we know something, it is easy to lose sight of our initial discomfort and/or striking insights. We may also forget that our perception is based on our notions of who we are, how we look, our vantage point for looking, even our preceding experience. There is no one real way to see the world. The Native American story about how tides were created feels very comforting when I struggle to make changes in myself, to learn new skills, or to approach familiar tasks using alternative possibilities.

How Tides Were Created

In the beginning, Raven created the world and the people who live in it. When it was time for him to rest he visited a community close to the great waters. When the people saw Raven they crowded around him and told him of their troubles with the great waters. "Sometimes the water is far from where we live and we can easily collect the fish in our baskets," said one.

"But," said another, "sometimes, just as we are gathering the fish, a huge wall of water comes and overturns our boats and kills our people. We never know what we will find."

"Will you not help us? We can learn to find fish in water that is deep or shallow. What we do not know is how to fish in shallow waters that suddenly become deep." Raven felt their misery and helplessness, and promised to help even though he did not know about these sudden changes.

He flew over the great waters looking for some explanation but met no one who could help. Then, just as he was resting on a log, a huge wall of water crashed down on him. Only his quick flight saved him. "Hey!" he yelled. When the waters calmed down he flew down to the log again and the same thing happened. Seeing nothing, yet irritated at being so badly treated, he flew about, looking for the cause of his sudden drenching.

He noticed a huge giant standing in the water. Raven watched the giant for a long time, so long he began to get sleepy. The only place to rest was on the giant's shoulder. As Raven settled on the giant, the giant shrugged his shoulders trying to get rid of the intruder. When Raven dug his claws in, the giant sat down quickly, the waters rose, and once again Raven almost drowned.

"Hey!" yelled Raven. "Do not do that!"

"Why not?" complained the giant. "This is what I always do."

"Well, maybe it is, and maybe it is not," said Raven grimly, "but you have to stop. You are killing the people when they go to fish."

"Why should I care about people I have never met? I will do what I have always done." And he stood up in a hurry, causing all the water to funnel in against him like a tremendous whirlpool. Raven had to hold on with all his might to keep himself from being sucked in.

"Stop moving so fast," complained Raven. "Why not bend and rise more gently?"

"I do what I have always done in the way I have always done it," whined the giant. "Now leave me alone." He plunked himself down and the waters suddenly rose.

"You must move more slowly," commanded Raven. "Otherwise the people will drown."

"No!" wailed the giant. "I will do what I have always done. Leave me alone." He quickly stood up and created another whirlpool.

Raven grew angry and determined. "If you do not stand and sit slowly I will peck your face."

"But," cried the giant piteously, "I am only doing what I have always done."

"Too bad," said Raven. "I will not warn you again." When the giant plunked himself down Raven pecked him with his sharp beak."

"Oh. You hurt me. Why are you hurting me?" wailed the giant.

"You are hurting yourself," reminded Raven. "All I asked you to do was to stand and sit gently." When the giant absolutely refused to listen, Raven pecked him again.

"Please, do not hurt me any more," begged the giant.

"It is up to you. Sit and stand slowly as I ask, and all will be well." Raven hovered while the giant began to move. Slowly and gently, he rose. Slowly and gently he sat. Satisfied, Raven said to the giant, "You have done well. I am sure the people appreciate your help." Then he flew to the village to see how the people were managing.

"Oh Raven, you have kept your promise to help," they cried. "The waters now move more slowly. We have time to gather fish safely."

Pleased, Raven flew to the giant. "Thank you for your help. The people are now able to fish in safety."

"What are you talking about?" asked the giant. "This is the way I have always moved. This is the way I have always been."

As teachers we must not forget that whatever now seems comfortable, normal, or habitual to us was once strange and unfamiliar. There is no way to learn without recognizing what we don't know— often a most uncomfortable experience. This is why I think it is important and useful for teachers to be continually learning new skills, to keep us honest and compassionate—aware of how easy it is to feel frightened and insecure when we don't know how to answer a question, find a passage, or make inferences as quickly as we are called upon to do so. This is why I occasionally share what I am currently working on with my students. The minute or two I take away from class material serves to remind them and me that learning can be a complex struggle. The more we stretch our capacities the easier it is to feel bad about ourselves. When teachers share appropriate experience about their learning with their class, students are more likely to trust their teacher's capacity to be kind and compassionate.

It is seldom easy to change established patterns of behavior, especially when we have administrators, parents, and fellow teachers expecting us to do as we have always done. But when we have the courage to explore new ideas and behaviors we also have the possibility of feeling most alive and vital.

So, how do we make changes given a fixed curriculum, clearly defined administrative expectations, statewide tests, disinterested students, unsupportive colleagues, and perhaps our own anxieties and doubts? Slowly!

I have found that when I am trying a new technique or approach I achieve more satisfactory results if I share my plans with my students than if I just do it to them. For example, the first time I brought finger paints to use in class I was rather nervous. Fifteen-year-olds have too recently left their childhood activities behind to feel comfortable with "childish" media. I debated how to approach them thinking up all sorts of educational benefits, arguments, defenses—even, I'm sorry to say, attacks. In the end, I found myself saying to my class, "I'd like your help. I think we need to find a way to help you feel comfortable speaking up in class, especially when you're struggling to find words or ideas. I've brought in some finger paints and paper towels." (Howls of laughter.) "Yes, I know this sounds funny. We associate finger paints with little children. But who is to say that finger paints are good for children in kindergarten? That first-graders must use crayons or that third-graders need to draw with colored pencils? What makes a particular medium childish?" (Shrugs, smirks.)

"I've been doing some finger painting in relationship to a book I'm writing, and I've discovered that the images I make help me know what I think. I'd like you to paint as part of our exploration of *The Scarlet Letter.* This approach is not about making art. It is not about being an artist. It is merely one way to explore knowing without being totally dependent on words. I'd appreciate your help." (Silence.) "I also want to stress that I will not interpret, analyze, or judge anyone's images, now or ever." (A few looks of interest.) "I will give you very little time to make an image, less than a minute. Probably it will feel like too short a time. Don't worry, just do the best you can." (Snickers and comments I can't make out.) There was nothing more I knew to say so I gathered my courage and began.

I handed out a set of six pots of paint for each group of three or four students and told them to paint an image of the marketplace as the book opens. I kept a running account of the time, and after one minute I told them, "Time's up. Let's look at what we have. Who'd like to share their image?" (No one. Silence. Everyone becomes intensely interested in the floor or a fingernail or a piece of dirt on their clothing. The silence builds like a wall.) I repeated myself keeping my voice calm, "Who's brave enough to go first?"

The class clown came to my rescue. Using a voice deliberately intended to make the class laugh he said, "Vat ve haff here is a veddy clear example of zuh marketplace landscape. Look veddy closely, and you vill see amazing sights. Step right up and take a look. Only fife cents a peep!" He grinned as the class exploded in laughter. I kept my voice neutral, "Thank you. Who's next?" No one. "OK," I said. "Let's put our images in that corner of the room so we can look at everyone's at the same time." Students got up and reluctantly placed their images on the floor. "Anyone notice anything?" I kept my fingers crossed. "Look at the images as a group. Any patterns that catch your attention?" I prepared my strategies in case no one spoke; I would ask them about their choice of color and size of image.

One girl said, almost without noticing the group, "I think it's kind of interesting how many of us put black paint in the center of our images."

"Yeah, I noticed that," said another student.

A boy who seldom spoke in class said, "It's like there's something bad happening—too many rules." More silence, but this time it felt OK.

"Makes me feel funny." Now it felt as if the class was really looking.

"Like it's not a good place to be." Heads nodded in agreement.

A few more comments pierced the silence before I asked students to take their images and return to their seats. They looked at me, as if waiting for me to comment on their remarks or participation. Instead, I asked them to share a passage from the first two chapters that caught their attention and to think about why they chose it. One student read the passage, "But, on one side of the portal, and rooted almost at the threshold, was a wild rose-bush, covered in this month of June, with its delicate gems, which might be imagined to offer their fragrance and fragile beauty to the prisoner as he went in, and to the condemned criminal as he came forth to his doom, in token that the deep heart of Nature could pity and be kind to him." (Hawthorne, p. 46)

She said to the class, "That rosebush makes me think of Hester Prynne, blooming in the midst of all those rules, made by men probably, who could do anything they wanted as long as they didn't get caught." Not bad for a first attempt. I noticed some of the students were looking at their images.

"Write down whatever thoughts come to mind about your image, and don't forget to date it. Later on you might want to remember your initial thoughts about *The Scarlet Letter.*"

About two minutes before the end of the period I thanked the class for participating and expressed hope they would be willing to make more images—in paint and in clay. I saw a few nods and shrugs. I found it hard to interpret what they thought, but I decided to take their grunts as a sign of consent.

Towards the middle of the semester, after they were more accustomed to painting and using clay, we talked about this first experience.

"I thought you were nuts."

"I hate getting finger paint under my nails."

"I was amazed at how much I wrote about after I made the image."

"It was a change."

I asked the big question, "Shall we continue using imagemaking?"
"Yeah."
"Why not?"
"It's different—breaks up the routine."

Considerations When Working in New Ways

- Start slowly. Focus on one change at a time.
- Be clear about what you're proposing to do and why.
- Share your concerns with your students. Ask for their help and participation.
- Reflect on the process after students have had some experience with the new techniques or material.
- Don't give up if your first attempt is less successful than you would wish. Think of your attempts to change as a learning experience for you and your students. How you handle "failure" gives students an opportunity to see you learn in public.
- Separate the process from the performance. You and your class probably need to experience the new techniques a few times before you decide its worth. Be gentle on yourself and the class when you reflect. It takes time, patience, courage, and a good sense of humor to make changes in established routines. No one ever rebuilt a house without a mess.
- No matter what happens, remember why you are making the changes, the goals you want to achieve, and their value and benefits for students.

Beginning: Issues and Problems

None of us come to the classroom with a clean slate. We're worrying about what we said yesterday, wondering what will happen tomorrow, thinking about what we have to do this evening. How you feel about the group, how they feel about you, past experience, present expectation, future worry, group dynamics—all affect classwork. How do you help thirty people to create a learning community? How do you establish trust quickly enough to allow learning to occur? How do you persuade students you care about them? How do you convince a class to talk about what matters? How do you keep educationally damaged students from damaging your class? How do you keep going when nothing you do seems to work?

There are no simple answers. We have to start from where we are. We have to teach the students who appear in our classes. All we have is who we are. No one teacher will ever reach every student. No one technique will ever interest every class member. But good preparation, genuine interest in students, delight in sharing interesting material, and careful student-teacher reflection help make good teaching and learning a reality most of the time.

Ignore or Confront?

Essentially a teacher has two choices: to ignore what is happening and hope it goes away or to confront the situation and hope that this depotentizes the problem. I have found that ignoring a predicament only makes it worse. It's as if everyone knows what is going on, but nobody can or will talk about it. In effect, this reduces communication to all but the most mundane matters. And, when the teacher tries to talk about personally important issues, the students know it's not safe to talk freely and openly.

The safest way to approach a troubling situation is also the most effective. Everyone, including the teacher, needs to talk about what is going on in terms of "I think, I feel, I wish, I hope . . ." No one is allowed to talk about someone else's experience, nor is anyone permitted to comment on another's words.

If the group is in very bad shape, I often use an old technique of passing the stone. A largish object is designated to be the permission-to-speak object. When you have it you may talk; when you don't, you have to listen. I also separate problem from solution. If the group is very upset, I tell them, "Today we are going to talk about what we think and feel is going on among the group members and within ourselves. Tomorrow (or the next class period) we will consider possible solutions using the same technique of passing the stone. We will not choose a solution at this time. During the next subsequent meeting we will reflect on all the issues, problems, and solutions and begin to explore the solution that seems most effective for all of us." I don't usually devote a whole class period to this and sometimes I set time limits of one minute per person or even thirty seconds if the group is very large. I do give them time to think beforehand, and I tell them to consider the essence of what they want to say. I ask for a volunteer to be the timekeeper. If the group really needs more time, we go around again. Of course I obey the same time limitation. When the class is satisfied that all the issues are on the table, it's not very difficult to move to working with a text or doing drama. Students comprehend the structure and are generally content to put it aside, knowing they will have another chance to talk during the next class meeting. Separating problem, solution, and choice of solution allows students to talk among themselves, reflect on personal and group needs, and to think more clearly without reflexive reaction. I have also found that students are relieved that I am not afraid to talk about what is going on. By providing them with a clear and workable structure that helps them to address issues, they also learn about effective negotiation and strategies to explore diverse opinion, culture, feelings, and experience.

Discomfort and Embarrassment

What teacher hasn't been confronted by students giggling when no joke has been told? Stony silence when the class is asked a question? Hysterical laughter when a person is asked to try a new approach? Eyes rolled up when embarrassment reaches crisis proportion?

As part of my introduction to class work I talk about the notion of comfort zone. When we walk or talk at our normal pace, do what we like or know to do, work with people we like, we are operating from within our comfort zone. Moving out of our comfort zone is very easy. It can be as simple as walking or talking faster or slower than the pace to which we are accustomed. It might be having to work with people we don't know or trust. We certainly feel uncomfortable when asked to act in unfamiliar ways or eat strange foods. The degree to which we venture into the unknown is the degree to which we feel uncomfortable. The further we move out from our comfort zone, the more likely we are to blush, feel uncomfortable, hyperventilate, lose our ability to communicate, become angry, or act quickly to protect ourselves. The more uncomfortable we are, the less likely we are to learn. However, if we never leave our comfort zone, we never learn, because learning requires venturing into the unknown. We have to step outside of our comfort zone to learn or try something new, and we have to do this carefully and with awareness of the process. I liken this work to preparation for job interviews or dealing with unknown situations or people. The more resourceful we are, the more likely we are to approach life with the sense that we can manage, no matter what. The practice of making unusual choices when working in role is excellent preparation for the constantly changing demands of being alive.

To help empower students to be more in control of their learning process, we practice moving in and out of their comfort zones in small ways such as walking faster than normal, speaking more quickly than usual, or keeping their eyes on the floor. We try a variety of activities until they sense an area where they're a bit uncomfortable but willing to stay because they understand the dynamics of learning, knowing they can move in and out of their comfort zones at will. For example, one student who reads poorly agrees to read a paragraph out loud as long as the class promises to help if necessary. It's not uncommon for a student to tell me, "I'm too far out of my comfort zone." Although I discourage commenting on comments that involve inappropriate judgment, I do encourage the class to come to the aid of any student (or teacher) who asks for help. At this point I often ask the class to make suggestions to the working student, and, in the process, the whole class becomes involved in learning how to learn. Occasionally, when I'm teaching a course for the first time, I tell students that I'm out of my comfort zone, that I welcome their suggestions on particular issues. What I'm after is something of a paradox, feeling comfortable with one's discomfort in the service of learning.

When we create drama and students work in role, many become embarrassed and easily lose their concentration and focus. To help them recover their center I ask them a series of questions that can be answered simply but require that the student image the character: "What did your character eat for breakfast? What kind of shoes is your character wearing, if any? If not, why not? What does your character like to do? What is your character's favorite color? How come?" I encourage students in the group to ask similar questions. The student answers in role using "I" to image the character and become more articulate and aware of character choice. Sometimes a shy student is asked to play a blustering role and has no idea how to approach the required behavior. Articulating where the student is and what the character needs begins the process of negotiation. Students practice using more space, talking more loudly, using their arms, demanding attention. Always, the class is there to help, encourage, and provide practical suggestions. We reflect on the difficulty of creating a believable character, of making choices we might not normally make. The more a student is able to image their character in their mind's eye, the easier it is to work in role and the less likely it is the student will continue to feel uncomfortable, embarrassed, or paralyzed.

Suggestions for Beginning

• Describe tasks so they have a clear beginning and ending. Students need to know what constitutes a finished task with no question of judgment, which is premature at this stage. For example, write a short story. "How short is short?" "Short

is however many words you need to tell your story." "Even one sentence?" "Even one sentence."
- Structure tasks so that students choose their own subject. If you ask students to describe their deepest feelings on the first day of class you're probably asking for trouble. If you ask students to look at the feelings of a particular character and to notice what life events may be important for character development, you may begin a workable dialogue.
- Encourage class members to help each other by structuring whole class consideration of individual class member's questions or problems. If a student is stuck, ask the class to think about ways to solve the problem and to suggest possible solutions.
- Avoid setting one person or group against another. If a person has a problem, put the emphasis on articulation of the problem and on universalizing the situation rather than keeping the focus entirely on one student. Encourage people to see how one person who is willing to share what is going on helps everyone to learn.
- Make space for people to express their feelings in safe, contained ways. The best way to do this is to insist that everyone who talks begins by saying "I" rather than "you" and talks only about personal experience. No one may talk about another's experience or for another person. Encourage silence between speakers for reflection.

Flexible Planning

We all know the saying, "The best-laid plans of mice and men oft go astray." Yet not planning can be a recipe for disaster. How do you plan well enough to provide structure yet at the same time remain open to the group? Students tell me they appreciate my unstructured approach when teaching, yet I am extremely structured. That they don't perceive the structure happens because I design the tasks to elicit their responses and factor in activities specifically designed to process their reactions.

What follows is a lesson that I planned for a class of twenty first-year college students who were studying *Siddhartha* by Herman Hesse. The session was the first of four devoted to the novel and occurred toward the end of the semester. The students were not used to working with finger paints but expressed their willingness to try. They were curious to see how, or if, making images could help them know more about their ideas. The comments in parentheses are my response to the class and the changes I decided to make.

Text:	*Siddhartha*
Time:	50 minutes
Focus:	Images of self
Paint:	On left side of paper, image of "self."
Write:	Words to describe a self.
Paint:	On right side of paper, image of "myself."
Write:	Words to describe myself.
Share:	Images and words. *(I intended this to take about fifteen minutes, but it generated a long discussion about the nature of self and the search for self in the student's lives and in the text's characters. The talking revealed bewilderment, fear, and concern about their selves and the development of self.)*
Paint:	Image of Siddhartha's notion of self at a particular point in the novel that interests/intrigues/irritates/excites you.
Select:	A passage that illuminates your notion of Siddhartha's self.
Share:	Images and passages. *(Because time was passing quickly, I asked for only two people to share, who had picked different points in the novel. Their choices evoked a lot of talk, and I used their interest to lead in the next task.)*
Create:	A brief (less than one-minute) monologue to describe Siddhartha's understanding of self at your chosen point in the novel.

Share: Monologues.
(I decided to ask for three volunteers who had each picked a different point in the novel.)

Discuss: How or if Siddhartha's understanding of self changed as he lived.
(I decided not to do this because the ideas emerged as the students did their monologues.)

Consider: Govinda (Siddhartha's friend since childhood) asks Siddhartha, "Give me something to help me on my way, Siddhartha. My path is often hard and dark." As Siddhartha, what would you give him? As yourself, what would you give him? If there are differences, what might account for them?
(Instead of talking I asked them to paint a gift from Siddhartha on the left side and a gift from themselves on the right side. I asked the group to hold up their images so we could see them. We processed them as part of the reflection. The gifts ranged from a lifetime pass to McDonald's—so he'd never be hungry!—to a portable CD player with all of Beethoven's symphonies. When the McDonald's gift was offered the class roared with laughter, looking at me to observe my reaction. Of course, I was laughing as hard as they were despite my initial snooty gasp of disapproval. One student commented that we were discussing important ideas, and he thought I was being rather flip. I asked him to tell us more about his ideas. He said he planned to be a psychiatrist and thought notions of self were extremely central to the development of personality. A classmate countered, "Do you think we're being flip because we laughed at the lifetime McDonald's pass?" The student admitted he felt the subject was too important for such levity. A third student objected and said that having a sense of humor was a sign of health. I suggested we think about the meaning of our gifts in relationship to our notions of the relationship between Govinda and Siddhartha and to share these during the next three classes.)

Reflection: On session and ideas evoked by the processes we used to explore the notions of self presented in the novel.

(Some students objected to the imagemaking as being irrelevant to "good thinking." Others passionately defended the experience, saying that they hadn't known what they thought until they saw their images. Another commented that the discussion was the best they'd had to date, so maybe the images were a good jumping-off place. Most agreed that the discussion was only the beginning, that they thought a lot about who they were and who they wanted to be.)

When I structure a session I take into account length of time of class session, number of people in group, relationships (among students, between students and teacher, students and course material), placement of class in regard to semester, difficulty of text, and ability of class. For example, the session on *Siddhartha* described above, which took place during the last third of the semester, was planned for students who were used to grappling with difficult ideas, who felt fairly comfortable sharing ideas or at least admitting when they didn't understand something. In this first session I wanted students to think about what we each mean by "self" and how our notions inform, describe, or affect our understanding of Siddhartha's development based on his life experience. I also wanted them to consider their ideas about their own selves and how this understanding might affect their life choices. The general plan was to go from the specifics of *Siddhartha* to the universal to the personal. In the process, we considered how psychology, religion, and culture affect notions of the self. Some students suggested that exploring notions of self would be a good way to begin the course, because the exchange of ideas provided them with a framework in which to think about and share complex ideas.

Teaching topics that are not only complex but powerful requires care and quick thinking. Recently I was asked to share some literature from the Holocaust with high school students ranging from first to fourth year. Class size ranged from twenty-two to thirty-seven; each class met for forty-seven minutes. I planned the following lesson; comments about one class are in parentheses. Although each class responded somewhat differently, I chose one class because of the response of a quiet fifteen-year-old who was a good student and generally cooperative.

Text: *A Scrap Of Time* by Ida Fink

Time: 47 Minutes

Focus: A child during the Holocaust

Introduction: Brief talk about the Holocaust following up on the film
Night and Fog, which students had seen the previous
week. These classes on the Holocaust were part of an
interdisciplinary approach to the Holocaust, designed
by the students' history teacher. He and I gathered
books, films, reprints of newspaper stories, and news
films from the thirties and forties, which he made
available to his students. I shared my Jewish
background—encounters with anti-Semitism as a
small child.
*(One boy said his parents told him there was no such thing
as the Holocaust, that the Jews made it up to get the Arabs
to give up their lands so the Jews could take over their
country. I let him talk, took a very deep breath and then
asked the class what they thought. Several of them said
words to the effect, "It was in all the papers. It had to be
true." [The teacher had provided books with copies of
newspaper accounts.] Others came to the boy's aid and
said that the Jews were very clever and could certainly have
made up a story to suit themselves. I showed him some
first-person accounts of survivors in some of the books their
teacher used as reference [Bauer, Frank, Friedlander,
Gilbert, Gotfryd, Hilberg, Meed, Miller]* and asked him to
consider what it would mean to him if there had been a
Holocaust. He said, "My parents would be wrong and
they're not." Several students commented that his parents
were wrong. Feelings ran high. I quieted them down by
requesting them to think about history, the writing, the
telling, the remembering. I asked them to remember a time
when they witnessed something and then saw it reported*

---

*I also appreciate the information given to me by the staff of the
Halina Wind Preston Education Center, 101 Garden of Eden Road,
Wilmington, DE 19803.

"wrong." Several people talked about car accidents and inaccurate police reporting. I made the transition back to the Holocaust by asking them to enter into the work I planned to do with them without judgment, to consider some ways of thinking about the Holocaust. I asked the boy if he could do this and he said, "Yes, but it's no use because it didn't really happen." At least I had his cooperation, and the class could continue.)

Paint: Images representing a pleasant town, a place you would like to live. Include trees or movies or places to go with your friends—whatever you think belongs. *(Students had large pieces of paper.)*

Draw: With a black crayon divide your town into four equal parts. Now take one square and divide this into four equal parts. Now take one of these small squares and divide them into four equal parts and then again, once more.

Imagine: Without warning, just before you are ready to eat your breakfast, there is a knock at the door. Armed men with guns drawn shove you down the stairs and force you to go to the smallest square. Your father has already left for work. Your mother has taken your smallest sister to school. No one is home. None of your neighbors come to help you though you saw some of them looking at you as you opened your door.
(Several boys spontaneously protested and said, "No way would I go. No one's gonna push me around." Others reminded them the Jews had no choice. Men with guns came suddenly and took the Jewish children, women, and men away. The Jews didn't know where they would be taken or what would happen to them. No neighbors came to their aid. Others complained that the square was too small, that no one could live in such a space, that it had no place to buy food and no where to sleep. I asked them what it would take to imagine being forced to go into such a place. One boy said, "It's really scary to think about.")

Reflection: What do you do? How do you feel? What is happening?

(I asked them to imagine themselves as particular people—their age, how they spent their time, if they had a job, the size of their family, how they got along with their family, how they might try to get word to their family. Most students said they couldn't imagine such a catastrophe, but one student offered his experience. He'd been in a boating accident and after regaining consciousness he didn't remember who he was. When police came to rescue him, he ran away because he was so confused. One of them fired a shot over his head, which so frightened him he just ran faster. Eventually he tripped and fell. When the police tried to hold him, he struggled, and they had to subdue him. Eventually he regained his memory and recovered. "But what I remember is how frightened I was. And these guys were trying to help me. In the Holocaust all the police wanted to do was to kill the Jews." I noticed the boy who thought the Holocaust didn't happen looking increasingly uncomfortable, but I said nothing to him at this time. I thought he needed time to think about his ideas and feelings.)

Read: "Splinter," by Ida Fink.

Write: Short note boy sends to girl after their encounter.
(We didn't do this because we ran out of time.)

Reflect: On session.
(A lot of students came up to me with questions such as: Why didn't the rest of the world help the Jews? Why did the Nazis pick on the Jews? Why do people refuse to admit that the Holocaust really happened? Why are countries still picking on the Jews?)

Assignment: Think about what you have seen, heard, and read about the Holocaust. Share your ideas by writing a short story in either first or third person.

The stories were collected and put into a book that was exhibited as part of the school's Excellence Fair. The boy whose parents told him that the Holocaust never happened wrote a story about a fourteen-year-old boy who is told by his parents that the German police who have come to town are his friends. In the story, the boy is knocked down and beaten because he is walking home from school with a schoolmate who is taken away by the German police. When he finally reaches his home, his parents yell at him for being a troublemaker. The last line of his story is, "The world is upside down."

About a month after my visits, the boy whose parents still insisted the Jews made up the Holocaust approached his history teacher. The boy, upset and confused, told him he didn't think he (his teacher) would lie but he didn't think his parents would lie either, and he didn't know what to do or what to believe. His teacher and I talked and decided to suggest that the student do research on how history is recorded/told/written as the topic for his term paper. We both agreed that the boy needed to come to his own understanding about politics and history, to decide how to form his own point of view, and what influences/ideas/experiences helped him to decide as he did. Both his teacher and I at times were tempted to tell him that his parents were wrong and we were right, but we knew this would not be in his best interest and kept silent.

I found that students who had experienced severe personal trauma, such as the death of a friend or family member, being in a car accident, or surviving a natural catastrophe like a hurricane, were more able to consider issues of powerlessness and sudden loss of rights arising from their study of the Holocaust. Although their personal experiences were of different size, proportion, and context, they often served as a connection to help the student to imagine what it might be like to face overwhelming mass murder and destruction.

Suggestions for Flexible Planning

- When structuring a class session, it is extremely important to keep each task separate and complete so that you can still create closure if you run out of time.
- Use the process of reflection as a way to tie up loose ends and to help students to think about what has happened during class and what will be discussed in the next class.
- Keep focused on your theme so that you can shape activity to it. Know where you'd like to go with your class and what you hope to leave them with. If necessary, state this explicitly so the class understands what they're doing, where they're going, and how the parts fit into a whole.
- When unexpected events occur, such as increasingly heated discussion or the sharing of powerful experience, try to

shape a transition that validates the students' responses and informs the work at hand. Suggest names of book titles and authors if people want to know more or to consider another possibility. Sometimes I bring books to class so that students can look at them and perhaps become intrigued enough to want to read further.

Teacher Participation and Connection to Process

To participate or not to participate, that is the question. When you participate you demonstrate to your students that what you ask them to do, you also do. On the other hand, participation means more than simply doing what you ask your students to do. Processing their responses and evoking ideas, questions, and responses is also participation. And, if you participate in the imagemaking, you run the risk of uncovering your own issues, which you will then have to process but which may not fit the class's agenda. Generally, I choose not to participate in imagemaking activity, especially when there are more than six or eight people in the group. Instead, I explain my understanding of my role as teacher and facilitator in the class. I liken myself to the ground in an electrical system—I keep the group safe by being both part of and apart from them, and my participation requires me to be the boundary keeper, the one who helps to focus the group on the task and issues at hand, the container and moderator. Sometimes I share my own work in progress to show students how I use imagemaking, rewrite drafts, and play with ideas just as I ask them to do. Occasionally I share a stuck place and ask the class for suggestions. Even though I keep these discussions short, students often give me valuable ideas. They tell me they learn a lot from the process of offering ideas in the form of asking questions because they learn how to suggest possibilities through questioning, and they see how a nondefensive attitude makes helping easier.

Suggestions Concerning Participation

- Define participation broadly. Active participation needs to be clearly distinguished from stale methods—the teacher knows, the students do not; the teacher speaks, the students listen. Create a climate where everyone knows and all can ask questions.
- Suggest ideas by asking questions of the person or group whose work is being shared. Discourage premature

judgment and disparaging comments. Encourage students to make connections by recalling events/ideas from previously read books or from their own lives. If a lot of students want to tell stories about their lives, one way to encourage them without taking a lot of class time is to have them write down their story, keeping it to one page. I often set a time limit of two minutes if they write during class. I would set a time limit of fifteen minutes if they wrote the story at home. I would share the stories of those people who wanted to do so using one of a variety of ways. For example, I might type them and put them in a book that could be borrowed. I might suggest they exchange stories with a friend or someone they would like to know better. I might suggest they keep a notebook of stories. The rationale is to honor their stories and to honor the students as storytellers.

- To focus on learning as process, teachers need to pay attention to student contribution in any form, especially when the student has helped the teacher to learn. When this happens, I publicly acknowledge how and what the student has helped me to learn. This exchange reinforces the idea of teaching/learning as dialogue with each person as contributor.
- Discourage premature judgment. If students don't know how else to react except to say something is good or bad, help them find responses such as "Your work makes me think about . . . reminds me of . . . is like. . . ." It is always helpful to suggest questioning as one way to deepen work.

Setting Personal and Professional Limits

I divide participation into three levels: *public, personal,* and *private.* The old stories, as well as the novels, autobiographies, and so on that we work with in class, are public stories available to anyone who reads the book or tells the story and can be told by anyone at any time. It is possible to talk about very intimate issues through the telling of public stories but using the context of old stories, novels, poetry, and the like, preserves privacy. The new stories created by participants are personal stories. These stories, written or told within the framework of a class and theme, are always appropriately shared. A personal story is not necessarily a private story. Memories shared by group members are private stories. Usually these are not shared unless a student feels there is an important connection to be made between

Groundwork

.... 51

the private experience and the common exploration. Generally, I focus on public and personal storymaking, but if a student chooses to share a memory he or she understands it needs to be in the service of the theme being explored. Many students who have shared private stories say that this kind of sharing is only possible when the teacher and class create a space that is safe for *all* stories and there is purpose to their telling. The phrase "wisdom of the psyche" suggests that when there is no force or persuasion, whatever is shared is appropriate. Often, it is not the story that is the problem but the group or teacher's response to the story. I think it is important for teachers to define their contract with the group. A teacher's responsibility is to extend and enhance skills such as reading, writing, and oral expression. Even when private stories are shared, the contract does not change. So what should be done about the sharing of painful memories? I have found the best approach is to be clear about the theme or subject under discussion and to shape my response or that of the group, according to this theme. For example, I was working with a class exploring the topic "an experience that forever altered the direction of my life." After students sculpted an image of "choosing a new path," each in turn shared the stories of their sculptures. Following a few stories that centered on new jobs, new step-parents, and new schools, a student told a tale of attempted suicide and the indifference of a pediatric hospital nurse. The story ended with the words, "I realized that if I didn't care about myself I would never get out of the place. I'd be in trouble all my life." There was a collective gasp and hush—everyone looked at me. I took a deep breath, nodded, and said, "Who's next?"

A student raised his hand and apologized, "My story isn't so dramatic."

I stopped him and said, "No comparisons please. What we're exploring are life-changing experiences." After making sure his story was really welcome, he told about changing a tire for the first time at night on an isolated road in winter, thinking that he might freeze to death before he could change the tire. Others told their stories, still shaken by the suicide story. As the class ended, the student who recounted the suicide attempt said, "Thanks guys, I appreciate you listening to my story without comments. It's the first time I haven't felt like a freak since it happened." At the end of the semester, in a discussion about the course, several students commented how powerful the suicide story had been. Hearing the story made many think about their life choices in new ways. As a group, we discussed what actually gave our lives purpose rather than experiences or institutions that were supposed to do so but did not. As for the student, being able to talk openly about what had happened enabled a healthy reconnection to peers, to getting on with life. Four years later the student graduated with highest honors and scholarship offers to distinguished graduate schools. Telling the suicide story opened the door to new perspective for the student and for the class, as several told me years later.

A teacher's choice of what stories to share are framed by the purpose of the course. I decided to tell my students that I am a member of a research protocol at the National Cancer Institute in Maryland, that I have a rare form of leukemia for which I give myself injections three times a week. I tell them this to provide a framework for my teaching and my changing levels of energy. Perhaps we spend three minutes on the topic, but I justify giving them this information about myself because the illness helps to define who I am and on what I spend my limited energy. Speaking out allows students to understand that even a life-threatening disease does not have to be the end of the world, that it's not a shameful experience. I also serve as a role model and source of information for students who have questions and fears about dealing with parents or friends who have cancer or other life-threatening diseases. They usually have worries and issues they don't know how to resolve. I encourage their questions and suggest services or places to which they can go for advice and support. Some colleagues have criticized my talking about the leukemia, yet when I ask students if they think my telling was a mistake, they usually answer no, that they appreciate my honesty. What they equally value is that I talk about it, ask for questions, and then get on to the business of the class without dwelling on the topic. For me, the three to five minutes we spend on the subject enables me to teach with greater authenticity. It enables students to see me as a real person who knows what it is to struggle with life-and-death issues.

Suggestions for Setting Personal and Professional Limits

- Clearly define the theme or topic for each class session.
- Clearly define the boundaries of time and purpose for each activity. The more powerful the idea, the more necessary is definition of limit. I actually bring a timer in to class when I don't trust my ability to keep to set limits. I wear a large watch with a very visible second hand.
- Make sure all talk or activity is in the service of the lesson's theme or topic. If personal stories tap into stories many

students want to share, I suggest they take two or three minutes to write their stories down and suggest ways to deepen and nourish their storytelling without demeaning their wanting to share. Sometimes we take a class session to share important experiences as they relate to or are invoked by the text we are using. Even in this instance, I ask them to connect their story to the text—to explain what idea is evoked by the text that elicits their memory.

- If a student becomes troubled by self-disclosure, it is important to respond quickly. Generally, I suggest the student focus on the topic at hand and explore connections evoked by the text or topic. Almost always the disclosure is appropriate, but the student is uncomfortable because he or she is not used to talking about important issues in a class setting. I help by framing their contribution and move it toward universal application. As often as possible I relate it to situations in the text so the student and class can use the information as part of the class's exploration of ideas.

- If the class responds in an uncaring manner either by inappropriate laughter, put-down remarks, or premature judgment, I stop the discussion immediately, talk about why I'm doing so, and ask the class to help restructure their response so the work can move forward. As often as possible I try not to focus on particular individuals. Instead I talk about creating an environment that helps us all to flourish. I also remind them how much easier it is to put someone down than it is to help someone up. I ask them about their notions of learning environment and how they want their class to be. Some colleagues tell me they don't have time to waste on such trifles, but I disagree. The heart of good teaching and learning is directly connected to the quality of the teaching and learning environment.

Creating and Facilitating an Effective Teaching and Learning Environment

We want our teaching to evoke student spontaneity and meaningful contribution, and we want and need to retain control. Are the two requirements necessarily contradictory? I think one depends on the other. However, student and teacher goals and perspectives are not automatically the same. Each has a role to play if the group is to work effectively and with connection. I use the following story from Iran to initiate a discussion about the nature of truth and the structure of our working together.

The Nature of Truth

A long time ago a King complained to Nasrudin, "My people do not always tell me the truth. This bothers me greatly."

Nasrudin answered, "It does not matter whether something is absolutely true or not. What matters is that something is true in relation to a particular idea or situation."

The King was not pleased. "This is just one of your tricks. A thing is true or it is not true. It cannot be true one day and not true the next."

The King thought of a plan to make his people tell him the truth. He had a gallows built just inside the city gates. He told the heralds to announce, "If persons want to enter the city they must first answer a question asked by the Captain of the King's Guards. If the answer is not the truth, the person will be hanged."

Nasrudin came forward. "I want to enter the city."

"Why do you come?" asked the Captain.

"I come to be hanged," answered Nasrudin.

"This is not true," said the Captain.

"If I am not telling the truth you must hang me," said Nasrudin.

"But this would make it the truth," complained the Captain. "I cannot hang you if you tell the truth."

"You must decide. Which truth is the real truth?" asked Nasrudin.

I ask my class. What is your truth? What is mine? Can we create *our* truth in order to develop a good working definition? So begins the business of creating a climate where learning is possible.

Each teacher decides what constitutes an effective teaching and learning environment each time a lesson plan is written and class structures are developed. Some administrators and teachers think the safest and best plan is the one where the teacher talks and the students listen (or appear to listen). The whip to make this happen is the test and the grade. Others want students to participate but don't know how to make this happen. Still others act as if nothing can be done to improve or change the class session. Some teachers complain: The texts are required; the students don't care; the students are not capable of active learning; control of the class is what matters. All of this is true—some of the time. But very often students don't care because they find the texts boring, the teacher's approach condescending, and the material covered to be of no relevance or interest given the lives they lead. I prefer to structure my class so the first order of business is to take the steps necessary to create student interest in the course material: This means making sure students understand that who they are matters to me; that I structure the class as a dialogue not a monologue; that there can be a diversity of points of view that are worth exploring; that I don't have all the answers; and that they know a lot more than they either know or are given credit for knowing.

Beginning a class session with the story about Nasrudin and the King enables me to evoke and demonstrate the collective wisdom of the class without being didactic or boring. I work hard to show students that by speaking their thoughts and feelings, they contribute to the quality of learning in very important ways. I reinforce the worth of each student's participation and encourage them to ask for help if they haven't quite focused their question by prefacing their remarks or question with the phrase, "It's something about . . ." The class is then invited to help the person to qualify and define the nature of the issue or idea through asking questions and suggesting possibilities. Although this may seem to some an unnecessary waste of time, the quality of discussion and contribution always improves when students feel it's safe not to know and equally safe to ask for help. The search for clarity is a worthwhile group process and an important part of learning.

Suggestions for Creating and Facilitating an Effective Teaching and Learning Environment

- When possible, arrange class in circle formation, or acknowledge that this is your preferred seating because you want everyone to be able to see each other and to talk face-to-face.
- Lay out classroom ground rules, and relate them to your philosophy of learning. For example, I ask everyone to use "I" when talking about ideas, responses, feelings, and so on, and I ask that no one speak for anyone else. This reflects my notion that only when we speak for ourselves do we come to know what we think or feel. Generalizing is a way of avoiding personal responsibility for one's thoughts and ideas. If we talk about other peoples' response or experience we keep them imprisoned in our notion of who they are. Not only does this make it harder for them to learn to speak for themselves, it also makes change and development much more difficult. Be clear that whatever

rules you make to facilitate learning also apply to the teacher.

- Don't allow comments on a comment. If one person says, "I think this book is terrible," and a second person comments, "You have no taste," a dialogue where each can learn is almost impossible. Teach students to respond to the first comment with questions such as, "What makes you think this?" or "What are you left with after reading the book?" or "How is it you feel this way?" Specific questions about plot, setting, characterization, point of view, and the like will help generate discussion and avoid the deadening effect of summary judgment.

- Don't allow put-down comments, sarcasm, or teasing. Be clear with students that these behaviors impede learning and have no place in your class. Of course, this applies to the teacher as well.

- If students are struggling, ask permission for you to help one of them in front of the class. Let everyone know you are aware that this is difficult, and you appreciate their willingness to work in front of the group. Engage the group's participation and help. Encourage others to talk about their learning difficulties, especially when they relate to the issue at hand. Be kind and gentle—but be firm. Always thank the students who have been willing to work in front of the class. Commend them for their courage. It's easy to legitimatize fears by avoiding issues. What students need is to understand, through experience, that being stuck is not a crime and asking for help is standard operating procedure in your class.

Maintaining an Effective Learning Environment

Just as a garden needs constant care and attention, so does the classroom. Each time a class meets, in some ways, it meets for the first time. Even after students learn to know and trust you and each other, crises occur. I try to maintain a frame of mind in which all situations and experiences contain within them blessings and curses. Therefore, no matter what happens, if I think fast and well enough, I can turn almost any apparently negative situation into one where all of us can learn. In order for this to happen I strongly suggest developing a personal, internal warning system that taps into your weak spots. When a student touches one of these places for me, bells ring, red flags wave, and sirens go off (in my mind). I remind myself to take a deep breath, think carefully, keep my classroom rules in mind, and when all else fails, be prepared to use an Akido technique of stepping aside. (In Akido, a Japanese martial art, the attacker's force is used against him as the person being attacked steps aside to let the attacker fall on his face.) I use this process when I say to the student, "Tell me more." This buys me a little time as I remind myself to stay centered, not to react defensively, not to attack, and not to judge. I find it necessary in difficult situations to keep in my mind's eye, an image of myself centered. An image that works well for me is a dove flying peacefully and perfectly up my spinal column.

I also feel free to separate feelings from judgments. For example, it is perfectly all right for a student to say, "I hate this class." It is not acceptable for the student to say, "This class is terrible." The difference has to do with the issue of personal responsibility and with speaking in a way that makes space for others to present divergent points of view. When a student uses "I" to frame opinions, I can then ask the person to explain or explore what she or he is experiencing and to engage the whole group when I think this is an appropriate issue for the class to discuss. Maintaining clear working dialogue doesn't happen all by itself. Students and teachers have to practice and learn what is at stake when they do or don't verbalize their ideas and feelings. It helps to do this before a crisis occurs, as a matter of regular classroom practice. I generally structure time around the mid-point of a course, after students have written evaluations of their class learning, to talk about how they feel, what they think, and why. But sometimes tension accumulates when I least expect this to happen, and I decide that it is necessary to confront the situation immediately. I plan to use the subsequent discussion not only to clear the air, but also to frame the issues being addressed into a viable dialogue where there is space to talk and listen.

Once, when I was working with a group of ninth-graders, one of the boys refused to respond to the task at hand. Instead, he said in a loud voice, "This class sucks." Some students laughed; others looked away. I tried to figure out how to avoid a power struggle while I got over my shock. We were working with the Grimm's tale, "The Fisherman and His Wife." (*The story tells of a poor fisherman who catches a talking fish who convinces the fisherman to release him. When the fisherman goes home empty-handed to his wife and tells her about the fish, she demands that he go and ask the fish for a gift, a small cottage. Subsequently, the wife becomes dissatisfied with each gift and each time sends her husband back to ask for more and more wealth and power. None of this makes the wife happy. Finally, she asks to be made Lord of the Universe and commands her frightened husband to ask the fish for this. The fish replies that she is now Lord of her Universe, and when the husband returns home, he finds his wife back in the hovel where they lived before the fisherman caught the talking fish.)*

I asked the boy, "Have you ever been asked to do something you don't want to do?" He looked at me as if I had lost my mind.

"Are you kidding? Happens every day."

"Like right now?" I asked, hoping for dialogue.

"Yeah, like right now," he muttered.

I took a chance, "So maybe you're feeling like the fisherman who has to keep going back to the fish to ask for another favor for his wife even though he doesn't really want to go?"

"Yeah, something like that," he admitted.

At least he was talking to me. I asked, "What would it take for the fisherman to say no to his wife?"

"Are you kidding? The deck's stacked against him. He has this godawful wife who's never satisfied and this stupid fish who keeps giving her what she says she wants. But nothing satisfies her and the husband just keeps going back, feeling worse and worse about himself."

He seemed a little interested so I took a chance. "Let's say, for the moment, you're one of the Grimm brothers, and you have the opportunity to change the story. Where would you start?"

He looked as if he was going to refuse, but one of his friends called out, "At the beginning. I'd never tell her I caught a talking fish."

A girl volunteered, "Look, she's working too. She has to live in a hovel with no money and no attention. Her life's not so great."

The boy sneered, "She's got it easy. He's the one who has to go out every day and find food for them. All she does is cook what he brings home. And, if he doesn't bring anything home, he's a shit."

I ignored his choice of language even though we all knew it was not supposed to be used in the classroom. I think this gave me an opening with him because he looked at me and seemed relieved when I said nothing about his vocabulary. Instead, I asked the students, "Divide into groups of three with each person choosing to be the Fish, the Wife, or the Fisherman."

"Do we have to? What if we all want to be the Fish?"

"Fine," I said. "Decide if this is one fish with three voices or three fish with three voices. I'd like you all to create a minute of dialogue about an issue evoked by the story that you consider important or irritating or stupid or whatever. Think about what has happened to each of the characters just before your scene takes place. When you're finished, I'd like you to title your scene."

They began to work intently, and I looked at my watch; we were almost out of time. I spoke quickly, "We have five minutes left before class ends. I'd like you to take three minutes to work on your dialogue, and then we'll share the titles. We'll start with the scenes in the next class." When I stopped them to ask for the titles, they looked annoyed and complained they weren't finished. I assured them they would have a few minutes in the next class to rehearse and then repeated my request for titles. We barely had time to go around the class when the bell rang, but at least they seemed interested. When we met the next time everyone got into their groups and began talking without any direction from me. The boy who said the class sucked was as involved as any of his classmates.

After the scenes had been played, and we reflected on the process and story issues, I asked the class to talk about their experience and to share what they really wanted to learn. I made no reference to the boy and tried not to look at him. There were many suggestions before he said, "I like it when we get a chance to do something interesting." The group agreed.

I always feel when a situation like this happens I've had a narrow escape, that I've been very lucky. Yet luck is not the only factor. What I did was to take his obvious discontent, connect it to the story, and get him to talk about his own issues using the story's frame. Of course not all students are willing to cooperate. Had he chosen not to answer me I would have had a harder time. Yet I would still have tried to connect his feelings with those of a story's character and situation. By doing this I demonstrate that I value his feelings, that there is a place for his feelings and his ideas in the discussion or exploration of the story.

Suggestions for Maintaining an Effective Learning Environment

- Teach from a personal sense of being centered. When chaos erupts, pay first attention to your own internal state to avoid making a situation worse. Take a deep breath, remain calm, image whatever helps to center yourself, and remember that no one is perfect. I always remind myself that crisis provides a time for new learning.
- When a class situation becomes tense, defuse the tension by listening to what the student(s) have to say without

interruption. If a lot of people want to talk, establish a time limit for each person to talk. Avoid becoming defensive. Rather than attacking the speaker, try to separate out the issues, problems, and solutions and clearly frame them for the class. Avoid personal panic by attending to your own breathing. Suggest the class do the same. Sometimes, it helps to ask for a minute of silence so that everyone can think about what is happening without mindless reacting. Contain the situation by being clear about boundaries and time. When people are very agitated I suggest they use the next two to three minutes to write down on paper what they think and feel is going on. I ask them not to sign the papers. I tell them I will collect them, although handing them in is optional, and I will read their thoughts to organize the issues so we can deal more effectively with them in the next class. If a class is really upset, I might tell a story that I think reflects the issues under consideration and ask people to explore what is happening to a particular character. Drama is an extremely useful tool because it safely encourages the expression of passion in a learning context. Making a group story that is then shared also helps to focus the group on issues and strategies.

- I generally take a minute or two in the beginning of each class to ask students if there are comments, complaints, or questions—"any news for the good of the company." I briefly establish a connection between events in the last class and what I've planned for this one. This helps students to put aside thoughts of other classes or life events and to focus on the work at hand. I use the process to reinforce the idea that our classroom is a community of learners.

- I always take time at the end of class to spend at least a minute or two on the process of reflection. Even if no one speaks, the time is well spent. Often it takes time for people to gather their thoughts and feelings and to test whether the environment feels safe enough for them to voice their ideas or responses. At the very least, it helps students mentally to finish this class and prepare to go to the next.

- I "take the temperature" of the class at random times by asking how they're doing, what they're learning, how they're feeling, and giving them a bit of time to respond. I continually repeat my genuine concern for their well-being and their interest in the work. Often students feel their teachers don't care about them or the course of study, and it's necessary to remind them that you do care by establishing processes for dialogue, reflection, and contribution in each class. It is also necessary to stress that you want students to talk directly to each other rather than always going through the teacher. I often have to remind students to look at the class as well as me, that I'm only one of many. For many students, other students have no value in regard to learning—only the teacher matters. This is not a useful mind-set and must be changed as quickly as possible. Telling students to talk to each other isn't enough to change long-held views. What is needed is interactional classroom experience that reinforces the importance of student contribution.

• At least once a semester I share my own work in progress and ask for students' comments as one way of letting them know that what's good for them is also good for me. I show them comments colleagues have written on my papers and ask their permission to try out bits of speeches I'm preparing. I tell them the kind of feedback I'm looking for, depending whether I'm still in the first stages, trying to define ideas, or I'm at a later stage where I'm cutting and shaping to fit a prescribed time or page limit.

Critical Thinking and Active Learning

Much is written about students who don't care or won't work but I find that many are simply dying of boredom. They know they have no input on their curriculum and no sense that they matter as individuals. Whether they come or go, the lecture remains. Even bright and capable students who perform well are actually turned off regarding real thinking or involvement with learning. They listen for the key words that tell them what will be on the test, what is required for the grade, what they need to do to get an A. If teachers want an interactive learning environment, connection to and with students is the first task. But be prepared! When you change your ways, students won't always thank you, especially in the beginning. One of my students informed me "being in your class gives me a severe case of culture shock."

"Why?"

"You don't explain how to get an A. You give us something to do like write a story, but you don't say how long it should be, or what it should be about, or how it will be graded."

"I don't give grades until the end of the semester."

"I know. That's the point. Everything you do is a surprise. We never know what to expect."

"So, what's wrong with that?"

"Look, we've figured out how to get what we want, and it works pretty well in every class but yours. We ask, 'What should we write?' and you never answer the question. You ask, 'What interests you?' If we ask if we're doing the drama right you ask us to repeat what you've asked us to do."

"So?"

"You just don't get it, do you? You never tell us how we'll know something is right. You keep on asking us, 'What was the task? Have you completed what was assigned?' Don't you have standards? How're we supposed to improve if we're always trying to figure you out?"

"Maybe you need to spend less time trying to figure me out and more time figuring out what you want." Groans. Sighs. Mutterings. "Well, at least you aren't bored." More groans. Big sighs. Eyes rolling upward.

By putting the focus on understanding and completing an assigned task I accomplish several objectives. Students have to decide what it takes to complete an assignment successfully. They have to take responsibility for their solutions. They have to create and satisfy standards that develop and deepen as the work progresses. And, most problematic of all, they have to connect who they are with what they do and how they do it. This means they can't be on automatic pilot, and they can't participate meaningfully unless they pay attention—to the text, to the task, to their inner lives, and to their classmates.

By refusing to repeat mindlessly, I put the burden on students to make decisions and to act on them. I require that students be present in class, each class, all the time. Initially, this process takes time to set up and reinforce, but by the middle of the semester most students are significantly involved. When students don't recognize the focus of an assignment they ask me to repeat it, hoping that I will say what they expect to hear. I don't like repeating myself so I state the assignment in terms of the task I expect them to accomplish. They listen. When they ask me to repeat the assignment I focus on the task. Eventually, most students stop listening for what they hope to hear and hear what I actually ask them to do. Sometimes, when I think I could be more clear I begin to elaborate what I mean. Students often stop me saying, "The more you explain, the more you complicate the task. Keep it simple and let us do what we think is right. We can talk about it afterward." They're right. When I give explanations to illustrate possible task solutions, I'm actually thinking about my ideas and what interests me. If I stay focused on the task, they are free to interpret the assignment as they see it, offering interesting and unexpected ideas that make the ensuing classroom conversation exciting and challenging for all of us.

Saying the right words matters, but common practice often undermines good intentions. For example, the simple technique of asking, "Who can guess the answer?" lets everyone know there is one right answer and a lot of wrong ones. Instead, asking, "What do you think?" "Why?" or "How?" gives everyone a chance to explore from his or her own perspective. If you think an answer is incorrect, you don't have to suffer in silence, simply offer questions for the class to consider. Sometimes I hear myself saying, "I have a problem with . . ." Students listen, ready to pounce on me, if I don't use "I" and follow the same classroom procedures I ask them to employ. Sometimes there is a right or best answer, but we come to this conclusion only after a lot of discussion, reflection, and exchange of ideas. This is quite a different procedure from one where the teacher is the one who knows and students are those who know nothing.

Probably the most important aspect of collaborative learning takes place during the process of reflection. I focus the group by asking questions relating to the topic at hand. For example, after a session on the Holocaust with high school students I asked, "What do you know or feel now that you didn't know or feel at the beginning of class? What happened to make this learning possible? Did you learn anything in class today that was a surprise or a new way of looking at information?" There were a few minutes of silence before the first student spoke. Gradually several students voiced their opinions, but the conversation grew lively only when they disagreed with each other and realized they could challenge each other. This is a good time to talk about critical thinking and perceptual awareness because students are already involved, and many are genuinely interested. To empower students I ask them to become aware of how they know what they know, where they might go to find additional resources and information, and how they evaluate the validity of source material. I don't want them to take my word just because I'm their teacher. What I do want is that they understand how to evaluate and process knowledge, both to further their own and to strengthen their understanding of what constitutes expertise.

Suggestions for Fostering Critical Thinking and Active Learning

- Be sensitive to the dynamic where only the teacher asks questions for students to answer. Instead, offer students the opportunity to ask questions of each other. Spend time uncovering issues, looking for questions under questions in order to understand the significance of issues and ideas.
- Sensitize students to look at each other rather than focusing only on the teacher. This helps to emphasize the notion of a community of learners.
- Use the question, "How else might we look at . . . ?" as a way to broaden perspective and point of view. Explore how who we are affects what we know and how we know it.
- Examine ways in which imagination is affected by experience (or lack thereof). Look at how imagination can be stimulated by adapting alternative points of view.
- When giving assignments suggest students create more than one response. Look at cultural notions of paradox and dichotomy. Explore how the tendency to think this or that affects ideation compared to a culture where knowing exists on a continuum.
- Admit when you don't know the answer. Explain what it might take for you to find the necessary information. Give the class a chance to answer the question or explore what is at issue.
- If you think students are bored or unresponsive, ask what's going on. Give them the opportunity to talk about what they want to learn, what they care about. Even if what you hear isn't what you choose to hear, emphasize the importance of the dialogue. Have students engage characters in the text as part of airing their complaints. When a student said *Robinson Crusoe* was boring, I asked two students to play Crusoe and Friday. I said to the bored students, "Go ahead, tell them why you dislike the book." The role playing became so lively other students wanted their chance. After, reflecting on the process, one of the students said the role playing "made me think about what I take for granted. Like telephones and TV and ice cream and hot showers." Another student said, "I didn't know I was objecting to his tone of voice more than I was to his way of dealing with his experience."

The Dynamics of Teaching and Learning

Teaching a class is much like conducting an orchestra. Sometimes it's like conducting electricity. Like the conductor, the teacher needs not only to know the material but has to be sensitive to pace, nuance, rhythm, volume, and variety. Too much time in any one mode creates student restlessness or boredom and trouble for the teacher. Shakespeare knew what he was doing when he created the night watchman's scene in *MacBeth*. After so much intense conflict, the audience needs a bit of humor to release tension and restore its capacity to take in the rest of the play. Had no humor been provided, the audience would find its own relief by laughing at inappropriate places.

When structuring a class session, look at its overall configuration. Occasionally plot the shape of your lesson by graphing points of intensity and release, noting the percentage of class time each activity takes. If in drawing your graph you come up with a flat line, you need to reconsider your choice and timing of activity so that material requiring intense concentration is followed by more playful or more physical activity. Generally when the primary mode of teaching requires that students sit, listen to a teacher, and take notes, students will become restless more quickly than when they are active participants. Naturally, the better the teacher is at lecturing, the longer students will listen, but the problem of attention remains.

A colleague teaching business asked me to sit in on his class; he felt his students were not responding to the material as he hoped they would. The first thing I noticed was that he spoke in a quiet, monotone voice, with no eye contact with any student. He recited lists of tactics, which students copied into their notebooks with no comments, questions (on his part or the students'), or anecdotes to liven up his delivery. After ten minutes I was struggling to stay awake. Later, when he asked me to comment on what I had noticed, I was troubled. In my judgment almost all his choices were poor, so what could I say that would be honest yet encouraging? I dodged his request and asked him, "What do you like best about teaching?"

Surprised, he thought a bit and then answered, "Nothing. I'm tired of what I do and even more tired of students who don't care. This is a course for majors—their livelihood is at stake, yet look at them! Nothing. No response!" Remembering my struggle to stay awake, I took a chance.

"How about using some drama to liven up the classroom?"

"I teach business, not acting."

"Business people are always interacting with new clients. Perhaps the experience of role playing would be useful when they're out in the world."

"There's too much material to cover as it is. If I take time out to give them acting lessons, they'll miss important ideas."

"Give me some idea of the material you plan to cover in the next class and I'll figure out how to incorporate role playing into their learning."

"They won't participate. I've asked them to do stuff. They won't."

"Look, all you have to do is watch, I'll do the work. You'll have one less class to plan."

"What if they won't do what you ask them to do?"

"I'll worry about that when I need to."

The next class session, I laid out the material needing to be covered. Although students had been assigned readings in the textbook I doubted that any had completed the assignment, so I couldn't depend on them having the necessary information. On the board, I listed their suggestions as to who might need to know the information being studied. Then we made another list of situations in which this knowledge might be crucial. When students asked me questions (most of which I couldn't answer even if I wanted to) I listed the questions on the board for consideration. I gave them a few minutes to look over their notes and texts before dividing them into groups of four. I said, "Create a business situation where one person wants to sell something to another. Decide who each of you in the group will be. Think about the kind of people you are. Do you easily accept new ideas, or are you a hard sell? Are you self-important, or are you open to new concepts? Do you have the necessary authority to make decisions, or do you have to consult colleagues? If so, how many? I'll give you five minutes to plan." I was actually pleased when students complained I wasn't giving them enough time. But I said, "Don't worry. You'll have all the help you need." Soon the class was buzzing with students arguing and discussing.

Before the groups shared their work I asked two people to go to the board to write down issues and questions that emerged from our drama work. Then I asked for volunteers to work in front of the class. No group raised their hands. I tried not to look at their teacher, but his smirk was unmistakable. I waited, looking at each student who immediately looked away from me. The tension increased. I noticed I wasn't breathing very deeply. I took a chance and decided to pick on one group who were sort of looking at each other. "The four of you look like you have some ideas; how about sharing them with the rest of us?"

Groundwork

.... 67

The group giggled nervously, and one of them said, "We have a situation, but we don't know who we are." That was good enough for me.

"Fine, let's hear the situation, and all of us can help to suggest characters." I had to stop them when I heard them trying to solve the problem without knowing who they were. I asked, "Let's identify the problem and put it on the board." After some internal arguing, the essence of the situation was agreed upon and noted. I asked the class, "Who might be involved in this situation?" A lot of good suggestions were made, and I had an idea. "How about if we all work with this situation for awhile with each of you choosing different characters? This way, we'll have a chance to explore a variety of possibilities."

"But, Ma'am, how will we know which is the right way?" Hah! The root of the trouble.

"What we're looking for are ideas regarding strategies. How can we possibly know ahead of time if there *is* one right answer? Maybe none of them will prove to be workable; that's the point of exploration." Overtly ill at ease, the groups took a few minutes to decide who they were, then the first group did their role play. Everyone's eyes were on me when the group finished. Smiling sweetly I said, "If any idea intrigues you or if you have a question, write it down. Next group." Uneasily, several more groups shared their work. I looked at my watch and saw we were running out of time. I suggested that the groups who had not had their turn could work in the next class. I took the rest of the time to have them read their questions and consider the issues that the two students had listed on the board. I invited their teacher to join us as we shared ideas. Eventually, as part of the discussion, some responses emerged as more effective under certain conditions than others, but I refused to let the students actually judge the worth of any idea.

Frustrated, one student asked, "What have you got against judgment?"

"Nothing. But when we're just beginning to look at possibilities we have to consider as many as we can imagine before choosing. We need to know our criteria for selection and research information about each possibility before we can make sound judgments. So I leave you with the questions: What do you need to know in order to achieve success? How might the people you interact with affect your outcome? What strategies might you need to have in reserve if your first choices don't work as you anticipate?" Students argued with each other as they left, convincing classmates of the worth of particular choices.

The teacher wasn't immediately convinced that his tone of voice and choice of teaching strategies were a large part of why his students behaved as they did, but the difference in student response troubled him. "So, they participated, but I'm not a drama teacher. I can't turn my class into an acting company."

No, but no one was asking this of him. Had the class been a course in acting, students would have spent considerable time on the techniques of acting. But role playing is a method that enables students vicariously to explore ideas, information, attitudes and strategies and to learn and respond thinking on their feet. Techniques such as speaking clearly and articulately, using effective body language, and responding to verbal and nonverbal cues are discussed and explored as part of the total learning experience, not taught separately to make the students better actors.

Using drama to teach business or literature or even math may seem like heresy to theatre people. So what? The important issue is to involve our students in their own learning and encourage them to become active learners. One colleague framed the issue, "I used to think my job was to give information. Now I think my primary task is to help students learn where to find information and to know how to evaluate its worth." Drama requires participants to enter into the world of information under consideration. Once students enter into this world, there is no hiding place. Action and reaction deepen knowing and students learn what matters as well as what and how they think and feel about the issues.

Suggestions Regarding the Dynamics of Teaching and Learning

- When students regularly don't respond, check your voice, behavioral mannerisms, interest in the topic, enthusiasm, curiosity, regard for student participation, and energy levels.
- Vary the dynamics of the class session by alternating longer activities with some that are shorter. Give students opportunities to be active rather than passive.
- Find appropriate ways to use humor, although this doesn't necessarily mean telling jokes. One can tell funny stories about one's self that allow students to see you as a fallible human being.
- Avoid sarcasm, picking on one student, or setting students against each other by giving them unequally difficult tasks. Encourage class members to acknowledge when they're having trouble so they can help each other.

- Stories and anecdotes are excellent techniques to use to integrate disparate bits of information. Students remember stories better than lists of issues or ideas. Helping students to create stories through telling or drama engages students and enhances their interest in the material being studied.
- If students have been sitting for a time, give them an opportunity to improve their circulation by standing up and stretching. Encouraging students to yawn helps to increase oxygen supply and feel refreshed.
- Pay attention to student response. Don't assume lack of reaction is due to student laziness, disinterest, not caring, or boredom. Encourage them to talk about what is or is not going on, what might improve the situation, and what their interests are. Even if they say they are totally uninterested in the book or topic there are ways to pique their interest if they are required to become active participants.
- Pay attention to your level of interest. If you're bored, the chances are good that your students feel the same way. Explore what makes you curious, excited, interested, and involved. Use the same techniques to engage your students. Let them know what's at stake beyond a test or a grade. Help them to imagine how knowing can enrich their lives.

Welcoming and Using the Unexpected

Twenty-five students walked into the crowded room where I had tried in vain to create a circular seating arrangement; sat down, looked at me, and waited. Handing out the syllabus, I told them what my expectations were for the public speaking course and asked if they had any questions. No one raised their hand. No one spoke. I waited for a few minutes and then said, "This is a class where you will improve your capacity to speak in public, what are you interested in talking about?" No response. I waited. And waited. And waited. Panic gave way to anger. My job was to teach them public speaking, but I wasn't about to tell them what to say. I looked at my watch and noticed we still had forty minutes before class ended. I decided I was not going to cajole, pick on someone, or beg. Either they talked or they faced the consequences. After thirty-seven minutes of silence someone asked in desperation, "Who do the Yankees play today?" Several people made quick comments about the baseball season, but after less than a minute we were once again sitting in silence.

Just before the bell rang a furious young man barked, "You're the teacher. You're supposed to teach. So teach!"

I shot back, "I have nothing to teach if you have nothing to say. I'm here, willing and able to improve your public speaking techniques, but I can't and won't tell you what to talk about."

"Who cares what we say? It's just a dumb old speech class," chimed in another angry student.

"I care," I said calmly.

"Well, it'd be better for us if you cared less and taught more," said the class clown evoking peals of nervous gasps and laughter.

"Caring less and teaching more is a contradiction in terms as far as I'm concerned." The bell rang. People jumped up and ran out. No one stayed.

Before the next class meeting I talked with colleagues, most of whom told me I was wrong, and the students were right. In their view, the issue was not what students wanted to talk about but how to improve their speechmaking ability. They told me I should have introduced the course by lecturing about the different kinds of speeches students would give, giving them suggestions about how they needed to prepare their talks. I felt misunderstood and misjudged. I didn't look forward to the next class meeting.

When I entered the room for the next class students carefully avoided looking at me. In front of my desk was a noose suspended from the ceiling with a bar stool underneath. Catching my breath, I moved the bar stool away from the noose and asked, "Who would like to give an impromptu speech persuading us that vigilante justice works better than following established legal procedure?" One student with defiance in her eye volunteered.

I suggested she set the scene: Who were we? Where were we? What crime had the prisoner committed? Why did the community feel it necessary to operate outside of the law? Rising to the occasion, she addressed the class, "Fellow citizens. Out here in the plains we don't need anybody to tell us wrong from right. We know, good as anyone that walks on two legs." She continued for a few minutes, describing the crime and the effect it had on the community. When she finished, I asked if anyone was willing to speak for the defendant. Some people tittered nervously, but most students were involved.

A short young man with a slight lisp volunteered. "I got to speak my piece. I know what it's like to be laughed at just cause you ain't like everyone else. I say being different ain't a crime." Several others spoke until the atmosphere was charged.

While I was wondering what to do next, a large student strode up to the front of the room and said, "I'm the sheriff from the next county. What you got here is a defendant who ain't been charged with a particular crime. In my town we charge defendants, put 'em on trial, and let a jury decide if they're guilty or innocent. So I'm takin' him with me, and I'll see he gets a fair hearing. But if any of you thinks you're gonna stop me, think again." He twirled an imaginary gun, took the imaginary prisoner, and sat down.

I was totally dumbfounded and unsure what to do. When in doubt I tell myself to ask the class to reflect on the process. So I said to the class, "Let's think about what happened for a minute, and then we'll share ideas about the situation." No one volunteered. I asked the class, "You saw the noose before I did. What did you think I would do?"

"Yell," said one.

"Turn us in," said another.

"Be real mad," said a third.

"But that didn't happen. What's going on?" I asked, praying for a real conversation. The gods were kind.

A girl with long blonde hair spoke, "I'm sort of interested in why you didn't scream at us. What we did wasn't so nice."

When in doubt, I tell myself, speak the truth. "I was too shocked. Then I thought to myself, 'I asked for participation, I got participation. Now use it.' The speeches you gave were persuasive speeches . . ." The class was off and running.

After spending many years deciding what to do when unexpected events occur, I began to notice that when I was able to use the situation to deepen class interaction about the topic under discussion, not only did many students participate quite remarkably, they also remembered the event as being a high point of the course. Naturally it's easier in hindsight to make great decisions during a crisis, but knowing that retaliatory response generally doesn't move the learning process forward makes it easier for teachers to come up with an imaginative reaction. At the very least, one surprising benefit of using an unpredictable situation wisely is that students are enabled to react in unforeseen ways. Usually, they're grateful for the change of pace and the unusual opportunity to explore nonhabitual response.

Teachers who develop the resourcefulness to use whatever happens for the benefit of their students will have an inner security that makes teaching more challenging and less routine. We have all experienced times when activities that looked simple and predictable on paper provoked unexpected reactions in practice. An inexperienced teacher, thrown by the startling response, may decide that the answer is to use less imagination and exert more control. But this solution never works for me. All I achieve by my retrenchment are bored students and an unhappy self. If teachers take for granted that they can never know exactly how a group will respond, then we can be more open to the actual response. Like theatre, where every performance of the same play is always different, genuine interaction with students is always unpredictable, which helps to make teaching so stimulating.

When evaluating a lesson it is useful to examine what was expected and what seemed to come out of nowhere. The unpredicted elements offer valuable insights into the work of individuals and the class as a whole, revealing their relationship not only to the subject but also to each other. Examining assumptions also proves valuable when reconsidering the presentation of subject material. This is why it is important to be clear about the focus, as well as the topic, of any specific lesson. Even if the prepared plans go awry, the teacher still has the planned focus to serve as guide for choosing new activity.

If you feel too many unexpected situations are arising, consider the degree to which you are clearly presenting assignments and tasks. Observe your class and confront signs of rebellion and distress as soon as possible. Waiting usually compounds the difficulty of the problem. I take student protest as a sign of involvement and would welcome it a hundred times over student passivity and disinterest.

Suggestions to Welcome and Use the Unexpected

• Before responding make sure you are breathing evenly. Center yourself as best you can using imagery, or counting to ten, or whatever crisis-centering mechanisms you have devised for yourself ahead of time, to be used in difficult situations.
• In addition to planning a lesson, be clear about the focus so you can adapt quickly to newly developing situations without losing your path. For example, suppose the class is studying *Robinson Crusoe,* and the plan calls for students to write letters home to England after the first ship has been sighted in over a year. The focus might be: taking stock and considering help. But when the students are asked to write these letters, they barely respond. It might be wise at this point to scrap the planned letter and ask half the students to prepare a plan to attract passing ships and the other half to consider what they would take with them as proof of their

story as well as to think about what faces them after returning to England. Dividing the group in half gives them a choice. Changing the activity may spur their interest, and the planned focus remains as guide.
- Crisis is always a blessing and a curse. Check your habitual inner reaction. Do you habitually panic, become authoritarian or defensive? Can you enjoy the interest evoked by the turmoil to use it to the class's advantage? Do you have a smorgasbord of possible responses to get you through the initial muddle?
- When the unexpected occurs, involve the class. Keep them informed as to what is happening. Create a response that supposes a partnership rather than dictatorship.

Success and Failure: Evaluation and the Learning Process

For three years I asked students in an honors program to list their three biggest fears in order of importance. For almost every student, fear of failure was their number one fear followed by their fear of being alone (no family or community) and their fear of death. Many of these bright young people feel like frauds and think that it is only a question of time before someone important finds out that they aren't as good as they're supposed to be. For many, their focus on getting an A keeps this moment at bay. It postpones but does not prevent their day of reckoning.

This knowledge caused me to ask myself, "How do I define failure? What constitutes success? What is the essence of evaluation?" I subsequently asked students the same questions and was not shocked to learn that "you're a failure if the teacher fails you, and you're a success if you get an A." When I asked students for their definition of failure and success most laughed as if the answers were obvious, although some felt that if a person tried hard, that should count in the final grading.

But grading is only part of the failure/success issue. One's definition affects much teacher–student interaction. I define failure as a lack of response, rather than a faulty one. Success involves grappling with issues and ideas, to be able as the result of experience to make more effective choices. I find it absolutely necessary to involve students in the evaluative procedure in order to help empower them, to sharpen their powers of observation, description, and decision making. This is no easy task. When the teacher makes all evaluative decisions, the student bears responsibility only for the work done, not for consideration of its quality. My students often prefer not to partic-ipate in matters of evaluation; they say it's my job, not theirs. Some complain that they've never had to evaluate themselves before, why should they have to do it now?

Each term, as part of their written midsemester and final evalua-tions, I ask students to develop criteria for their grade, defining what constitutes an A, B, C, D, and F. If their criteria are not specific I help them to focus on particular outcomes and to decide how they differ-entiate between an A and a B. We discuss this issue in class, and students are encouraged to help each other evolve satisfactory defini-tions. This is the beginning, rather than the end, of the process of student empowerment, for the issues of failure and success permeate every moment of their class existence. To limit ideas of failure and success to the issue of grading is to miss an important learning opportunity.

Yet students have to learn how to learn in a classroom where grades play only a small part in the total learning process. In order to begin helping students to become active learners, I generally ask them to paint an image of an abstract idea that connects to some issue in the text so we can begin sharing ideas using the images as a starting point. I welcome diversity, but they do their best to try to figure out what I want so they can be right instead of thinking about what they think or feel. For example, when reading *Robinson Crusoe* I asked students to paint an image of Crusoe in England on the left side of the paper and an image of Crusoe shortly after he arrived on the island on the right. Immediately several hands went up, and one student asked, "Do you mean when he was a boy or a grown man?"

I know this routine so I reply, "What is the assignment?"

A good student, he knows the task, "To make an image of Crusoe in England and an image of him on the island."

I keep my voice neutral, "So? What is the problem?"

He's becoming a bit defensive, "Well, you didn't say when."

I remain impassive, "What do you think this means?"

He's clearly annoyed with me, "I don't know."

I sidestep his annoyance and remain friendly, "Yes, you do."

He's upset that a simple question evokes so much dialogue, "I guess it means we all have to decide for ourselves."

I smile, "You got it."

In the beginning of a course, similar exchanges are common, but once students understand that I value exploration, the pressure to figure out what teacher wants is greatly reduced. In the above exercise some students made images of Crusoe as a child, others as a young man, still others at the moment he boarded the ship, which began his adventure. As I ask them to consider their choices, I make sure they understand the evidentiary material required to support their selection. As the semester progresses, they learn to choose textual passages that support their ideas and to question each other regarding difference in choices. At some point a student usually asks, "Isn't there ever a right or wrong answer?" I am always pleased when the question is asked, and I generally turn it over to the class for consideration.

My favorite answer came from a student who had, up to then, never volunteered. "I guess it depends on the size of the question. Small questions have right and wrong answers. Big questions raise too many issues for simple answers." This discussion enabled us to talk about what constituted the criteria to decide effectiveness and to know how to gather support information, from the text as well as from personal ideas and experience.

By creating a collaborative environment where students are encouraged to consult each other, competition is reduced, and ideas of failure and success can be defined more broadly. This does not mean students take their work less seriously; quite the opposite. When students realize you want them to consider their ideas and experiences as being important, their attitude about learning often changes radically. I have had many students taking a course with me for the first time tell me they hate to read and they hate to write. After they have been in class for awhile and trust that their ideas matter, that they don't have to read with me looking over their shoulder, many come to enjoy reading and writing as part of coming to know themselves more deeply.

Feelings about failure are greatly influenced by the responses of important others. It's easy for a teacher to make someone feel stupid by asking, "How could you possibly think . . . ?" If the question is reworked so that it becomes, "Tell me hcw you came to think . . . ," the student can look at how the ideas evolved and what information was employed to form the answer. Creative people in the arts and the sciences admit that they learn more from their failures than from their successes. If you learn a lot from an experience, how can it be labeled a failure?

Suggestions Regarding Success and Failure

- Encourage the class to define failure and success in terms of their own learning and the requirements of the class and components (papers and projects) that make up the final grade.

- When reading students' papers consider asking them questions as part of your commentary rather than giving them a grade, especially on first drafts and papers written early in the term.
- When questions about right and wrong or good or bad arise, encourage the class to discuss their ideas and feelings. Encourage students to develop criteria that they can use to make decisions. Talk about where to find information or support to become more broadly educated.
- Teach students how to focus on what they aim to learn when writing a paper, designing a project, or giving a talk in class. Then, after the presentation, when you and/or the students discuss the work, the talk can focus on what was attempted, what was learned, what might need deeper or further exploration, or changes the student might want to consider in view of original or restated goals.
- Every professional I know says she or he learns more from failure than success. As a student I seldom had professors give more than lip service to this truth. I believe students benefit greatly when teachers help them to learn from their failures rather than merely criticizing them for their shortcomings.

Exploring Issues/Solving Problems

All of us feel at times that we lack resources or have nothing to offer when it comes to suggesting ideas or solving problems. This story from Mexico has helped many of us to restore and nourish our depleted selves.

Even the Least Valued

In the time before the sun shared its warmth with the creatures of the earth, there was only darkness. The gods gathered to decided which of them would make the sacrifice to bring the blessing of light to those on earth who were struggling in the dark and cold. One by one, each god declined, offering excuses, until it came the turn of the littlest god, covered with sores and scabs. Ignored by all the other gods, the scabby god spoke quietly, "I offer myself."

The largest, most handsome god did not want to see the scabby god receive all the praise so he volunteered, "Such a sacrifice requires the presence of two gods."

Each god made preparations. The scabby god was too poor to buy anything and used earth, branches, and flowers. The handsome god was very wealthy and made his preparations using the finest jewels and gold treasures.

When it came time for the sacrifice, the gods built a huge fire. Each of the gods sat around it waiting for the two to throw themselves into the dancing flames. The rich, bejeweled god stood, "I will be first." He walked a small distance, then ran to throw himself into the burning pyre. But as he felt the heat his legs refused to carry him further. Three times he tried. Three times he collapsed. Three times he failed.

The scabby god, covered with earth, branches and flowers, stood up, ceremoniously bowed to the assembled gods, and walked calmly into the fire. The rich god was so shamed, he threw himself into the flames. Thus did the blessings of light come to the creatures of the earth.

Even though I select and tell stories because the tale speaks to a particular issue, I never moralize or explain what my point is when sharing a story. Invariably, a student will propose an explanation or meaning that none of us has heretofore considered. One technique I have found useful as a way to begin student/student dialogue is to have each of them paint an image of a telling moment, a place in the story that grips, annoys, irritates, engages, or even angers. By discussing these images and talking a little about their choices, students come to understand personally the notion of diversity and the value of sharing ideas without worrying about right, wrong, good, or bad. This technique builds confidence in students' expressive capabilities and makes it easier for them to share responses and ideas when we read longer literary works such as novels or plays.

But there are times, all too many of them, when students stare at the floor or the window with nothing to say or at least no desire to speak. At such moments their withdrawal generally worsens when I ignore the signals they are sending. Despite tight schedules or material to cover, I usually find it necessary to ask what is going on. If I'm lucky, they answer my question. Some complain they don't like the texts or what we're doing with the material. Others are turned off school, adults, the world. These are the hardest to reach, and my ingenuity is often stretched to the limit. Sometimes, the best I can achieve is that they agree not to bother those who do want to learn. As one person, no matter how caring, I can't repair all the damage they have sustained. But, a surprising number of students, after testing me and the class, do begin to participate when they sense there is an audience for their ideas. Their interest deepens if they sense someone cares about them.

If they find a required book boring, even though I can't change the text, I can help them to become articulate about why it's boring and to use these criteria when reading books they find more appealing. When possible, I take their reactions into consideration when future texts are selected. Once, when faced with a virtual student rebellion, I asked them to read the books and to note why they hated them so they could write letters to the principal. Most students refused, saying no one cared about what they thought or felt, but a few decided to do as I asked, as much to show me how useless their actions were as to be given more interesting books to read. Much to their astonishment, the school principal came to the class, thanked them for their willingness to tell him how they felt about the required books, and asked them what kinds of books they might like to read. Even though many never read voluntarily, they talked about situations, people, and ideas that interested them. Matters weren't settled by one visit or one talk; I encouraged the principal to continue the dialogue. Despite his busy schedule, he and the class met two more times and came up with the idea to have student readers as part of the selection committee, bearing in mind the texts required by state and national exams. What began as a difficult situation became a fine learning experience for all concerned. Some of the most vocal class members were students labeled by administrators as "troublemakers," or "uninterested in learning," or "not bright enough to bother with."

Perhaps the best technique to encourage active student participation is the quality of listening on the part of the teacher. Most students assume the only person of value in the room is the teacher and often have little patience or attention when classmates speak. If the teacher makes it a practice to listen carefully and to encourage other students to enter the dialogue, giving them time to think as well as speak, there is a good possibility that students will become more active more of the time. Like all of us, students want their voices to be heard as well as to be heeded.

In my experience, the more I tell, the less students listen. This doesn't mean I don't talk in class, but it does mean that I risk turning students off when I don't engage them in the learning process. A good way to get students to participate is to ask them to brainstorm questions raised by their reading of a text. I list these questions on the board, as many as I can evoke, with no commentary. When students can't think of any more questions I structure a bit of silence to contemplate the questions on the board, keeping the list on the board for the length of the session. They add new questions to those listed as thoughts occur. Sometimes, I ask them to copy down the list. Other times I go around the room and ask each student to select the question that interests them the most, saying why. Even though I seldom spend much time answering the questions, students say they learn a lot about the text and their views through the question-asking process. In addition, students learn how to formulate and articulate their concerns with no risk of being labeled for asking stupid questions.

Suggestions for Exploring Issues and Solving Problems

- Establish and maintain good contact with students by articulating and confronting unsatisfactory student response as it happens. Don't hesitate to compliment a class when you are pleased with their work.
- Create procedures whereby students are encouraged to explore issues and solve problems so that the burden of class maintenance does not fall exclusively to the teacher. Incorporate this process into the curriculum.
- At predictably difficult times (exams, holidays, and so on) acknowledge the problem; ask the class to suggest ways to deal with what is happening. These procedures will serve teachers and students at times of crises.
- There can be great joy when exploring ideas or solving problems. Discussing concepts can be challenging and engaging. Choose your approach with care, being mindful of your presentation to avoid boring, dull procedures that do not excite or stimulate response.
- When students suggest ideas you have not thought of, be sure to give them credit. A little generosity goes a long way.
- If students respond in ways that make no sense to you, give them a chance to explain by admitting you don't understand. Ask them to tell you more or ask specific questions to help them become more articulate. Focus on the learning process and how thoughts are clarified and expressed.

Sharing and Showing Work: The Process of Growth and Development

How or if students display their work to others can only be decided within the context of the educational philosophy and practice of a class or school. But I define *sharing, showing,* and *performing* as they are used in this book to suggest the importance of careful consideration when adopting a particular course of action.

Sharing involves the presentation of work with others who are similarly participating in the same process, usually in the same class. This is the most informal way of working with an audience. The emphasis when sharing is the encouragement of additional, more focused exploration, the development of new ideas, the deepening of capacity, and on discovering whether intention is matched by action.

Showing consists of the presentation of work to others who could be doing a similar activity but at a different time or space, generally a separate group such as one class presenting work to another class in the same school. This presentation differs from sharing in the amount of shaping and polishing that occurs before the audience sees the work. Because this presentation is more formal and diverse classes operate with dissimilar rules for response, care must be taken to protect those presenting from thoughtless criticism or judgment. Each class may have distinctive criteria—it is the teacher's role to establish parameters when talking with the audience to safeguard students, to enable them to receive useful feedback consistent with established classroom practice. Teachers need to decide the purpose and the usefulness before work is shown to any audience.

Performing is the most formal way to present work to an audience, although its range includes everything from improvisation to totally planned, scripted productions. Here the emphasis is on meeting the needs of an audience, and all too often students get lost in the shuffle of trying to make the work perfect.

To encapsulate the difference, work is shared *with,* shown *to,* performed *for.* There is nothing inherently good or bad about any of these categories. What helps to make them a negative or positive experience has to do with teacher–student preparation, doer–watcher arrangements, and the connection between process and presentation.

When a beginner first starts to paint, no one expects that the result should be framed, but when inexperienced students explore movement, music, dance, or drama, many expect a finished performance. Should beginning students be encouraged to present their work to people not involved in its creation? Teachers considering the scope and nature of presentation need to ask themselves, "Who will see this work? Why? How will the students benefit?" In order to accomplish a specific goal within a fixed period of time, it usually becomes necessary to sacrifice experimentation and to eliminate possibilities without full exploration. Beginners need to concentrate on themselves and their group, developing skills and confidence. Premature exposure does not speed or facilitate this development. If the school play has to be performed, stress the communication of feelings and the development of process so that students are not sacrificed to meet some vague notion of school spirit or community relations needs. Egos of the director or teacher must not be the determining factor in structuring the presentation.

When presenting material to provide students with new educational opportunities, teachers need to structure carefully the environment to minimize self-consciousness and emphasize the nature of this particular learning experience. Limit comments by asking people to speak only from their own experience, "I think," "I feel," "I see," "I hear," or even "I wonder." Encourage those who wish to comment on the quality of what has been seen to put their opinions in question form. "What would happen if . . . ?" or "How would it be if . . . ?" are useful ways to frame concerns. Consider widening the viewing audience only when a group can openly and confidently share work with peers and has good rapport and well-developed internal monitoring systems that allow participants to match intention and action.

Suggestions for Sharing, Showing, and Performing

- Before deciding the level of presentation, consider the skills, needs, and maturity of the class. Structure presentation so that it arises from the activities of the class and informs their experience.
- Be clear about the kind of response the class needs so that you can structure comments that support, deepen, and extend work. Focus comments to meet the needs of the class during each presentation.
- Structure reflection to include contemplation about the process as well as the presentation. Encourage diversity of opinion. Sometimes dissatisfied or unhappy students feel no one wants to hear their comments, yet much can be learned from them when each person uses "I" to express feelings and talk about issues.
- Resist pressure to have unprepared students present work under inappropriate circumstances where there is unproductive pressure to sacrifice learning to impress outsiders. If there is a compelling need to have students present work, keep it informal and casual, at the level of sharing.

• Engage students in the decision-making process. Listen carefully to their concerns. Encourage the group to explore ways to make all presentation experience consistent with their needs and abilities.

• When problems arise, talk openly about them with the class. Acknowledge their feelings, frustrations, wishes. As a group, try to create more satisfactory solutions, if not for this experience then for the next.

• Focus learning by helping the class choose goals for each opportunity in front of an audience to make new learning experiences possible. This is particularly important when a group repeatedly presents the same material. Talk about specific ways to deepen characterization, character interaction, and script interpretation.

Conflict Resolution

How teachers resolve conflicts is determined in large measure by their personal background as well as their professional skill. When a group experiences conflict and feelings are in turmoil, calm consideration of the problem is often difficult. I tell the following story from Russia as much to achieve a bit of time as to suggest new ways of thinking about conflict.

The Troubadour's Song

There was once a king and queen who lived happily until the day the king decided to try his skill in battle. Although he was a fearless knight, commanding brave troops, his small force was soon defeated. The king and his men were taken prisoner and treated very cruelly.

After three years, the king sent his wife a message that commanded her to raise a large army to pay his ransom and secure his release. The queen decided this plan would take too long to carry out and would cost more money than the kingdom possessed. She devised her own plan and immediately set it in motion.

Without telling her advisors, she changed her clothes from those of a royal woman to those of a troubadour. She took her lute and began to walk. After a short time she met up with a group of pilgrims and walked with them in safety. When her path diverged from theirs, she joined a group of merchants. In time, she left them, climbed the steep mountains, and entered the country where her husband was being held captive.

She approached the castle and began to play her lute. Singing in a fine, sweet voice, she soon attracted the guard's attention. In a very short time, she was standing in front of the king who held her husband in his dungeons.

At his command, she sweetly sang of love and loss. Much taken with her, the cruel king asked, "Sweet troubadour, from where do you come?"

The queen, disguised as a man, answered, "From far away. I wander as I will, earning my living by my song and my lute."

Touched by her performance, the king said, "For seven days, play and sing for me. When you leave, ask of me what you will. I will grant your request."

At the end of the seventh day, the queen said, "The mountains of your country are steep. The road is often dangerous. Perhaps you will allow me to take one of your prisoners to keep me safe company."

And so, when the queen was ready to leave, she was taken to the dungeons where she found her husband. Because she was disguised as a man he did not recognize her.

Safely home after an arduous journey, the queen changed into her queenly garments and welcomed her husband home. But, he was displeased. "You did nothing to secure my release. I asked you to raise an army and a king's ransom. You ignored my commands. Had it not been for a brave troubadour I would still be languishing in a cold, dark prison."

The queen excused herself and returned in her troubadour's garments. Once more she approached the king. He greeted the troubadour with grateful ceremony. Then the queen stood before the king, removed her disguise, and revealed her true identity.

The king did not understand.

The queen plucked her lute and sang about the time and effort the king's plan required. She sang of missing him too much to wait so long. She sang of wanting a kingdom with full coffers and healthy people to greet him on his return. She sang of the plan she devised to rescue him without having to raise an army and the money for his ransom. She sang of a new plan to rescue those still imprisoned. The king bowed his head and begged her forgiveness.

The king understood.

Conflict in the classroom creates a difficult situation because time to resolve issues is limited, and the teacher holds most of the power. The best time and way to resolve conflicts is before they happen. During my first class meeting, I begin to establish procedures whereby students are empowered to resolve problems whether they concern me or other students. I do this by de-emphasizing blame and judgment and emphasizing the importance of issue definition and the separation of problem from solution. At the end of each class, as we reflect on the session I ask, "Any comments? Complaints? Ideas for the good of the company?" Often, if I sense a problem is brewing I ask this at the beginning of the session as well. My goal is to establish procedures that make conflict resolution part of the normal learning experience. I give students opportunities to practice negotiation among themselves and with me, and I let them know that I expect people to get along, to respect difference, and to welcome diversity. Always, I talk about mindfulness, the process of being mindful as the most important guiding principle.

If a conflict does arise between two people, role playing may help, especially if the issues can be depersonalized and given more universal framing. Whatever the solution, teachers need to avoid the role of judge. As a friend wisely said, "The person in the middle lives in a muddle." The responsibility for resolving the issue, if the two people are unable to reach a satisfactory compromise, needs to be shared with the class. Sometimes matters can be helped by having the antagonists work on a new problem or activity so they can work out their differences in a face-saving manner. At times, isolating the troublemakers allows the rest of the class to work in peace and shows those who are fighting the damage they are doing to themselves and the group.

Occasionally two students who don't get along reflect a division within the class and receive support from their respective sides for causing disruption. This is a difficult situation to negotiate because the apparent cause is only the symptom of a deeper problem. Before devising any solution, notice spatial relationships. Often there will be a clustering of factions around the two leaders. At times it may be useful to ask the class to freeze in their positions and to exchange the ringleaders, placing each in the center of an alien cluster. This will probably externalize the conflict and can be the initial catalyst for change through negotiation by an open discussion in which participants avoid personal slurs or accusations.

Although asking for cooperation by itself is generally ineffective, discussing the basis for cooperation may yield helpful insights for both class members and teacher. Asking people to keep a diary noting when and how difficult incidents begin may help to change the environment from adversarial to collaborative. Collective observations, noted over a period of time, will suggest patterns and help to clarify underlying attitudes and imbalances. Having several people read their version of a specific incident will enable students to gain insight into the nature of conflict and how personal issues and experience color perception. Discussing these differences without blame or judgment may provide a healthy basis for coming to a working agreement.

Perhaps the most difficult conflict is that between the teacher and one or more students. Teachers, although human, are often ashamed or unaware that they dislike particular students. Discovering what kind of student or behavior triggers your buttons generally facilitates resourceful reactions. Once the source of the conflict is at least partially known, solutions are more readily found. For example, I have always had difficulty with students who whine, "I don't know . . ." My first response, which I have learned to keep to myself is, "Neither do I . . ." in my most sarcastic tone of voice, that accomplished nothing except to make the student more upset with me. Now, when I have the wherewithal I tell the student I have a difficult time listening when someone takes no responsibility for their own learning. I don't tell them I have trouble with whining (which I do) because the response I got was defensive, "I'm not whining." This can only degenerate into a "Yes you are/No I'm not" discussion, which goes nowhere fast. Now, when I hear the whine I see a red flag in my mind's eye and recognize I'm in dangerous territory. If I cannot think of anything helpful to say or suggest, I try to remember to rephrase the problem and to ask the class for help. I begin this process by requesting the student's permission to share the problem with the class and then, afterward, thank the student for being willing to learn in public and the class for being so resourceful. Occasionally, if the student is having a conference with me and this behavior surfaces, I tell them truthfully that I have difficulty with whining and apologize for my lack of resourcefulness. I also suggest how to reframe the response and recommend alternative ways to ask for help. At least this puts the burden where it lies, my difficulty with whining.

All experienced teachers know they do not like or work equally well with every student nor does every student respond equally well to every teacher. This being so, all we can do is to heighten our awareness of behavior we particularly find difficult and develop means whereby we soften our personal prejudice or bias and construct techniques that will be more helpful for our students and ourselves. I find that when I admit my part of the difficulty out front, I often help students to accept that they have choices and don't necessarily have to act habitually. Most important, a well-developed sense of humor is a great asset for teachers.

Suggestions for Conflict Resolution

- Establish procedures for resolving conflict as part of ordinary class business, before any conflict arises. Help students practice ways of speaking that reflect personal responsibility for what they say and feel. Teach the difference between description and accusation.
- Incorporate the conflict into the learning, and use materials from the text to help reframe and universalize the issues. Use plays such as *Romeo and Juliet* to help underscore the tragedy of people not willing to talk to each other about their differences. Underscore the importance of listening to each other without interruption or attack.
- Help students accept conflict as a normal part of interaction so that procedures to deal with it are not seen as extraordinary or shameful. Encourage students to take note of conflict resolution in novels, short stories, plays, and current events.
- Defuse tense situations by exploring issues in generalized rather than personalized terms. Help students avoid blaming, which inflames rather than reduces tension.
- It is important to remember that the tenser a situation, the more calm the teacher needs to project. Deep breathing is a useful technique for everyone.
- I find unraveling tangled yarn a useful metaphor for resolving conflict. When I untangle yarn by pulling hard I generally make the knot more difficult to unravel. What works best is to open up the tangles and gently guide the yarn through the knotted areas. Find a metaphor that works for you and gives you guidance in a time of trouble.

Outside Influences

Teachers do not teach in isolation. Students do not leave their troubles at the classroom door. Recognizing where a teacher's responsibility begins and ends is a continually difficult balancing act. Ultimately, all a teacher can do is to provide intellectual nourishment and emotional and psychological support for learning and personal growth, helping to create a learning environment where collaboration and cooperation are more important than competition. Part of teaching involves empowering students so they leave a class more aware of

Groundwork

.... 87

inner and outer resources. If teachers are successful, their students develop skills and positive attitudes as they explore textual issues and ideas and discover how social and cultural experience affects self-worth and personal ingenuity. There are many serious problems, such as drugs, homelessness, and devastating family relationships, about which teachers can do little. Yet teachers can provide opportunities for students to shape their experiences into poems, essays, and short stories that may provide a different perspective. However this process needs to be encouraged: Forty-five-minute teaching periods, student resistance, and lack of sufficient faculty encouragement by school administrators often discourage even the most conscientious teachers. Still, recognizing the difficulties and valuing the process of imaginative expression is a first step in nourishing students' expressive capabilities.

Another factor working against our use of imagination and creativity is the amount of television we watch as our primary source of information and entertainment. Our imaginations and ideas are shaped by what we watch and experience. Constant television viewing tends to deteriorate a person's capacity to form images, to create stories, and to assign meaning. Teachers need to be aware that watching so much television can be a serious impediment to learning if they want students to express original ideas. I recognize that in some cases, the only common culture students have is what they watch on television. Although it may be helpful to use television as a way to begin, I find that sharing stories allows students to expand their imagination and helps to create a common culture in the classroom.

Telling students not to watch so much television is a waste of time and breath. For many, it's a legal way to stop the world. What teachers can do is to teach students techniques that help them to regain access to their own imaginations. Because many students do not read for pleasure they are unaccustomed to imagining characters, creating a physical setting in which the story can take place, or devising a plot that is not heavily influenced by one they've seen on television. Sharing old stories is one way to create community—all students hear the same story though they do not all respond in the same way. Working with a story that may be only a few paragraphs long is a good way to begin the development of access to imagination. The more stories students hear or read, the less dependent they will become on television plot and character portrayal. The following story from Cameroon provides many opportunities for character and story development.

The Bride-Price

There were once two brothers. The older brother worked very hard, saved his money, and secured a bride with a fine bride-price. His younger brother was astonished to discover his brother had given his wife's parents two bags of gold for their daughter to become his wife. The younger brother, who was called Smallboy, said, "I would not give more than a halfpenny for mine."

The villagers laughed at Smallboy and called him a fool. His older brother said, "Take this halfpenny, and do not return until you bring home a wife."

Smallboy was allowed to leave with only the clothes on his back and the halfpenny given to him by his older brother. He walked until he was hot and tired. When he saw a woman selling fruit he asked, "Will you trade me a piece of fruit for my half-penny?" She felt sorry for him and made the trade.

Smallboy took the fruit and walked until he came to a house. He asked the owner of the house, "Will you let me rest myself in your house until morning? It is very late, and I am tired." When the man agreed, Smallboy asked, "Will you put my fruit where your chickens cannot eat it?" The man took the fruit and put it in a safe place. They all went to sleep. In the morning Smallboy asked for his fruit. The man saw it had been pecked and apologized. He gave Smallboy a chicken as compensation.

Smallboy continued on his journey. Towards evening he arrived at the house of a man who had many goats. "I am very tired. Will you let me rest myself in your camp until morning?" The man took pity on Smallboy and let him enter. "Will you put my chicken where your goats cannot eat it?" asked Smallboy. The man took the chicken and tethered it in a safe place. They all went to sleep. In the morning Smallboy asked for his chicken, and the man saw it had been trampled to death. He gave Small-boy a goat to mend matters.

Smallboy thanked the man, took the goat, and continued on his journey. He arrived at a camp where there were many fine cattle. He asked a herdsman, "Will you let me rest myself in your camp until morning?" When the herdsman consented, Smallboy asked, "Will you put my goat where it will be safe from your cows?" The herdsman agreed and they all went to sleep. In the morning Smallboy asked for his goat. The herdsman saw the goat was dead and gave Smallboy a cow in exchange.

Continuing on his journey, Smallboy noticed some people digging a shallow grave to bury a young girl who had just died. "Stop!" shouted Smallboy. "This girl deserves better treatment. Please take my cow in trade for her body." Bewildered, the people agreed. He carried the dead girl all day long. Towards dusk, he walked into a small village and went to see the Chief of the compound. "I am very tired and my young wife is already asleep by the side of the road. Will you allow us to rest ourselves with you until morning?" The Chief agreed and told Smallboy to carry his wife to the hut of his daughters where she could rest safely until morning. Smallboy carried the dead girl into the daughters' hut and covered her with a blanket before he went to the men's hut to sleep.

In the morning Smallboy walked to the daughters' hut and asked, "Please wake my wife, and tell her it is time for us to leave." The girls tried to wake his wife and discovered she was dead. The Chief was very upset and asked Smallboy to take one of his daughters to make up for the loss of his wife.

Smallboy chose the girl who most appealed to him. They left the compound with gifts and food for their journey. Laughing, he returned to his village with his bride. He met with his older brother, "Look! This young woman is my wife. Is she not as wonderful as your wife?" His brother agreed and congratulated Smallboy. Smallboy was content.

SUGGESTIONS FOR EXPLORATION

Reflect: It is one year since Smallboy returned from his travel. He is the father of a child and decides that Smallboy is no longer an appropriate name. He decides to hold a contest to see who can give him a new name that best fits him.   1

Write: Smallboy's criteria for new name.

Divide: Into groups of four.

Decide: How your group will hold the naming contest. How will the contest will be judged?

Create: The drama of naming Smallboy in your group.

Share: Dramas.

Choose: Name for Smallboy as a group.

	Create:	Naming ceremony for Smallboy.
	Reflect:	On issues which contributed to selecting his name.

2

Reflect: Smallboy is now a member of the Village Council and is known as a very wise man. Many people come to him to ask him answers to important questions. Smallboy always finds an answer that satisfies the questioner.

Write: On a small piece of paper an important question you wish to ask Smallboy.

Collect: Questions and redistribute them to class members.

Write: Story that answers the question as if you were Smallboy.

Divide: Into pairs. One person asks the question, second person answers as Smallboy. Reverse roles.

Share: Questions and story answers with class.

3

Reflect: Smallboy's children ask him about his life.

Create: An episode from Smallboy's life that he chooses to share with his children. Decide how old the children are and why they want to hear about their father's life.

Divide: Into small groups. Make a short drama that shows the episode. Decide from whose point of view you will make the drama. Perhaps it is Smallboy's mother or father who sees what is happening. It could be a young friend or a village elder. Think about how the choice of point of view affects the drama and the tone of the action.

Share: Dramas.

Create: An episode from Smallboy's life at a particular age. $\boxed{4}$

Share: Episodes. Decide where and when the sharing is taking place.

Reflect: On the episode as if a period of time had passed.

Consider:
- What subsequent changes in Smallboy's life affect his memory of the episode?
- What effect did the episode have on his life after the episode?
- Why did he remember this particular episode rather than another?

Reflect: On the process of remembering.

Suggestions for Dealing with Outside Influences

- Create a way to begin class that helps focus students, such as standing in a circle and holding hands for thirty seconds in silence.
- Encourage students to suggest ways to integrate what is happening outside the classroom with what takes place inside the classroom.
- Pay attention to how the students enter and leave your class. If the class generally enters noisily and suddenly comes in quietly, take the time you need to find out what is going on. Students are pleased when a teacher notices them, when they feel that they matter.
- Even if a teacher cannot change or improve events in students' lives, encouraging the sharing of concerns may alleviate some distress.

Sourcework

A Way of Thinking

I title this chapter "Sourcework" to describe my hope that the material in this chapter will be used as a map for readers to find their own approach to teaching language and literature. I suggest possible strategies because I know the importance of sharing ideas and examples. Ultimately, teachers need to develop their own structures based on who they are, where and whom they teach, and their specific administrative and faculty goals. What I intend is to nourish the processes and resources by which teachers are empowered to create and express ways of teaching language and literature that connect students to the text, the self, and the world.

In my use of storymaking and drama I follow certain guidelines that make it possible for students, regardless of age and experience, to begin, despite fears, worries, anxieties, or doubts. I share these ideas to give teachers a way to reflect on selected works of literature so they can make their own choices based on their particular situation and personal preference.

I divided the class sessions into segments of forty-five minutes, knowing this is the maximum time many teachers have to teach. However, teachers can choose to work in shorter segments as long as they appropriately introduce and bring closure to the lesson.

Guidelines for Storymaking and Drama in the Classroom

- Storymaking and drama are tools to facilitate comprehension, expression, and communication.
- All tasks are structured to promote community and collaborative rather than competitive learning.
- The initial task is to establish dialogue between students and teacher and among students.

- Everyone who speaks must preface comments by saying "I" rather than "You"—for example, "I think," "I feel," or "I wonder."

- No person may comment on another person's comment. Each person speaks from her or his point of view. This sometimes makes no sense to students until I explain what I mean. Suppose a student says, "I think the character in the story is stupid and should be thrown out of school." The next student says, "What a crazy idea!" Soon people are shouting at each other, defending their ideas and attacking everyone else's. No one is listening to anyone or reflecting on possibilities. So, if a student says, "What a crazy idea," I stop the person to ask, "How do you think the character should be dealt with?" or "What might be your solution to the problem?" I encourage the student to be articulate and concise. If there is disagreement about outcomes and consequences I *focus* the discussion so we are all clear about the topic and its relationship to the text at hand.

- I give students very little time in which to paint, write, sculpt or role play, perhaps thirty seconds or a minute to paint or sculpt an image and never more than five to ten minutes to write a page of dialogue, a poem, or a short story. I do this to encourage their spontaneity and to discourage self-censoring and premature judgment. I accept their discomfort and, in some cases, anger with little or no comment, because I know their attitudes, feelings, and sense of time will change as they gain experience and trust. I never analyze or interpret their work.

- When students begin to talk about their imagery they often feel tentative and unsure about what to say. To ease their discomfort, I limit their time by suggesting each person take thirty seconds to share or to describe an aspect of the image in one sentence. If they don't know what to say I may ask a question about color choice or ask the class if they have questions. Sometimes the barrier is shame—a student is afraid to talk. Trust takes time. To break the ice I ask them to say one sentence about their process of imagemaking.

- If I have students who seem to talk forever I challenge them, in a friendly tone of voice, to limit their remarks to two or three sentences. I liken this practice to making clear, articulate statements when they write essays or answer exam questions. Students find it useful to consider the essence of their ideas and how to express them more economically. If a student is unable to do this I sometimes give the person all the time she or he needs to express the ideas and then ask the class to suggest ways to focus and tighten the utterance. I explain how we are using the technique of collaborative learning to solve a problem all of us occasionally encounter.

- I do not allow people to denigrate their work or the work of others. I am very firm about how people introduce their work. If someone says, "Well, I'm not very good at painting, but . . ." I stop the student and ask that he or she begin again without the self-criticism.

- If people laugh in ways that I feel reflect self-consciousness or feelings of discomfort, I use the occurrence as an aid for learning and ask the class to consider their laughter and the source from which it comes. I work with the group until the class can respond more comfortably. I avoid being judgmental and focus my description to what I perceive is happening, why I think the response does not promote learning, and how we can use the experience to consider new possibilities.

- If no one volunteers to share their work I may ask people in turn and go around the room, especially in the beginning of the course. Sometimes I ask the person who has just shared to select the next person to share, prefacing the selection with, "I'm curious about . . ." or "I'd like to know about . . .'s work." If I feel a problem is causing the silence I ask why no one is volunteering. If no one answers I describe how I feel about their reticence and suggest possible solutions. If the silence continues I may talk about ways I acted in the past that have included enduring the silence for however long it lasts or giving notice that if no one volunteers I will leave, which I then do. (I don't recommend leaving, nor is it possible for most teachers to do so, but it makes for a good story and usually helps me to stimulate class discussion about why people are having difficulty sharing and what's going on in and among group members.) I remind the class that for me the essence of teaching and learning is dialogue, not mono- logue. I need and want to know what the group is thinking and feeling in order to help students engage in dialogue. Although this process takes time, ultimately it makes more effective student interaction possible, especially when the class realizes how much I value spontaneous participation.

- If a topic is controversial I structure the discussion very carefully to make sure everyone who wants to talk has the chance. Equally important, everyone is encouraged to listen to each other. Response tasks (tasks that people do in response to the activity of one member or a small group) provide focus, as does a bit of silence before the next person speaks. Writing the essence of each person's idea on the board gives everyone a chance to reflect and allows the speaker to make sure she or he has been heard correctly.
- Periodically I take the pulse of the group to check out how people are feeling, if there are issues we need to discuss, and any suggestions students might have to improve, develop, or enhance the class experience. I do this even when I think the class is going well. This gives students a chance to vent concerns or share ideas before a crisis occurs and demonstrates my concern for them.
- I always invite students to share a relevant monologue, paragraph, stanza . . . just to whet our appetites. This encourages students to bring material into class without having to be responsible for a whole play, story, or novel. I also encourage students to share their own work in process and carefully structure the feedback to inspire the student to deepen, expand, extend, or hone—to feel appreciated.
- I offer selected and appropriate anecdotes about my life as a way to encourage students to feel more comfortable when talking about themselves. I explain the nature of sharing personal response as the difference between "One" and "I" and explain my use of the levels of sharing: public, personal, and private. In some cultures the level of discomfort when sharing anything about one's self is so high that students refrain from saying anything. I help students understand the importance I place on sharing and explain the notion of the wisdom of the psyche, that what is shared voluntarily is appropriate.
- I actively encourage diverse interpretations and am careful not to suggest mine is necessarily best or right. Students are expected to talk about why they think what they think and how they arrive at their conclusions.
- I carefully structure the beginning and the ending of class so that I am aware of issues that may affect closure and can make necessary last-minute choices. What matters is that

students leave class feeling that we have reached a place
where it's OK to stop and they are ready to go to their
next class.

The Power of Imagemaking

"Words, words, words! I am sick and tired of words. Why do we have
to talk so much and say so little?" said a disaffected tenth-grader.
"What else do we have?" asked a classmate. The response was
silence, a few shoulder shrugs. This was school, high school. What
else could there possibly be?

For teachers willing to explore nontraditional techniques, there
are many alternatives to enhance and deepen learning. Since the day
I shared the tenth-grader's frustration I began to discover the truth of
what is often mentioned in textbooks but not so often practiced, that
our sensory mechanisms differ. Some of us learn best through visual
means, others through auditory stimulation, still others through
kinesthetic approaches. Therefore, including two- and three-dimen-
sional imagemaking (paints and clay) as part of a multifaceted
approach to teaching language and literature naturally follows. There
are many benefits. Sharing images is a fine way to encourage dialogue, especially among shy or self-conscious students. Looking at
images makes connections possible between and among people who
might otherwise have thought they had nothing in common. Observ-
ing a group's imagery gives individuals a sense of the whole and,
perhaps, their place within it. I remember the day I asked students to
paint a talisman image to keep them safe in times of danger. A few
painted religious symbols, which were immediately recognizable, but
most painted abstract images that intrigued and puzzled the class. As
we went around the room sharing our paintings one student
observed, "I didn't realize how many of us feel unsafe." She had
noticed the number of students who painted a small self in a large and
frightening world. Her comment evoked many responses including
words to current pop songs. This experience led us back to the text
and a deeper understanding of the main character's struggles.

One of the crucial issues in imagemaking is how the teacher and
students process and reflect on what is produced. Every student feels
vulnerable, and no one wants to be judged, even though most expect
criticism. Because it takes time to build trust and to heal old wounds
about not being good enough, I encourage teachers and students to
begin simply. When a student doesn't know what to say and mumbles,

"I have a lot of red in my picture," I nod and may ask if he associates red with a particular idea. Usually, in the beginning, there is no answer, but gradually, almost imperceptively, students have more to say and more to ask.

Once, when asked to talk about her image, the student responded, "This is my image, and I have no idea what it means." Across the room another student said, "Your image reminds me of the first day of spring—kind of cold and bleak, but still—the first day of spring." The student looked at her work and smiled, utterly contented.

Materials for Imagemaking

When I take out the little pots of finger paints students' reactions run the gamut from, "Oh great! I haven't painted since I was a little kid," to "Oh no! I hate to get my fingers dirty," to "This isn't kindergarten, why are we using kids' toys?" However, given no choice but to begin, most students come to value paints as an opportunity to express ideas and feelings in a way that does not depend on words. Throughout the course students keep their images, which are dated and titled in notebooks, to refer back to when they have to write papers on specific texts. The collected annotated images also act as a kind of journal, recording personal responses in color, shape, and line. Many students have worked their way through writer's block by painting images of what they think and feel but for which they currently have no words. Imagemaking doesn't replace words; it augments, enhances, and provides a way of knowing, particularly when the main mode is stuck. Putting one's fingers into little jars of paint is very different from using an implement. Precise images are almost impossible to make, yet the nontraditional material enables participants to evoke ideas and feelings, knowledge that they did not know they had. If you plan to use finger paints make sure everyone has access to a minimum of six colors (red, blue, brown, black, green, and yellow). Some students buy sets that include only red, blue, yellow, and green thinking these are enough. Yet inevitably, strong feelings emerge that require black and brown, and the other colors just don't satisfy, nor are they able to get the colors they want just from mixing the colors they have.

When I'm unable to use finger paints because none are available or there are too many students in the class, I use fat crayons or pastels and try to ensure that each person has access to the same minimum of six colors. I'm not exactly sure why pens, pencils, fine brushes, and felt-tip markers don't have the same liberating effect that finger paints have; but I think it has something to do with our association of pens and pencils with words. The thin unforgiving lines of felt-tip markers and the inability of many to paint fulfilling images with thin water-color brushes makes these materials less satisfying. However, if these are all that is available, use them or pens or pencils rather than avoiding imagemaking. Occasionally, the surprise students feel when asked to paint or draw images makes possible new responses to old subjects.

Relationship—to people, objects, or place—is a key factor in the study of literature. Working with clay enables students to use space, shape, size, focus, and texture to explore relationship. Working three-dimensionally encourages students to discover how characters relate to (or ignore) one another in a particular scene or context and to make their ideas concrete in a flexible, changeable medium. I often ask students to sculpt an image of how two characters relate to one another at the beginning of the text. I then ask them to select a point in their reading where these relationships change. Sculpting a second image allows for reflection. What caused the changes? How do the characters feel about these changes? Perhaps we sculpt these same characters at the end of the text. Having all the sculptures available enhances a focused discussion where differences are explored and examined. Whether the sculptures are concrete or abstract, the ideas evoked by the making of a clay image create an exciting way of talking about a piece of literature. I am constantly surprised by the power of clay to liberate words in people I have previously, and erroneously, thought of as inarticulate or even worse, shallow thinkers.

I have used clay that never hardens as well as clay that can be baked in an oven and saved; both have advantages. Generally, my students and I prefer the nonhardening clay because it lasts longer and is easier to manage. Regardless of their initial reaction to working with clay in the classroom, in very little time, many students begin to manipulate the clay as soon as they enter the class. Most tell me they find it relaxes them and helps them to focus better. Some have taken balls of clay into exams to use when they cannot think of an answer on a test. No, they aren't hiding answers in the clay, but somehow, playing with the clay aids in their process of remembering.

Both paint and clay provide nonverbal opportunities to evoke ideas and feelings. These experiences frame the discussion or writing that follows and enable students to explore ideas using many sensory possibilities. Although their use takes time, the language use that follows is rich and complex. Even bright, articulate students who have good access to their knowing learn more about what they think and feel when they paint and sculpt as part of their classroom activity. Sharing images supports and helps to develop independent thinking and subsequent expression.

Structuring a Class Session

I divide my class planning into four parts: selecting a text, choosing a focus, developing activities, and evoking reflection. I make my choices so that I am clear about where my class is going even though I never know exactly how we will get there. It's a tricky balancing act. Too much direction leaves no room for students to affect their learning; too little direction makes it difficult for students to begin. Only experience and a too-large number of mistakes help to hone teacher effectiveness.

Selecting a Text

I generally select the text, if I have a choice, based on what my students are ready to read, but it is always a text I enjoy. I take into account what is appropriate for their grade, age, and experience as well as issues that concern them. But sometimes, if I sense trouble brewing, I may choose textual material that will help me and the class to discuss underlying issues. For example, if a class is worried about exams, I might use an old story such as "A Community of Knowing" (see "Knowing How and When to Begin," p. 26) to talk about ways to defuse their worries and strategies for successful test taking. I may not spend the whole period on this text, but I use the primary theme to segue into the next text. Occasionally, I come across a short poem or story that moves me so much I decide to share it with the class for the same reason I occasionally share a personal anecdote. It's a way for the class to know me a bit better and a way for me to share literary pieces that move me. Sometimes my enthusiasm and excitement move a student to ask for the title of the book. The literary works I selected to use in this book reflect my wish to explore a variety of style, authorial experience, and cultural diversity.

The texts that I have chosen for this book exemplify material that interests me and my students. The myths and tales scattered throughout these pages are stories I find personally meaningful and, at the same time, enable me to explore ideas without becoming didactic. I chose the two novels, *The Joy Luck Club* by Amy Tan and *When The Legends Die* by Hal Borland, because they are powerful and compelling works that offer students an opportunity to experience complex and intriguing lives. *Romeo and Juliet* is a play that students

Sourcework

.... 101

enjoy and, at the same time, it enables them to talk about important issues that often affect their lives. In the section on autobiography I chose texts to which my students and I continually returned, always finding something new or important to share or question.

Choosing a Focus

My choice of focus for a particular session evolves from a phrase, image, or concept that is evoked by or comes from the text. I look for a theme that is large enough to encompass diverse and complex ideas and feelings. Selecting the focus takes me almost as much time as planning the activities that follow from my choice. If I'm working with a large work like an autobiography or a novel, I teach from a new focus each period, but when I put them all together, all foci form a whole. Choosing an evocative focus takes time and experience, but I believe the process is worth the work because it clarifies all subsequent work and helps me to direct subsequent discussion. Given all my preparation I am always amazed when students and faculty tell me, "I really like that you're so unstructured!" I guess it's the difference between beginners and professionals; the professionals make everything they do look spontaneous, no matter how difficult the task.

Before I plan any activity the focus acts as a beacon, helping me to organize our class journey. Although I don't usually share the focus with the class, it's not a secret. If I'm asked, I certainly say what it is and, if asked, how I came to select it. I don't routinely share the focus I've selected because students then tend to censor themselves by asking: Does this fit the focus? Or, is my question relevant to the focus?

What affects my choice of focus is the process of paring a piece of text to an essential idea or phrase. However, experienced teachers do not always choose the same focus. In a sense, whatever focus stimulates, challenges, or excites the class tends to be a good choice. I often use the focus as the first image to be painted or sculpted. I may also use it as the title for a poem, short story, or piece of drama that I ask my students to create. I generally use the focus to frame the reflection that comes at the end of a session as a way to weave together all the individual strands and aspects we have explored as a group.

Developing Activity for a Class Session

Generally, the first activity is designed to center students' attention on a theme, image, or concept with which we will be working. I often begin by asking students to paint or sculpt an image to help them particularize their thoughts and feelings. The activity provides the basis for everything that follows. I alternate thinking and doing so the class is able to recharge its batteries and regenerate resources, a process similar to Shakespeare's use of comic scenes in tragedies such as the gatekeeper's scene in *Macbeth*, the skull scene in *Hamlet*, and the comic sexual scenes of Nurse in *Romeo and Juliet*.

Each subsequent activity alternates personalized response with group sharing to allow both individual and group points of view to emerge and to stress the importance and power of diverse ideas and experience. I also teach collaborative learning techniques by structuring activity where the large group helps an individual or small group to deepen, extend, develop, or change the work that has been shared. I always encourage individuals and small groups to ask for help from the large group to provide individual learning in a public arena. This reinforces the notion that it's good to ask for help, to admit when one is stuck, and to openly enter into a dialogue with others about one's work where there is no premature judgment or hindering criticism.

If the group looks bewildered by the task they have been given I stress the specific task and address all questions to the task. For example, I asked a class to sculpt an image of "me" and "not me." I was bombarded with questions such as: "Do you mean what I think of me or what others think of me?" or "Do you mean what I know is not me or what I hope is not me?" To these and other questions I repeat the task and remind them that their responsibility is to define their answer as long as it satisfies the given task. I sometimes have to point out that what they really want to know is what will satisfy me, and what satisfies me is a response that addresses the problem in a personally fulfilling manner. This takes time, but the time is worth the effort. When students trust that the teacher wants honest responses, which are treated respectfully, their work can often be spectacular. If I sense that what I've designed isn't working because I've miscalculated, I change direction. If I think the class is not working well, I address the problem of their response. If I'm not sure, my choice depends on the rapport I have with the class, the pressure we're under to finish working with the text, or my intuition.

Evoking Reflection

Although all parts of any session are integral to learning, most often when we reflect as a class ideas make sense, and connections to self and text are made. I may ask a direct question: "What do you think of today's work?" or "How do you feel about character . . . 's choice?" or

Sourcework

.... 103

"Any comments, questions, or suggestions about what we've been exploring?" I allow silence for personal reflection before probing. In the beginning many students resist sharing anything. They consider their response to be too personal or inappropriate. I find I have to keep questioning, supporting, reinforcing, and gradually, the class responds. There is no set time, nor do I insist everyone say something. I encourage everyone to talk about what's going on for them at least once a week. I remind them that only through sharing can we know how we are reacting, what we are feeling and thinking.

If all else fails I might go around the room and ask everyone to use one sentence to say what's going on. At times I have asked a class to paint or sculpt their response or to title their reaction to the class. I am often asked why it matters so much that they speak up even when they might prefer to remain silent. I respond by sharing highlights from my years of experience and tell them that the groups who have learned how to reflect in class are those who often make the deepest connections between their inner and outer lives. They begin to value their singular response to a text and gain confidence in their capacity as readers and makers. Very often it is only during the process of reflection that students come to understand the deep and complex meaning that underlies their symbolic paintings and sculpture.

In order to encourage active student participation I might ask if anyone has a question to ask, either of the group or of a particular person. In the beginning there are usually few questions, but once the ice is broken and the questions emerge, the resulting discussion and exchange stimulates and challenges everyone.

Routinely saving time for reflection creates an opportunity that students learn to welcome, if only because it allows them to go to their next class with the sense that the work in this class is finished, that they are more, rather than less, ready to go to their next class.

Working with Poetry

Jeanne Walker wrote a series of poems based on real and imaginary headlines from the *National Enquirer*. Afterwards, she said to me, "I've been writing a lot, but I'm not quite sure what I've written." When I read them I thought they sounded like dramatic monologues and suggested she have a reading to hear the power of her words spoken out loud. Her puzzlement was caused by the contrast between the form in which she was expert—poetry—and the dramatic monologues she had created, which were more drama than poetry. She subsequently incorporated the monologues into a play and some of them were included individually in her poetry collection *Coming Into History*. I chose to use four of her poems to exemplify ways in which I work with poetry because I find her poems powerful, evocative, and stimulating. Each time I read them it is as if I am reading them for the first time.

Poems, like any piece of literature, are not automatically meaningful to every reader. All too often, the only time students read poetry is when they're required to do so for English class or to pass an exam. It's difficult to make a person understand, connect to, or like a particular work just because someone some place has decided a particular work is important. Good teachers know that it isn't enough to teach poetic form, that we have to help students to connect their own experience to that of the poet so the students' experience resonates with their inner life. When we do this our students are more likely to be turned on by the idea of reading poetry. I have selected to share the way I might explore these four poems because I think they will appeal to students and teachers alike, a necessary starting point for any meaningful work with poetry. Equally important, I hope this approach to working with the selected poetry will suggest ideas to help teachers to make required poetry reading less of a treatment and more of a treat. I offer four ways to work with each poem, creating a different guiding center for each structure. When I teach, the idea that I select to frame the session comes from my reading of the poem and my understanding of my class's needs, but many others are equally valid and possible. I encourage teachers to plan each session keeping in mind the importance of connection—of students to the text and of students' inner lives to their outer worlds. All directions are for the teacher to give to the students.

Human Boy Found in Indian Jungle Among Wolf Pack

He had apparently been nursed by a she-wolf and
taught to hunt with the males.
For Derek Davis

I'll be your subject till the rainy season.
I stay in these white rooms because I want to.
But what you have taught me takes root in my brain.
Now I picture myself dressed and sitting
on your chair, talking. I like to push
my finger across the little insects you say
spell my name in your essays. I like
to see how the world is hardly any bigger

than a green melon and how one hand can make
it spin around. Now I believe the days
have names and that they live on a piece
of paper. Every night I practice loving
this blouse you gave me, which smells like a
human woman. But her smell quarrels
with the odor of my mother's stinging fur.
Inside my brain they fight like two cheetahs.

My mother taught me to run on all four legs.
I could follow the pack of silver fur
through the brushwood of the timberland,
flying after a fox like a ray of light
the moon had hurled into the stupid dark.

The snarling jungle vines were my veins.
I circled the bitter bark of the banyan tree
quiet as a python. My skin became
the nine different roughnesses of moss.
My joy was fluent as the underwater brooks.
Lying belly down on the steaming ferns
I could hear the scree of the small green bird,
almost out of range of human ears,
above the bellowing mountain waterfall.

It isn't grief, exactly, that I feel.
Doesn't grief finally loosen its claws,
fly off and let its victim rest?
But this goes on and on. Beyond my wall
I see the amber streetlights burn like violent eyes
that want me again. I go out and howl,
but they never come. Tell me, is there
a time when it gets too late to go back?

SUGGESTIONS FOR EXPLORATION

Time:	45 minutes	1
Text:	Human Boy Found in Indian Jungle Among Wolf Pack	
Focus:	A territory with no map	
Read:	Poem out loud.	

Paint:	Image of boy in jungle.
Write:	Words that describe his feelings.
Paint:	Image of boy in the white rooms.
Write:	Words that describe his feelings.
Share:	Images and words.
Select:	A sentence that moves you. Write it down. Think about why it is important to you.
Share:	Sentences in whatever order feels meaningful to you.
Reflect:	On what it means to be in strange territory without a map.

2

Time:	45 minutes
Text:	Human Boy Found in Jungle Among Wolf Pack
Focus:	Grief with no name
Read:	Poem out loud.
Sculpt:	An image of grief.
Write:	Words that you associate with grief.
Share:	Images and any words you choose to share.
Create:	One sentence to describe your grief as if you were the boy.
Share:	Sentences.
Reflect:	On ideas of grief evoked by poem.

Time: 45 minutes   **3**

Text: Human Boy Found in Indian Jungle Among Wolf Pack

Focus: A collision of cultures

Give: Each student a copy of poem.

Divide: Into pairs. One partner takes the role of Boy, the other
               takes the role of You.

Boy: Reads poem to You.

Create: Short monologue for You to respond to Boy.

Share: Monologues.

Discuss: As a whole group, issues raised either in role of Boy
               or You.

Reflect: On incidents of culture clash students have
               experienced. Consider how these events compare,
               contrast, or resonate with the boy's experiences in
               the poem.

Time: 45 minutes   **4**

Text: Human Boy Found in Indian Jungle Among Wolf Pack

Focus: When late becomes too late

Sculpt: Image of possibility.

Write: Words evoked by sculpture.

Share: Images and ideas.

Read: Poem out loud.

Sculpt: An image of the Boy's possibility.

Share: Sculptures.

Reflect: On the life of the Boy. What would you like to see happen to him? What do you think will happen to him?

After working with the poem using a variety of approaches, I might ask the class what they think of the poem, what the poem evokes in them, and how (or if) they are affected by the poem.

Woman Picked Up by UFO, Flown into Black Hole

Hello, it's Lettie here. How're you doing, Wanette!
You saw my picture in the paper? I know.
My hair looks weird. It turned white.
The air in the black hole burned it, somehow.
Like getting a permanent when you're pregnant.
Well, I have trouble believing I'm alive,
so I figure who cares about the hair?

I'll tell you about it if you have the time.
I was just parking in the Acme lot,
twelve thirty on the worst day of my life.
The night before, Hank came home as mean
as a Tom Cat with his tail on fire.
His boss rides him. He drinks. When he comes home,
he slaps me around. He got me on the ear
and I could hear church bells all morning.

It took me down. For one thing, see, I love him.
I tried to leave Hank once, last summer.
You didn't know that? Well, I thought I'd go
this time for sure, right after I got him groceries.
I worked myself up, crying, missing him.
And that's when I got zapped. Outside the store
like a tornado—a black funnel cloud,
huge as the fist of God. It sucked me up.

Don't ask why telling the story helps.
It's like putting something into the black hole.
Once you've been in, you have to find some way

Sourcework

.... 109

to occupy yourself. Like knitting, the way
Betty always knits, but with my mouth.
I wait for folks to call. The piece in the paper's
got me a few calls. But they don't call twice.

No I didn't hear no voices, just this wind
like a monster vacuum cleaner coming down.
Some mouth organ sobbed the blues inside my head.
I never saw them. The story got it wrong.
Who could see anything? My whole head was
black as the high school auditorium
that day the movie stuttered, then struck and tore
and Cooney couldn't find the right light switch.
Remember we got dizzy from the dark?

That's what a black hole is. Nothing. Nothing,
like I am without Hank. No job, no friends,
no self-respect, like being turned inside out,
like disappearing, first one finger up to
the knuckle, then everything. Being eaten.
This is personal, I know it is. Wanette!
Give me one minute. Wanette! Wanette?

SUGGESTIONS FOR EXPLORATION

1	**Time:**	45 minutes
	Text:	Woman Picked Up By UFO, Flown Into Black Hole
	Focus:	Telling my story
	Consider:	A time in your life when everything changed.
	Paint:	An image evoked by this experience.
	Write:	Some words that come to mind when you think about your story.
	Read:	Poem out loud.
	Write:	Letter to Lettie. Tell her who you are and why you are writing. You can write as yourself or as a character in her life.

Share:	Letters.
Reflect:	On the issue of what it means to tell your story.

2

Time:	45 minutes
Text:	Woman Picked Up By UFO, Flown Into Black Hole
Focus:	A black hole
Sculpt:	Image of you in relationship to black hole.
Share:	Sculptures.
Discuss:	Meaning(s) of black hole.
Read:	Poem out loud.
Write:	Two diary entries, one before Lettie is picked up and one after she is picked up. They can be from any time period. Include feelings, thoughts, sense impressions.
Share:	Entries.
Reflect:	On the image of the black hole.

3

Time:	45 minutes
Text:	Woman Picked Up By UFO, Flown Into Black Hole
Focus:	Shape-changing experience
Give:	Copy of poem to each student.
Read:	Poem out loud.
Select:	One sentence that attracts your attention.

Sourcework

.... 111

Paint:	An image of the sentence you have chosen, which becomes the title of your painting.
Share:	Images and titles.
Discuss:	Why you have chosen the sentence you selected. Think about why this sentence matters to you. How does it make you think about your own life?
Reflect:	On shape-changing experience in poem.

Time:	45 minutes	4
Text:	Woman Picked Up By UFO, Flown Into Black Hole	
Focus:	Being in a black hole	
Paint:	Image of black hole.	
Write:	Words that come to mind.	
Share:	Images and words.	
Read:	Poem out loud.	
Role play:	As Lettie, create a short monologue that describes her life in the black hole.	
Share:	Monologues using "I."	
Reflect:	On black hole as a metaphor and as reality.	

After the class has explored the poem I might devise some activities using two poems. For example, what might Lettie say to the boy found in the Indian Jungle about her black hole experience? How might the boy respond to Lettie were she to end up in his white rooms? Make a sculpture of Lettie and the boy in relationship. What information do you use to make your sculpture?

Meteoroid Falls in Farmer's Back Yard

Hold the check. No price you fellas quote me
will get you my quarter acre for your Park.
I'm writing to you—whoever gets this letter
at the Department of the Interior—to say
I could shave and put on my suit and drive
to Farmer's Mutual Bank and have
the young Wilson kid withdraw enough to keep
me till I'm ninety. I don't believe in taking
from the State. Or giving to it, either.
I think a man should keep what is his own,
even if it's no good to him and the only thing
that he can do is stick it six feet under.

But what I wanted to say when I began—
I believe I saw this star when I was fourteen.
I grew up on this farm. I had a black pony
named King, and one August at sunset
my mother sent me for Virginia Slade,
the slow midwife down the road a ways.
My youngest sister was struggling to be born.
I didn't go back to gawk at women's business.
I swam, against the rules, in Johnson's pond,
where a broken stone slashed my left foot.
It bled like a stuck pig. I couldn't go home.
All night I lay in an alfalfa field,
smelling dust and greenness. I was naked.
Black, lumpy dirt clotted under my back
and the nettles scratched my forearms. But
what has stuck with me is that queer star,
how I had to squint a certain way
and lie on my side to get it. I thought
I'd seen a new star, that everything would change,
a clean sweep, that I would be important.
I was eating blueberries, sweet little worlds
one after another, till I was full and sleepy
as someone who had conquered everything.
After that I worked and planned and saved,
too crowded to inquire what star I'd seen.
But I carried it the way a girl would carry
a thorny white rose pressed in her pocket.

It pierced through everything I ever did,
my little sister's birthstar. She was my
favorite. She's been dead sixty years.
She died of whooping cough. And I turned out
to be an ordinary farmer. This star
in my back yard, this gravelly piece of ash
seems like, by right, it should belong to me.

SUGGESTIONS FOR EXPLORATION

Time:	45 minutes	☐1
Text:	Meteoroid Falls in Farmer's Back Yard	
Focus:	Keeping what is mine	
Paint:	An image of birthstar.	
Title:	Image.	
Share:	Images and titles.	
Give out:	Copies of poem.	
Read:	Poem out loud.	
Create:	Short monologue that the farmer shares with his sister.	
Share:	Monologues.	
Reflect:	On what it means to "keep what is mine."	

Time:	45 minutes	☐2
Text:	Meteoroid Falls in Farmer's Back Yard	
Focus:	The presence of the past	

Read:	Poem out loud.
Sculpt:	Image of farmer as boy.
Sculpt:	Image of farmer as man at time of poem.
Share:	How the past has shaped who the farmer is now. Use lines from the poem to support your ideas.
Reflect:	On the issues evoked by the presence of the past.

3

Time:	45 minutes
Text:	Meteoroid Falls in Farmer's Back Yard
Focus:	Making connections
Read:	Poem out loud.
Divide:	Into groups of two. One person plays farmer as a boy of fourteen. The other plays man at time of poem.
Create:	Dialogue. Consider: What are the boy's questions? What are the man's questions? How does the boy live within the man? What might the man tell the boy he was were he able to have a meeting?
Exchange:	Roles.
Share:	What strikes you as important from the experience? Use part or whole of dialogue to enhance your telling.
Reflect:	On the process of making connection: between past and present, with self and a specific other.

4

Time:	45 minutes
Text:	Meteoroid Falls in Farmer's Back Yard

Sourcework

.... 115

Focus:	Saying no and saying yes
Read:	Poem out loud.
Write:	Letter farmer writes to the Department of the Interior.
Share:	Letters.
Design:	Memorial in clay or with paint that farmer creates for his land.
Share:	Designs and ideas that sparked them.
Reflect:	On poem and issues around saying no and saying yes.

After working with this poem the teacher might ask for questions that students have after reading and thinking about the poem. Instead of answering them, put all the questions on the board. Ask students to reflect on the nature of the questions and which, if any, they would like to address, and why the question interests them.

Beauty Queen Has Monster Child

*She has vowed to reporters she
will keep the child. . . .*

I've saved my beauty against the name they call you.
Monster. I gave up caring about beauty—as though
one day the rhinestone button on my coat
grew wobbly. One thread gave up and then
one more, until the button was hanging
off the coat. Finally, I ripped it free.

I can still feel beauty when I want to,
small and hard as a button in my pocket
underneath my finger tips. I'll give it to you.
May it be all the looks you'll ever need,
my face fixed in magazines and films—
the high cheekbones, gray eyes, the mole
above my lip, my skin as soft as cornsilk.

This beauty is like a mask that traps me.
I've struggled against it lately like a deer
who thrashes its eyes out in a hunter's snare,
or an opossum who will gnaw its leg off
to get free. But now, with you here,
your face off center, barely but terribly wrong,
I see how to escape.

I'll go with you as you make your way
from that fixed beauty, as the milky way
spins away from earth, like flock on flock
of buttons, cut loose together, spiraling upward,
opening out to everything imperfect, deep and
promising. I want to learn to spin away
from those old finished pictures of myself
to wheel into the darkness where you are,
breathing further and further out, passing
winking stars that no astronomer
has thought of, till I get to the last,
brightest star, which is your face.

SUGGESTIONS FOR EXPLORATION

1	**Time:**	45 minutes
	Text:	Beauty Queen Has Monster Child
	Focus:	On being designated Beauty Queen
	Write:	Qualifications for becoming Beauty Queen.
	Share:	Qualifications and write them on the blackboard.
	Read:	Poem out loud.
	Paint:	Image of Beauty Queen with monster child.
	Reflect:	On being designated as beautiful and having a child labeled monster.

Sourcework

.... 117

Time:	45 minutes	2
Text:	Beauty Queen Has Monster Child	
Focus:	The meaning of monster	
Paint:	Image of monster.	
Write:	Words that come to mind.	
Share:	Images and words.	
Read:	Poem out loud.	
Imagine:	Being in a school yard surrounded by hundreds of chanting children who scream "monster" at you.	
Write:	A short chant or poem to help yourself feel better.	
Reflect:	On what it means to be called monster. Share chants or poems as part of the reflection.	

Time:	45 minutes	3
Text:	Beauty Queen Has Monster Child	
Focus:	Beauty as a mask that traps	
Sculpt:	Image of beauty as a mask.	
Share:	Sculptures.	
Read:	Poem out loud.	
Imagine:	Being beautiful. Think about what it might mean to your life.	
Reflect:	On how what we see affects our judgment.	

4

Time:	45 minutes
Text:	Beauty Queen Has Monster Child
Focus:	The last and brightest star
Read:	Poem out loud. Give everyone a copy.
Select:	One sentence of the poem that intrigues, angers, stimulates, or makes you wonder. Think about why you have chosen this sentence.
Paint:	Image of title.
Share:	Images.
Reflect:	On knowledge of self as the last and brightest star.

After working with the four poems the teacher might read (or have four students read) all the poems out loud. Reflect on the poems. Think about the nature and power of poetry. Ask students to look at poems—in books or songs or those they have written—and to share some poems that have moved them.

Since English teachers want to, and are probably obligated to, teach formal aspects of poetry and interpretation, I suggest they do so after whatever exercises they have chosen have enabled the students to make connections between themselves and the poems. Then teachers can explain—and students may well be interested to learn—just how the poem does what it does.

Working with Short Stories

I use two kinds of short stories in my classes, old stories that have no known author (legends, folk tales, myths, and fairy tales) and new stories that are written by a particular author. I have selected two old stories and two authored stories to exemplify techniques to help students become actively engaged in the process of reading, reflecting, and expressing ideas, thoughts and feelings generated by the stories.

Old Stories

Stories that have come down from the past, retold and collected, have no authorial voice. They are tales told by generations, storytellers who preserve the core while elaborating the story's edge. Usually the characters in these stories have no names and no identifying personal characteristics other than, for example, the third brother is a fool, the first sister is greedy, or the youngest daughter is beautiful. Also, there are few descriptions of motives, analysis, thoughts, and feelings. Old stories focus on action with little or no explanation. Working with old stories from around the world allows a group of disparate students to develop a sense of community as they share stories from a variety of cultures and times. The best description of the value of old stories comes from an eleven-year-old-girl who was taking my course, "Creating Theatre From Myth." In a discussion of the plays the group was creating she said, "I really like these old stories we've been using, they're so roomy. The ones we use in school are all filled up, there's no place for me inside them."

Old stories are seldom time- or place-specific—"In a time long ago" or "In a place far away" are common beginnings. In my experience, they provide a good way to help students learn to make connections between themselves and the character, issue, or conflict expressed by the story without having to deal with authorial voice or the specifics of time and place. Although they often contain powerful and profound ideas, the stories are usually simply told without elaboration. I include two old stories that have proven to be effective with many students; the first, "The Journey to Home," is Native American, and the second, "Coins of the Realm," is Japanese.

The Journey to Home

The people were bumping around in the dark and the cold. This was the life their parents had led, and this was the life that they would lead. Still, in time someone asked, "Is this all the world there is? Will we never have a better life?" But no one could answer the question.

One day, a strange creature appeared, burrowing its way to where the people were gathered. Someone asked the creature, "Is this all the world there is?"

Mole, for that was the creature's name, answered. "Well, sometimes I go to a place that feels different." Mole prepared to leave. The people were anxious and uncertain.

One of the people asked, "Mole, will you take us to the place where it feels different?"

"Yes," said Mole, "but remember that I take the earth from in front of me and I put it behind me. You must do the same. If you come with me you will never be able to return to the place you have known." The people argued and worried but in the end, they decided to follow Mole. They took the dirt from Mole and passed it along to the last person who put it behind all the people. It was a long, hard journey.

Suddenly, with no warning, Mole said, "This is where I must leave you. This is the place that feels different." The people begged him to stay but he said, "I am blind. I dig beneath the earth. I cannot stay with you."

After Mole left some of the braver people walked toward the warmth, stepped outside, and screamed with pain. They ran back to the others and said, "Let us go back. At least we were used to living in the dark and the cold." But they knew no way to return to the life they had lived.

At last they grew silent and listened to a tiny voice that spoke to them, "My children, do as I tell you, and your eyes will not hurt." She told them how to cover their eyes with their hands and to gradually open their eyes until their eyes were used to the new light.

When they were able to see they asked her, "Who are you? Can you help us? We are lost."

"Of course, my children. Do not fear. I am your Grandmother Spider, and if you follow my advice, all will be well. If you look to the east you will see Red Mountain. If you go there you will bleed to death from the wounds of the wild creatures who live there. If you look to the west you will see Black Mountain. If you go there you will starve to death, because nothing grows in that darkness. If you look to the north you will see White Mountain. If you go there, you will freeze to death from the cold. If you look to the south, you will see, very far away, Green Mountain. If you take this journey you will live to have children."

"But how will we know we have arrived?"

"You will see a creature you have never seen. Although it is not Mole, it will remind you of Mole. Although it is not Grandmother Spider, it will remind you of me. When you see this creature you will know you have arrived at the place of your new life." So the people huddled together during the long night, waiting to meet their first dawn.

With the coming of the sun, people grew restless. Some of the people said, "Green Mountain is too far away. Let us go to Red Mountain. We are brave enough to kill the creatures who would

Sourcework

.... 121

kill us. We will go. When we return, we will tell you what we found." The people who went to Red Mountain never came back.

A few, unwilling to follow the advice of Old Grandmother Spider, said, "Let us go to Black Mountain. We know how to live in the darkness." No one returned.

And many others, too impatient to walk to a place they could barely see said, "Let us go to White Mountain. Surely we can make our way." They left, but no one returned.

And now there were only two people, a woman and a man. They decided to follow Grandmother Spider's advice and began the long journey to Green Mountain. They walked, and they walked, and they walked but Green Mountain seemed no closer. They grew tired and discouraged and thought of stopping. But they remembered the people who had gone in other directions and not returned. They did the only thing they knew to do—they walked and kept on walking. They walked toward Green Mountain.

As they were walking, the woman noticed a creature she had never seen. The man urged her to keep away from the danger. At first the woman heeded his words, but her curiosity grew too strong. She walked closer to it and watched the creature stop and pull its head into its shell so it could not see. The woman laughed and said, "That creature reminds me of Mole."

The man joined the woman and noticed the pattern on the shell. "Oh! Those markings remind me of Grandmother Spider." They looked at each other and smiled. They had come to the place that was home.

SUGGESTIONS FOR EXPLORATION

Time:	45 minutes	1

Text: The Journey to Home

Focus: Is this all there is?

Tell: The Journey to Home.

Paint: An image of "Is this all there is?"

Write: An entry in your diary, as if you were one of the people who were bumping around in the dark before the arrival of Mole.

Share:	Images and diary entries.	

Share: Images and diary entries.

Create: In pairs, a dialogue between two of the people before the arrival of Mole.

Share: The essence of a few of the dialogues.

Reflect: On what underlies the question, "Is this all there is?"

2

Time: 45 minutes

Text: The Journey to Home

Focus: Choosing your own path

Tell: The Journey to Home.

Paint: A series of images of the journey of one of the people in the story. Consider the dangers, the possibilities, the reality of what the person encountered.

Title: Your series of images.

Share: Images and titles, using "I," as if you were the person whose journey you painted.

Sculpt: A memorial statue in honor of the person whose journey you painted.

Reflect: On the notion of choosing your own path using your sculpture as a reference point.

3

Time: 45 minutes

Text: The Journey to Home

Focus: On leaving what you know

Tell: The Journey to Home

Sourcework

··· 123

Sculpt: An image of "no way to return to what is known."

Share: Images.

Paint: A talisman image to help you through the dark times.

Write: Some soft words for some hard times.

Share: Talisman images and soft words for hard times.

Reflect: On what it might mean not to be able to return to what
                you know.

Time: 45 Minutes   4

Text: The Journey to Home

Focus: Changing perspective

Tell: The Journey to Home.

Paint: An image of a moment on the journey as if you were
                one of the people in the story.

Title: Image.

Write: What your thoughts and feelings are of this moment as
                if you were a person on the journey.

Consider: It is now twenty years later. Think about the moment
                you selected. Think about your life now.

Write: How you think and feel about this moment now that
                twenty years have passed.

Share: Initial thoughts and feelings after twenty years.

Reflect: On how (or if) your perspective is affected by time and
                experience.

Coins of the Realm

There were two laborers whose custom it was to take a short nap after lunch. Usually both men quickly fell asleep as their work was hard and the day was long, but one day one of the men could not sleep. As he lay on the ground listening to his friend snore, he noticed a bee fly into the sleeping man's nose. Astonished, he watched until the bee flew away, and the man woke up saying, "What a dream I have had."

After hearing the dream his friend said, "That is a wonderful dream. I would like to buy it from you." The second man laughed. But the first man persisted, "Please, let me buy your dream." The second man finally agreed; he was too poor to turn down such a gift.

That night, when the first man went home he told his wife what had happened. She asked, "Are you crazy? We have barely enough money to feed our children, and you spend your money buying someone else's dream? What was so marvelous about this dream?"

Her husband said, "The dream was about going to Osaka, finding the richest man there, digging in his garden, and un-covering a vase full of gold buried among the roots of the tallest tree. Is this not a wonderful dream?"

His wife said, "Yes, it is a fine dream, but dreams are only dreams. And, this is not your dream, it is a dream you have purchased."

"It is my dream now. If only I can find the money to go to Osaka, I will dig in the garden of the rich man where the tall tree grows and uncover the vase filled with gold. Please go to your parents, and ask them to lend us the money. When I return we will have enough money to live on for the rest of our lives."

His wife finally agreed to help, went to her parents, and told them about the dream her husband had bought and his desire to go to Osaka. They laughed at her and the foolishness of her husband, but finally they lent her the money.

Early the next morning the husband set off for Osaka with only the clothes on his back and a bit of food to eat as he walked. The journey took four days, but the man's spirits were high. Upon entering the city he asked five people to give him the name of the richest man in Osaka, and each person gave him the same name. Convinced, he knocked at the man's gate and asked to speak to the master of the house. The servants refused to admit him, but the man persisted. When the master heard about the jar of gold he told the servants to tell the man to return early the next morning. "If there is a jar of gold under my tree why should I share

Sourcework

.... 125

it with a poor man? I will dig up the vase and take the contents. He can have the vase."

The servants and the master went out to the tallest tree in the garden and began to dig. At first they found nothing but roots but when the hole was deep enough for a man to stand in, one of the servants uncovered a bit of the vase. Eagerly, the master pulled out the vase and opened it up and looked inside. It was empty! Annoyed, he had the servants replace the earth. The next morning, when the man returned, the servants told him he might dig and explained that the soil around the tree had just been loosened to plant new flowers.

The man paid the servants his only coin in return for their help, digging carefully to avoid hurting the tree. Joyfully he dug out the vase and sat down to look inside. When he found the vase was empty he knew his wife had been right, that he had been a fool to think a dream could be more than a dream. He thanked the servants for their help and left, exhausted and despondent.

As he walked toward his home he wondered what to do. "I ought to jump in the river and put an end to my life. I am not worth the air I breathe. But my wife deserves better than to sit and wonder why her husband has not returned." And so he walked home, thinking he should end his life and worrying about his wife and children.

When he came to the edge of his village he had no strength to go home. He sat and cried, wishing he had had the courage to drown himself. Two children found him and shouted, "Here he is! He is home!" He heard his wife's cries of happiness and his children's voices welcoming him home. They pulled him up and walked joyfully besides him. He tried to tell his wife he had no gold. He told her he was more than a fool, but his voice was lost in the excitement.

He stood in front of his little cottage, ashamed to share his disappointment with those whom he loved. But no one paid any attention to his unhappiness. They pushed and pulled until he was once more standing in his own doorway. His wife grabbed his hand and pulled him inside. There, all over the walls and ceiling and floor, were more gold coins than he had ever dreamed.

SUGGESTIONS FOR EXPLORATION

Time: 45 minutes   1

Text: Coins of the Realm

Focus: The reality of a dream

Tell: Coins of the Realm.

Paint: An image of the story that is most vivid to you.

Title: Your image.

Share: Images, titles, and issues evoked by story.

Write: On half a piece of paper, a dream you have had or a dream you would like to have. On the other half of the paper write what it would take to make your dream come true.

Reflect: On dreams and dreaming as a kind of reality. Share any part of your dream you choose to share as part of your discussion.

---

2 **Time:** 45 minutes

Text: Coins of the Realm

Focus: On following one's dream

Tell: Coins of the Realm.

Sculpt: An image of the man before he heard the dream.

Sculpt: An image of the man after he heard the dream.

Share: Sculptures. As the man, using "I," talk about the differences, if any, between the two.

Reflect: On what it took for the man to follow his dream, on what it takes for each of us to follow our dream(s).

Sourcework

.... 127

Time:	45 minutes	3

Text: Coins of the Realm

Focus: On perseverance in the midst of bad times

Tell: Coins of the Realm.

Divide: Into pairs.

Create: A one-minute dialogue between the man and a character he meets on the road, either going to or returning from Osaka. Focus on the essence of the difficulties the man is experiencing.

Share: Dialogues.

Reflect: On issues evoked by dialogues and the inner and outer qualities we need to have to keep going when our life feels more difficult than we can manage.

Time:	45 minutes	4

Text: Coins of the Realm

Focus: Valuing life

Tell: Coins of the Realm.

List: On board, questions that the group would like to ask the man.

Divide: Into small groups.

Imagine: You are the man visiting a small group of people. They have invited you to talk with them about your life.

Create: A discussion. Decide who you are, where you are, why your question matters to you, and how you feel about the man.

Reflect: On issues evoked by the various discussions. Focus on what it means to value life.

I chose two authored stories, "Homecoming" by Árpád Göncz, a Hungarian author who writes in English and Hungarian, and "The Woman from America" by Bessie Head, an African author who emigrated from South Africa to Botswana, to exemplify some of the ways I work with these short stories. Although very different, the two stories continue to resonate inside me long after I originally read them—an important factor when I choose a piece of literature with which to work.

"Homecoming" by Árpád Göncz

"And see that you don't stop at the first bar and get soused," said the prison guard, as the man closed his watch and put the wedding ring on his finger. For the first time in six years, he didn't answer.

Outside, summer raged. The colors. The sky was blue, the trees green, the streetcars yellow. Women were colored, exotic birds.

He stared in awe at everything and everyone; it's a miracle someone didn't give him a thrashing.

Those who once crossed over to the other side in order to avoid him now crossed over to greet him and shake his hand.

"My dear man, I hear you had a little inconvenience . . . believe me, I only escaped it by the skin of my teeth . . ."

Here he wasn't protected from them by the prison's clear-cut black and white set of norms.

His wife took him on an outing one Sunday. Him and the little boy. The boy who was six months old then and is almost seven now.

In the woods on the trail, the little boy said, "Daddy, you lead" and he closed his eyes. The boy understood his hand; for over a minute he stepped, blindly, around stones, branches, puddles, tracks. Then the little boy opened his eyes and said: "Now I lead, Daddy." He closed his eyes and took almost ten steps blindly. He, too, understood the little boy's hand.

Then he opened his eyes and, from the corner of his eye, he saw an almost smile on his wife's lips. The wife noticed that he saw.

The sky was blue, the foliage green, and through the leaks in the green foliage, thick, rich sunlight poured onto the stones, the branches, the puddles.

Sourcework

.... 129

SUGGESTIONS FOR EXPLORATION

Time: 45 minutes   ☐1

Text: "Homecoming"

Focus: From incarceration to liberation

Sculpt: Man's relationship to self in prison.

Title: Statue.

Sculpt: Man's relationship to self just after his release.

Title: Statue.

Share: Sculptures and discuss ideas about what you think is going on
               in this man's life. Consider:Why was he in prison? How does
               the man feel about being freed? Select a passage from the
               story to support your ideas and feelings.

Reflect: On what is gained and what is lost as the man leaves prison
               and reconnects with his family and his life.

Time: 45 minutes   ☐2

Text: "Homecoming"

Focus: Seeing your old world with new eyes

Paint: Image of man in prison.

Write: Man's journal entry for one day in prison.

Share: Images and journal entries.

Paint: Image of man after he has been released.

Write: Man's journal entry for his day of release.

Share: Images and journal entries.

Reflect: On what it might be like to lose six years of your life. What issues might affect your ability to re-establish relationships with family, friends, and business, professional, and political acquaintances?

3

Time: 45 minutes

Text: "Homecoming"

Focus: Differing points of view

Paint: Image of man in relationship to those who once avoided him and who now greet him.

Create: Short monologue in which man chooses to acknowledge (or not acknowledge) a person who is now willing to greet him but who refused to talk to him when the man was in trouble. Think about your reasons for your choices.

Share: Monologues and greetings (if so chosen).

Reflect: On "inconvenience" and "six years" in prison. Think about the differing points of view.

4

Time: 45 minutes

Text: "Homecoming"

Focus: Homecoming

Sculpt: Image of homecoming.

Write: As the man, a letter to someone who matters to you, about your homecoming. Share your thoughts and feelings. Ask the person to whom you are writing a question of importance to you which you would like to have answered.

Exchange: Letters by putting all letters in a box. Each student selects a letter.

Answer: Letter as if you are the person to whom the letter is addressed.

Share: Letters. Return letters to original writer.

Reflect: On what it means for this man to come home, for you to come home.

"The Woman from America" by Bessie Head

This woman from America married a man of our village and left her country to come and live with him here. She descended on us like an avalanche. People are divided into two camps. Those who feel a fascinated love and those who fear a new thing. The terrible thing is that those who fear are always in the majority. This woman and her husband and children have to be sufficient to themselves because everything they do is not the way people here do it. Most terrible of all is the fact that they really love each other and the husband effortlessly and naturally keeps his eyes on his wife alone. In this achievement he is 70 years ahead of all the men here.

We are such a lot of queer people in the southern part of Africa. We have felt all forms of suppression and are subdued. We lack the vitality, the push, the devil-may-care temperament of the people of the north of Africa. They do things first, then we. We are always going to be confederators and not, initiators. We are very materialistically minded and I think this adds to our fear. People who hoard little bits of things cannot throw them out and expand, and, in doing so, keep in circulation a flowing current of wealth. Basically, we are mean, selfish. We eat each other all the time and God help poor Botswana at the bottom.

Then, into this narrow, constricted world came the woman from America. Some people keep hoping she will go away one day, but already her big strong stride has worn the pathways of the village flat. She is everywhere about because she is a woman, resolved and unshakable in herself. To make matters more disturbing, she comes from the West of America, somewhere near

California. I gather from her conversation that people from the West are stranger than most people; at least this woman from the West is the most oddly beautiful person I have ever seen. Every cross-current of the earth seems to have stopped in her and blended into an amazing harmony. She has a big dash of Africa, a dash of Germany, some Cherokee and heaven knows what else. Her feet are big and her body is as tall and straight and strong as a mountain tree. Her neck curves up high and her thick black hair cascades down her back like a wild and tormented stream. I cannot understand her eyes, though, except that they are big, black and startled like those of a wild free buck racing against the wind. Often they cloud over with a deep, brooding look.

It took a great deal of courage to become friends with a woman like that. Like everyone here I am timid and subdued. Authority, everything can subdue me. Not because I like it that way but because authority carries the weight of an age pressing down on life. It is terrible then to associate with a person who can shout authority down. Her shouting-matches with authority are the terror and sensation of the village. It has come down to this. Either the woman is unreasonable or authority is unreasonable. In reality, the rule is: if authority does not like you then you are the outcast and humanity associates with you at its peril. So try always to be on the right side of authority, for the sake of peace.

It was inevitable though that this woman and I should be friends. I have an overwhelming curiosity that I cannot keep within bounds. I passed by the house for almost a month, but one cannot crash in on people. Then one day a dog they have had puppies and my small son chased one of the puppies into the yard and I chased after him. Then one of the puppies became his and there had to be discussions about the puppy, the desert heat and the state of the world, and as a result of curiosity an avalanche of wealth has descended on my life. My small hut-house is full of short notes written in a wide sprawling hand. I have kept them all because they are a statement of human generosity and the wide carefree laugh of a woman who is always busy as women the world over about things women always entangle themselves in—a man, children, a home. Like this:

> Have you an onion to spare? It's very quiet here this morning and I'm fagged out from sweeping and cleaning the yard, shaking blankets, cooking, fetching water, bathing children, and there's still the floor inside to sweep, and dishes to wash and myself to bathe—it's endless!

Or again:

> Have you an extra onion to give me until tomorrow? If so, I'd appreciate it. I'm trying to do something with these awful beans

and I've run out of all my seasonings and spices. A neighbour brought us some spinach last night so we're in the green. I've got dirty clothes galore to wash and iron today.

Or:

I'm sending the kids over to get 10 minutes' peace in which to restore my equilibrium. It looks as if rain is threatening. Please send them back immediately so they won't get caught out in it. Any fiction at your house? I could use some light diversion.

And, very typical:

This has been a very hectic morning! First I was rushing to finish a few letters to send to you to post for me. Then it began to sprinkle slightly and I remembered you have no raincoat, so I decided to dash over there myself with the letters and the post key. At the very moment I was stepping out of the door, in stepped someone and that solved the letter posting problem, but I still don't know whether there is any mail for me. I've lost my p.o. box key! Did the children perhaps drop it out of that purse when they were playing at your house yesterday?

Or my son keeps getting every kind of chest ailment and I prefer to decide it's the worst:

What's this about whooping cough! Who diagnosed it? Didn't you say he had all his shots and vaccinations? The D.P.T. doesn't require a booster until after he's five years old. Diphtheria-Pertussis (Whooping cough)-Tetanus is one of the most reliable vaccinations I know all three of mine and I have had hoarse, dry coughs but certainly it wasn't whooping cough. Here's Dr. Spock to reassure you!

Sometimes, too, conversations get all tangled up and the African night creeps all about and the candles are not lit and the conversation gets more entangled, intense; and the children fall asleep on the floor dazed by it all. The next day I get a book flung at me with vigorous exasperation! 'Here's C.P. Snow. Read him, dammit! And dispel a bit of that fog in thy cranium.'

I am dazed, too, by Mr C.P. Snow. Where do I begin to understand the industrial use of electronics, atomic energy, automation in a world of mud-huts? What is a machine tool? he asks. What are the Two Cultures and the Scientific Revolution? The argument could be quaint to one who hasn't even one leg of culture to stand on. But it isn't really because even a bush village in Africa begins to feel the tug and pull of the spider-web of life. Would Mr. Snow or someone please write me an explanation of what a machine tool is? I'd like to know. My address is. Serowe, Bechuanaland, Africa.

The trouble with the woman from America is that people would rather hold off, sensing her world to be shockingly apart from theirs. But she is a new kind of American or even maybe will be a new kind of African. There isn't anyone here who does not admire her—to come from a world of chicken, hamburgers, TV, escalators and what not to a village mud-hut and a life so tough, where the most you can afford to eat is ground millet and boiled meat. Sometimes you cannot afford to eat at all. Always you have to trudge miles for a bucket of water and carry it home on your head. And to do all this with loud, ringing, sprawling, laughter!

Black people in America care much about Africa and she has come here on her own as an expression of that love and concern. Through her, too, one is filled with wonder for a country that breeds individuals about whom, without and within, rushes the wind of freedom. I have to make myself clear, though. She is a different person who has taken by force what America will not give black people. We had some here a while ago, sent out by the State Department. They were very jolly and sociable, but for the most innocent questions they kept saying: 'We can't talk about politics.' Why did they come here if they were so afraid of what the American government thinks about what they might think or say in Africa? Why were they so afraid? Africa is not alive for them. It seems a waste of the State Department's money. It seems so strange a thing to send people on goodwill projects if they are so afraid that they jump at the slightest shadow. Why are they so afraid of the government of America which is a government of freedom and democracy? Here we are all afraid of authority and we never pretend anything else. Black people who are sent here by the State Department are tied up in some deep and shameful hypocrisy. It is a terrible pity because such things are destructive to them and hurtful to us.

The woman from America loves both Africa and America, independently. She can take what she wants from us both and say: 'Dammit!' It is a difficult thing to do.

SUGGESTIONS FOR EXPLORATION

1

Time: 45 minutes

Text: "The Woman from America"

Focus: On fear

Sourcework

.... 135

Consider: "People are divided into two camps. Those who feel a fascinated love and those who fear a new thing. The terrible thing is that those who fear are always in the majority."

Paint: An image of fear.

Write: Quick answers to the following questions:
  • Who fears?
  • What is feared?
  • What remedy is there for the fear?
  • What are the consequences of confronting the fear?

Share: Images, questions, and answers.

Reflect: On how it was that the woman from America created fear among so many in the African community. What might have happened to allow the African woman to become the friend of the American woman? How might this friendship affect the African woman's relationships in her community?

  Have you experienced a situation where an outsider comes into your community and creates fear among some and a desire for friendship among others? How did you respond? Looking back, how do you think and feel about that time? If you had it to do over, what changes, if any, would you make? Why?

Time: 45 minutes   2

Text: "The Woman from America"

Focus: A stranger in a strange land

Sculpt: An image of the woman from America in her new African community.

Reflect: What are some of the differences she might experience? How might she cope with the strangeness of her new life?

Share: Sculptures and ideas about what the woman from America experiences in her African community and how she feels and copes. What do you think about her ability to respond with "loud, ringing, sprawling, laughter?"

Write: A letter from the woman from America to a person back home. Decide at what point in the short story she writes the letter and the circumstances that precipitate it.

Share: Letters.

Reflect: On what it might mean to be a stranger in a strange land for the woman from America and for you. What would be a strange land for you? What might you do to create a place for yourself in this strange land? What would you be willing to give up in order to fit into the new community? What would you be unwilling to do or be? How might you decide these issues? What factors might come into play?

3

Time: 45 minutes

Text: "The Woman from America"

Focus: Bridging barriers

Paint: An image of the African woman from the African community on the left side of the paper.

Write: Some words to describe her. Create some experiences that might have helped her to become the person we see in the short story.

Paint: An image of the woman from America on the right side of the paper.

Write: Some words to describe her. Create experiences that might help her to become the person we see in the short story.

Write: Some words that make it possible for the two women to become friends. Write these words to form a bridge that connects the two images you have painted.

Share: Images with a partner.

Choose: One of the two characters. If both choose the same character play them as alter egos. If males prefer to play male characters, each male student can choose to be one of the two women's husbands and continue the activity as one of the husbands. When choosing to be one of the husbands, consider how you envision the man and his relationship to his wife. What factors inform your choices?

Create: An incident, issue, or idea to talk about.

Reflect: On discussions, issues evoked, feelings revealed—points of friction, and places of agreement.

Time: 45 minutes   4

Text: "The Woman from America"

Focus: Extending the dialogue

Sculpt: One of the two women characters in relationship to a character of your choice. Select a character from the story or create a character who might interact with your chosen character.

Envision: What conflict, exchange, or interaction might occur between them.

List: On the board the conflicts, issues, exchanges, interactions.

Share: Sculptures. Talk about why you have chosen these particular characters and situation.

Select: A partner.

Choose: One character who interests you. (If both choose the same character imagine them interacting as alter egos.) Choose one issue, conflict, exchange, or interaction to explore.

Create: A dialogue with your partner and write down your script, which needs to be about a minute. Focus on one strong moment between the two characters. Consider the precipitating moment (what fuels the scene), each character's reactions to the issue, conflict, exchange. Particularize their responses so that every word contributes to the power of the scene.

Share: Script with another pair. Explore possibilities after each pair reads their script.

Reflect: As a class on problems, new learning, ideas to enrich scripts.

5

Time: 45 minutes

Text: "The Woman from America"

Focus: Playing the part

Paint: An image of your character in the environment of the scene you and your partner have written, paying attention to the character's feelings, perception of the scene, and response to the other character in the scene.

Share: Image with partner and reflect on the scene of your script from previous class.

Read: Script with partner to make any desired changes.

Share: Scripts with class.

Reflect: On scripts and the situations, character development, ideas and issues evoked. Explore how the scripts affect your understanding of the story and of your feelings about the characters and situation of the story.

After exploring these short stories the teacher might ask the class to look at the society and environment in each story and some of the ways in which the author creates the world of the story, the characters, and the conflict or theme. Students might want to consider what it's like to live in a closed world where outside influence is minimal. How does our culture affect our behavior, thoughts, and feelings? What role might our family and friends play in mitigating, exacerbating, encouraging, hindering, changing, and/or affecting our choices, wants, needs, wishes, and dreams?

Given the diverse background of many students, sharing a short story (which can be read or heard in one sitting) and exploring it through a variety of points of view and experience, helps to establish a sense of community within the class. Learning to pay attention to one's thoughts, feelings, and reactions is initially easier when reading a short story than when reading a novel or a play, but the tools are the same. I make student participation a high priority because it is only when everyone feels somewhat comfortable sharing thoughts, feelings, and responses, either asking for or giving help, that focused dialogue, questioning, and expression occur. One result of sharing is that students become more aware of their own issues and can learn to place them in perspective rather than automatically using the text as a projection for personal concerns.

Working with Dramatic Literature

For years scholars and theatre practitioners have argued about the best way to teach dramatic literature, especially when the play is a classic by Shakespeare or Sophocles. Many English teachers, with no theatre experience, prefer to treat the play as if it were a text to be read rather than spoken—a novel in a different form. However, dialogue written to be read silently can be surrounded by description that qualifies a character's thoughts or feelings. Spoken dialogue, by contrast, is based in action and must reflect, with no help from expository text, the character's thoughts and feelings. Even when a character does talk to the audience in a monologue or aside, there is no time or place for explanation or description that is separate from the action. Novelists understand that their words will be read silently, quite a different process from playwrights like Shakespeare who wrote his plays for a company of actors, often in a rush to meet the deadline of an evening's curtain or the company's need for money to pay creditors.

When teachers teach dramatic literature as if it were only a literary text, they miss the power and passion of characters enacting a vicarious reality using real time and space. When readers read a playscript silently, they can take as long as they choose. But, when readers read a role out loud, taking on the needs, wants, and urgency of a character, the dynamics change. Spoken dialogue demands immediate action and reaction. This spontaneous interaction calls into play the functions of nonverbal communication, blocking, the use of space, and, later—costuming, set, and light design. Changing any one of these elements can alter the meaning the text has for the actors and thus for the audience.

The difference between reading and speaking dialogue was brought home to me very clearly at the Oregon Shakespeare Festival when I was teaching English teachers who were enrolled in a ten-day summer course titled "Strategies for Teaching Shakespeare." Of the twenty high school teachers in the group, only one had had any theatre training or experience, and none of them used drama regularly as part of their classroom practice. Highly experienced and suspicious of acting out the parts as a viable classroom technique, they regarded any form of active dramatic participation as, at best, unnecessary, and at worst, a call for chaos in the classroom.

When I asked them to explore active script participation they balked, some refused, and all complained that I was wasting their time. Indeed, these teachers had been selected on the basis of school and district recommendation. Who was I to challenge their time-tested methods?

Our first few days together I felt like a marine drill sergeant dealing with unwilling draftees. They did what I asked them to do, grudgingly with as little involvement as possible. At least they were honest—when I asked them how many thought their students enjoyed studying Shakespeare, only two teachers raised their hands. I kept on sharing ideas knowing it would take a powerful event to change their minds. One can only hope!

All the course activities were built around attending the plays being performed at the Festival, talks with actors and directors, tours

Sourcework

.... 141

backstage, and classroom techniques designed to engage student interest. As part of my work with the teachers I showed them how to move into a text beginning with a nonverbal exploration. Since I was also serving individual directors by sharing ideas with them on ways to improve their actors' use of movement and nonverbal communication, I shared the ideas adopted by directors with my students. For example, in Shakespeare's *Measure for Measure* I pointed out that the director initially asked Isabella, when she first meets Angelo (the Duke's deputy), to kneel at his feet. I objected to this choice because it gives Isabella, a nun, no place to go as the play evolves and Angelo increases the pressures on Isabella to go to bed with him. If instead, Isabella bows in the doorway, as far from Angelo as possible, she demonstrates her distaste for her task, pleading for mercy for her brother convicted of adultery by Angelo's law. Given that Isabella is a nun who has relinquished all contact with men, what purpose is served by having her willingly enter and kneel at the feet of a man with whom she wants no contact? In class, I used this example to explore how blocking choices (movement of actors on stage) nonverbally set up the verbal action.

In another instance, in *The Merchant of Venice* the director asked Antonio to pat Shylock on the back to demonstrate their initial relationship. But Antonio would never voluntarily touch a Jew, and to do so sets up a false understanding about the place of Jewish merchants in the Venetian society at that time. Instead, I suggested that Antonio maintain a larger space between him and Shylock than he does with the non-Jewish population to emphasize Shylock's role as outcast. When the director complained this choice felt too constraining, I suggested it gave more latitude, because as the action grows more intense Antonio will find himself closer to Shylock than is comfortable for him. Antonio can then use this discomfort to fuel his anger at Shylock, who never really has a chance to prevail given that society's anti-Semitic rules. I asked the English teachers to select a short bit of dialogue between Antonio and Shylock and to play with how the words could be augmented, denied, challenged, or made less potent, depending on how space was used. Having the opportunity to watch me work with live directors and actors gave the teachers an occasion to connect theory and practice immediately, despite their lack of personal active theatre classroom experience.

I also demonstrated how to explore the meaning and dynamics of a scene using one key word. For example, when we worked with *Romeo and Juliet* I asked them to look at the scene where Romeo first talks with Juliet at the party given by her father. I include the text to provide a clearer sense of what it means to use key words.

Romeo (to Juliet):
If I profane with my unworthiest hand
This holy shrine, the gentle sin is this,
My lips two blushing pilgrims ready stand
To smooth that rough touch with a tender kiss.

Juliet:
Good pilgrim, you do wrong your hand too much,
Which mannerly devotion shows in this;
For saints have hands that pilgrims' hands do touch,
And palm to palm is holy palmers' kiss.

Romeo:
Have not saints lips, and holy palmers too?

Juliet:
Aye pilgrim, lips that they must use in prayer.

Romeo:
O then dear saint, let lips do what hands do.
They pray; grant thou, lest faith turn to despair.

Juliet:
Saints do not move, though grant for prayers' sake.

Romeo:
Then move not while my prayer's effect I take.
Thus from my lips, by thine, my sin is purged.

Juliet:
Then from my lips the sin that they have took.

Romeo:
Sin from my lips? O trespass sweetly urged.
Give me my sin again.

Juliet:
You kiss by th' book.

Here we have Romeo, probably dressed in disguise as a pilgrim, in the house of his family's enemy, talking to the woman his parents would least like him to know. Yet Romeo is dazzled by her. Just before he speaks to Juliet he says to himself,

Did my heart love till now? Foreswear it sight,
For I ne'er saw true beauty till this night.

As one way to begin working with this text I asked the English teachers to work in pairs, preferably but not necessarily male and female. I requested each of them to select one essential word or phrase that underscored their understanding of what is happening to their character in the text. For example some of the Romeos chose "saint" as their key word, while several Juliets chose the word "pilgrim." They spoke their word in role, moving closer to or further away from their partner depending on each pairs' understanding of the meaning of the text. Nonverbal action such as touching hands or kissing was then added to underscore how nonverbal choices (use of space, dynamics, and blocking) affect meaning. Finally, the English teachers read the full text, in role, enriched by the understanding derived from their work with key words and nonverbal communication.

With the knowledge gained from these two experiences, students were more likely to be engaged intellectually and emotionally when reading a scene. By the eighth day, one or two teachers were beginning to be genuinely interested in our work together, but most of the others were still adamantly opposed, taking their cue from a man who was Head of the English Department at a large and well-known California high school. He expressed his disapproval with eloquence and the weight of twenty-five years of experience. "My students score well on SAT exams and that's good enough for me."

I asked him, "Why is it an either/or proposition? Do you really think that I would propose to use methods in an academic classroom that diminish intellectual achievement? I consider the idea that one is either emotional or intellectual a false dichotomy. As human beings, we cannot divorce feelings from thoughts in any meaningful manner, nor do I think our best interests are served by attempting to do so."

"Your methods take time away from scholarship and that's what a classroom is all about—scholarship." And so it went . . . for nine days.

Othello, the last play we saw as part of the class, was a play few teachers taught and even fewer liked. In the production we saw, the actor who played Othello was tall, dark, and handsome, a sharp contrast to Iago who was short, light, and unattractive. During a discussion, our first class activity after seeing the play, the actors revealed how the director had used nonverbal means to create the changing power balance between them. In the beginning Othello is seen as central, dominant, and literally head and shoulders above Iago. As Iago's poison begins to take hold, Iago is seen talking to Othello from a step so that Iago appears to be gaining in stature as

Othello loses some of his certainty. Towards the end of the play Iago places himself so that Othello literally has to look up at him, thus physicalizing Iago's growing power and influence at Othello's expense. The Head of the English Department started to laugh derisively, "What you're saying is interesting, but it has nothing to do with the play Shakespeare wrote. All we need is the text and a few nice costumes. Who cares about all this psychological baloney."

Both of the actors playing Iago and Othello were stunned. To cover the silence I suggested an experiment where the two actors chose parts of three scenes that essentially demonstrate the changing power balance between Othello and Iago. I asked them to play the scenes twice, the first time with no physicalization but with all their normal vocal activity, and the second time, using the staging that supported their changing character images.

We settled in as the actors created a playing space, discussed which scenes to play, and briefly rehearsed the two approaches, agreeing to keep their vocal approach the same in both versions. The results astounded some of the teachers, but the majority refused to accept that there could be any value for students in the physicalization of a scene. After the actors left, I assigned the final project. They were to take a two-character scene from *Othello* and play the scene using one word and one prop for each character.

Among the first to volunteer was the Head of the English Department and his partner, a teacher from a small high school near his. They had selected the scene where Othello kills Desdemona; he used a thick stick as his prop, she used a handkerchief. They both decided to use only one word for their work, although some of the other teachers changed their words or phrases as their scene developed. His word was "kill"; her word was "love." As they moved through the scene, using their understanding of the words as the basis for their choices, his voice grew louder and more powerful. Her voice grew more insistent without becoming shrill or hysterical. Then something magical happened. As the Head of the English Department became more involved in playing Othello, he began to use his stick more actively, the growing thud underscoring his increasing anger. At the moment of the killing he smashed the stick into pieces next to Desdemona who crumpled to the floor while her handkerchief floated gently on top of her, covering her face and masking her last, soft, "love." The man playing Othello burst into racking, raspy sobs. Desdemona remained quietly in her final position. The class held its collective breath.

After regaining his composure the man looked at me, and then said to the class, "I was wrong. Dead wrong. I never understood that play till now. But I can't talk ... I need some time to pull myself together. I'll be back this afternoon." He left. Because it was close to lunch time I dismissed the group, but people seemed unable to move.

A few minutes passed in silence before one group member said, "I'm sorry we've given you such a hard time."

Woody Allen has always been a hero of mine, and I thought of him as I quipped, "Ah well, in the words of old Willy S., 'All's well that ends well.' "

That fall I received several letters from the course participants who asked for suggestions regarding the use of physicalization with the play they were teaching. One letter came from the Head of the English Department:

> I left the course with muddled feelings. On the one hand, I was immensely impressed with how my experience in our class greatly, and positively, affected my understanding of the play. On the other hand, I could not ease the discomfort I felt when I thought about using some of the techniques we explored in class. I am a man who likes order, reasoned discussion, and intellectual discourse. How do I let loose the passions without losing control? You know what you're doing. You have experience and confidence. I don't. Can you help me bridge the gap between what I'd like to do and what I know to do?

Some English teachers believe there is a dichotomy between passion and intellect, yet I think the division is false, serving the interest neither of student nor of teacher. For me, the real question is, "How do I engage the minds and hearts of students in ways that are consistent with good classroom practice?" There are many ways to address this question, depending on the rapport we teachers have with our students, the number of students in our class, the willingness of students to participate, the level of student engagement with the text, even the ability of students and teacher to explore the unknown. I always suggest that teachers begin by working with clear parameters, establishing specific guidelines, and carefully articulating each task and its connection to the text, especially when the text is a dramatic work. Often, students are not aware of how choices relating to nonverbal communication, blocking, and the like can affect meaning. When students are given an opportunity to explore this, they begin to appreciate the differences between dialogue meant to be read and dialogue meant to be spoken. If reading a dramatic text is not in itself sufficient to study a dramatic work, neither is merely reading or acting out the parts. Rather, we need to structure classroom experiences that begin with the text, enable students to explore the text and the meaning it has for them, and return them to the text with deepened appreciation and understanding of the work.

I suggest that teachers tell students when they are trying a new technique so that they can choose to react both as participants and as observers. This split focus is a bit like what actors do when they perform—constantly monitoring that they are heard and seen even as they act and react to other actors. After the lesson, during reflection, students are often helpful as they share their ideas regarding the shortcomings and benefits of a particular approach. Most students appreciate a teacher who cares about the members of the class as well as the literature being studied.

Teachers who help students to enter into the world of the text and to become aware of their responses to it when the text is a novel, short story, or poem often have difficulties presenting the material when the text is a dramatic work. The head teacher's question, "How do I let loose the passion without losing control?" is a core issue, especially when a teacher has had little theatre experience or training.

I have chosen here to work with *Romeo and Juliet* because it is a well-known play that deals with issues of potentially great interest to young people. Although students may initially find the language difficult, there are many exciting ways to engage their interest and their willingness to explore unfamiliar language. My way of working with this play exemplifies an approach to exploring dramatic literature that is based on the following principles:

• Students who have been brought up on television, film, and comics need to learn how to visualize a text before they read the text.
• Works written for the stage need to be spoken as well as read in order to be fully appreciated in the form intended by the playwright.
• Students can begin to understand a play by working with small units such as a scene or a short encounter between two or three people.
• When teaching a play, it is especially important to set the stage visually, in the mind's eye of students, to make the dramatic conflict come alive in students' imagination, before they begin to read the text.
• Students often prefer to use material such as video tapes or expurgated texts rather than to read the actual play. Teachers

Sourcework

.... 147

can help students enjoy reading the full text by focusing on the experience of exploring and entering into the text, rather than on the acquisition of knowledge about the text. For example, the first scene of *Romeo and Juliet* contains a lot of puns that students can learn to enjoy if they are properly encouraged and if they are helped to relish the rich use of language rather than feel estranged by its unfamiliarity.

- I believe the time that is spent to engage students' curiosity about the world of the text is amply rewarded when students begin to personalize the lives of the characters—their problems, their joys, and their issues, to experience the life of another human being vicariously.

- When students learn to enter into the world of characters in a play, they learn to penetrate the world of any text. Working with a dramatic text is particularly useful for beginning students of literature—written dialogue provides one clear entry into the thoughts, feelings, actions, and attitudes of a character that can be examined by working in role.

When working with a play, I initially focus on establishing the context through the exploration of questions such as: "Where are we? What has been happening? Who are the main characters? What is their relationship to each other? What conflict is brewing?" I spend a lot of time setting the stage because I know that if I can't engage the students' interest I will have a long and lonely time in class.

If the language of the play presents difficulties I work with short encounters and engage everyone in the process of speaking the language of the play, even if it means that fifteen pairs of actors are speaking simultaneously. It is important that students learn how to connect to characters who may initially appear to be very different from them. For example, I have seen many fine versions of *Romeo and Juliet* where the characters were dressed in traditional dress, yet when I saw a production where the young people in the cast were dressed as twentieth-century hoods, I was taken by surprise. The play took on an immediacy that made me look at it with fresh eyes. This is not to say that only by dressing characters in contemporary clothing can you reach a modern audience. Rather, the viewer does not separate character from clothing or setting: They are inextricably one and the same. Given my choice, I prefer students to see the play, whether on stage, television, or film, after we have at least partially explored it. This enables students to create their own visual images rather than to depend on someone else's ideas about how the play should look.

I divide my work with *Romeo and Juliet* into the following parts:

- Setting the stage
- Creating the context
- Entering into the lives of the characters
- Exploring the issues
- Making connections

My main purpose when designing class activity is to engage students, helping them to explore the play as vicarious participants, enabling them to care about what happens to the characters. Once students develop the skills to enjoy reading a play like *Romeo and Juliet,* they are more likely to be willing to read and view others.

Before I make plans for teaching a work I have to decide how much time I have, the interests of my students, their level of development, and their previous experience (if any) with Shakespeare. The classwork that follows in this text is based on exemplary ways to explore various aspects of dramatic literature. I hope these suggestions will stimulate readers to create their own meaningful approaches to teaching a play and encourage students to keep all their images and writings in a notebook for future use.

I often end discussion by asking students to ask questions about the reading itself, the reading in connection to previous reading, the reading in connection to themselves, the reading in connection with current or past events in their lives, or the reading in connection with their own work as creators (prose, poetry, painting, sculpting, music, dance, and so on). The questions are meant to stimulate—often deeper questions lie unasked because students have no way of getting to them. Occasionally, a question will be so important students ask to have it answered. If so, I help students to explore possible answers before I offer my opinion, carefully structuring my answer to evoke new possibilities, rather than answering as if I am the one who has the right answer and the final word.

In this exploration of *Romeo and Juliet* I stress issues and ideas that I consider important and meaningful, selecting lines that rivet my attention that I think will be of interest to my students. Other teachers may make different choices. However, in order to make ideas concrete, I suggest a use of passages to demonstrate effective ways to work with a dramatic text, enable students to enter into the world created by the playwright, become aware of their own inner life, and to connect the two in meaningful experience.

SUGGESTIONS FOR EXPLORATION

Time: 45 minutes

Text: *Romeo and Juliet*

Focus: Setting the stage

Read aloud: Prologue.

Chorus:
Two households both alike in dignity,
In fair Verona where we lay our scene,
From ancient grudge break to new mutiny,
Where civil blood makes civil hands unclean.
From forth the fatal loins of these two foes,
A pair of star-crossed lovers take their life;
Whose misadventures piteous overthrows
Doth with their death bury their parents' strife.
The fearful passage of their death-marked love,
And the continuance of their parents' rage,
Which, but their children's end, naught could remove,
Is now the two hours' traffic of our stage;
The which if you with patient ears attend,
What here shall miss, our toil shall strive to mend.

Paint: Image of two households both alike in dignity.

Label: One house Capulet, the other Montague.

Paint: Image of Juliet in the Capulet household.

Paint: An image of Romeo in the Montague household.

Divide: Into pairs each of whom have a copy of the play.

In pairs: Read aloud lines in Prologue which interest you.
                Discuss what each of you think is happening. Identify
                unfamiliar words.

Share: Ideas evoked by the Prologue. Put unfamiliar words on
                the blackboard. Discuss their meaning in the context

of the play. Talk about what the Prologue sets up in terms of conflict and action.

Reflect: On issues and ideas evoked by passage.

Assignment: Read Act One: Scene One from beginning to the end of the speech where the Prince says, "Once more, on pain of death, all men depart."

Ask: Students to suggest questions which the prologue evokes. If no one has any, the teacher might raise a few, not to answer, but to evoke questions from students. The point is to look at the issues, events, or feelings that evoke them.

2

Time: 45 minutes

Text: *Romeo and Juliet*

Focus: Creating the context

Sculpt: Image of Sampson and Gregory in relationship to Abraham and Balthasar. Think about what identifies them as friend or foe and to whom.

Share: Ideas or issues evoked by sculpture.

Read aloud: In role, the parts of Gregory, Sampson, Abraham, Balthasar, Benvolio, Tybalt, Officer, Citizens (at least two, preferably four), Capulet, Lady Capulet, and the Prince in the first half of Scene One.

When reading, ask readers to group themselves into those who belong to the Capulets and those who belong to the Montagues. Those who belong to neither house such as the Officer, Citizens, and the Prince group themselves as they see fit. The class may want to place characters as they appear. For example, characters like Gregory, Sampson, Abraham, and Balthasar give way to Benvolio, Tybalt, Capulet, and the Prince. How does who they are affect the space they take and the space they are given? The tone of voice they use to another character? The connection between comrades and the disconnection between enemies? As people read in role each person moves toward or away from others according to the action being taken by the character and the group (if any) to which the character belongs.

Discuss: What is happening in this part of the first scene in the play. Identify and define unfamiliar words, phrases, or ideas and write them on the board.

Read aloud: If time permits, read this part of the scene again using the same or different readers.

Reflect: On how Shakespeare translates the words of the Prologue into the actions of the characters. Consider the feeling tone of the scene and the nature of relationships created in terms of alliances, antagonisms, and power (peace makers, fighters).

Assignment: Read Act One: Scene One from Montague's speech, "Who set this ancient quarrel new abroach? Speak nephew, were you by when it began?" to Benvolio's speech "I'll pay that doctrine, or else die in debt." Ask for volunteers to read this part of the scene in the next class.

Ask: Students to design an armband that identifies them as Capulet or Montague. What do we need to know or decide in order to create?

Time: 45 minutes

3

Text: *Romeo and Juliet*

Focus: The Montagues and Romeo (entering into the life of a character)

Paint: An image of Romeo in relationship to his father (Lord Montague) his mother (Lady Montague), Benvolio, and any other kinsmen you choose. Paint the armband you have designed on each character to designate the House of Montague.

Identify: Lord and Lady Montague's concern about their son, Romeo. Talk as if you are a character in the play and have strong feelings either for or against Romeo.

Share: Passages from the second half of Scene One that describe their concern. Look at how he sees himself when he talks with Benvolio.

Reflect: On how the issue of enmity between the Montagues and the Capulets affects the lives of the young men we have met such as Tybalt, Benvolio and Romeo.

Assignment: Read Act One: Scene Two.

Ask: For questions regarding Romeo and what is happening around him.

4

Time: 45 minutes

Text: *Romeo and Juliet*

Focus: The party (creating a context)

Paint: An image of the Capulets using the armband you have designed to designate the House of Capulet.

Identify: Lord Capulet's concern about his daughter Juliet in relationship to Paris's suit.

Read aloud: In role, passages that describe how Romeo and Benvolio view the party.

Reflect: On the meaning of the party to Lord Capulet, Romeo, and Benvolio. Select passages that describe how each

sees the party. Notice that we have not yet met Juliet.
Why do you think this might be so?

Assignment: Read Act One: Scene Three.

Time: 45 minutes [5]

Text: *Romeo and Juliet*

Focus: Juliet and the House of Capulet (entering into the life
of a character)

Paint: Image of Juliet in relationship to Lady Capulet and
Nurse.

Share: Images and ideas evoked by images.

Read aloud: In role, Scene Three beginning with Lady Capulet's
lines,

Marry, that marry is the very theme
I came to talk of. Tell me daughter Juliet,
How stands your disposition to be married?

Reflect: Romeo is unhappy—his love for Rosaline is not
returned. Juliet is encouraged by her parents to marry
Paris. The Capulets are giving a party so that Juliet
may meet Paris. The Montague clan—Romeo and
Benvolio—plan to attend the party uninvited.

Ask: For questions that are evoked by what we know so far.
Try to have students ask as many questions as
possible with no worry about answering them.

Assignment: Read Act One: Scenes Four and Five.

Time: 45 minutes [6]

Text: *Romeo and Juliet*

Focus: Romeo's concerns (entering into the life of a character)

Read aloud: In role, Act One: Scene Four until Romeo says, "In bed asleep while they do dream things true." Read his last speech, "I fear, too early . . ."

Paint: An image of the party given by the Capulets, using armbands as much as possible.

Read aloud: In role, Romeo's first vision of Juliet (Act One: Scene Five).

> O she doth teach the torches to burn bright.
> It seems she hangs upon the cheek of night
> As a rich jewel in an Ethiop's ear;
> Beauty too rich for use, for earth too dear.
> So shows a snowy dove trooping with crows,
> As yonder lady o'er her fellows shows.
> The measure done, I'll watch her place of stand,
> And touching hers make blessed my rude hand.
> Did my heart love till now? Foreswear it sight,
> For I ne'er saw true beauty till this night.

The exchange following Romeo's speech between Tybalt and Capulet ending with Tybalt's speech,

> Patience perforce with wilful choler meeting
> Makes my flesh tremble in their different greeting.
> I will withdraw, but this intrusion shall,
> Now seeming sweet, convert to bitt'rest gall.

Reflect: On the change in Romeo's feelings. Consider Tybalt's enmity toward Romeo and the House of Montague.

Assignment: Read the Prologue and Act Two, Scenes One and Two.

---

7 **Time:** 45 minutes

Text: *Romeo and Juliet*

Focus: Romeo and Juliet's first meeting (entering into the life of a character)

Sourcework

·· 155

Paint: Image of Romeo and Juliet in the context of the
               Houses of Montague and Capulet.

Read aloud: In role, the first meeting of Romeo and Juliet, and
               continue to the end of the scene, adding the
               characters of Nurse, Benvolio, and Capulet.

Create: As a class, using ideas from the group, armbands that
               signify the House of Capulet and those that signify the
               House of Montague. Make paper armbands that people
               can wear when playing a particular role.

Discuss: How choices are made, colors and designs decided.

Reflect: On how the love of Romeo and Juliet flourishes in the
               midst of hate. Consider Juliet's speech, "My only love
               sprung from my only hate, Too early seen unknown,
               and known too late!" Think about how your lives are
               affected by the place or people from which you come.

Assignment: Read Act Two: Scenes Three, Four, Five, and Six.

Time: 45 minutes   ⑧

Text: *Romeo and Juliet*

Focus: Creating a play to understand a play (exploring the
               issues)

Divide: Into groups of two or three. Each group select an
               exchange between two or three characters. Using your
               own words, create the scene paying particular
               attention to what your group thinks and feels is the
               most important part of the scene. Each scene lasts no
               more than one minute. Feel free to incorporate some
               of Shakespeare's dialogue.

Play: The scenes taking no more than one minute for each
               scene.

STORYMAKING AND DRAMA

156 ··

Reflect: On issues evoked by scenes. List on board questions people have about what has happened, what has been set into motion, and clues we have about future action.

Assignment: Read Act Three: Scenes One, Two, and Three.

| **9** | **Time:** | 45 minutes |

Text: *Romeo and Juliet*

Focus: Love in the midst of hate (exploring the issues)

Paint: Image of one character we have met so far.

Write: One sentence as if you were your character regarding what has happened thus far in the play.

Read aloud: Prologue of Act Two.

Chorus:
Now old desire doth in his death-bed lie,
And young affection gapes to be his heir,
That fair for which love groaned and would not die,
With tender Juliet matched, is now not fair.
Now Romeo is beloved, and loves again,
Alike bewitched by the charm of looks;
But to his foe supposed he must complain,
And she steal love's sweet bait from fearful hooks.
Being held a foe, he may not have access
To breathe such vows as lovers use to swear;
And she as much in love, her means much less
To meet her new beloved any where.
But passion lends them power, time means, to meet,
Temp'ring extremities with extreme sweet.

Write: Your character's views on the matters described in the Prologue of Act Two.

Share: In role, your characters thoughts before and after the Prologue.

Reflect: On the Prologue, what it means, what it sets up. Why do you suppose Shakespeare wrote a prologue for Acts One and Two but not for Three, Four, or Five? Consider the lines:

> But passion lends them power, time means, to meet,
> Temp'ring extremities with extreme sweet.

Assignment: Read Act Three: Scenes Four and Five and Act Four: Scene One. Select a passage that intrigues, moves, angers, irritates, or otherwise makes you take notice. Be prepared to share your choice of text.

Time: 45 minutes

10

Text: *Romeo and Juliet*

Focus: The insufficiency of good intentions (exploring the issues)

Write: Three short diary entries for Romeo after he has been married, after his interference causes Mercutio's death, and after he unwillingly kills Tybalt.

In pairs: Share diary entries. Be prepared to share observations or powerful entries with class.

Share: Passages from your reading.

Reflect: On what has happened to Romeo despite his intentions not to fight. Consider Romeo's speech to Tybalt:

> Tybalt, the reason that I have to love thee
> Doth much excuse the appertaining rage
> To such a greeting—villain am I none.
> Therefore farewell, I see thou knowest me not.

Assignment: Read Act Four: Scenes Two, Three, Four and Five. Pick a speech that interests you. Be prepared to read it to the class and to talk about why you have chosen this speech.

11

Time:	45 minutes
Text:	*Romeo and Juliet*
Focus:	The power of love (exploring the issues)
Sculpt:	Ring that Juliet designs for Romeo as a token of her love.
Write:	A short poem that accompanies her gift. Include a line of Juliet's dialogue.
In pairs:	Share sculptures and ideas evoked by sculpture choices.
Share:	Short poems.
Reflect:	On the choices Juliet has and the choices she makes. Share speeches that support your thoughts and feelings.
Assignment:	Read Act Five. Choose one character, and be prepared to comment in role on the events of the play and how (or if) you think life will be different given the deaths of Romeo and Juliet.

12

Time:	45 minutes
Text:	*Romeo and Juliet*
Focus:	Dying to live (exploring the issues)
Paint:	Image of the character you choose to comment on the events of the play.
Write:	One or two sentences using "I" that reflect your deepest feelings about the play as the character.
Share:	Your views of the events of the play and how (or if) you think life will be better for the inhabitants of

Sourcework

.... 159

Verona given the deaths of Mercutio, Tybalt, Romeo, and Juliet.

Reflect: On the last speech of the Prince:

A glooming peace this morning with it brings;
The sun, for sorrow, will not show his head.
Go hence, to have more talk of these sad things;
Some shall be pardoned, and some punished.
For never was a story of more woe,
Than this of Juliet and her Romeo.

Time: 45 minutes   13

Text: *Romeo and Juliet*

Focus: Thee and me (making connections)

Sculpt: Memorial statue commemorating what you consider to be a telling moment in the play.

Share: Sculptures.

Write: What it is you take away with you after having read this play.

Share: Writings.

Reflect: On your experience of this play. How does it resonate with your life? What issues in this play are similar to those in your life? Would you recommend that someone you know and care about read this play? If so, why? If not, why not?

Working with Novels

Reading a novel makes it possible for us to live an invented life—vicariously experiencing events, facets of which remain hidden yet touch the reader's heart and mind. Entering into the world of a novel allows us to live imaginatively in a space we help to create and shape. When a class reads a novel, each person reacts and responds according to reader skill, personal vulnerability, life experience, and willingness to suspend or postpone judgment until the book is finished. For some readers, reading a good novel is a source of pleasure and stimulation. Yet highly successful students may consider reading to be a chore despite their academic prowess. How can this be? One student spoke for many who do not like to read and write when he said, "I hate having to guess what the teacher's going to ask on the test. It's like he's perched on my shoulder demanding that I read and remember according to what he says is important. And it's the same with writing, I never even get to think about my ideas—I'm so busy answering his questions. It makes me hate reading all together."

If we want students to read, if we want them to find pleasure in reading, we have to devise ways to help them enjoy the process. Pleasure may easily seem to be last on a teacher's list, that includes having to prepare students to do well on state and national tests, teaching more students than there is time to listen to their ideas—much less read their papers, and having to teach a curriculum that may have no connection to what teachers wish to have students read. A lot of damage is done if teachers have too many pressures put on them that work against helping students to enjoy reading. When teachers have to structure classwork around the demands of a test or to teach books that hold no interest for students, neither teachers nor students are well served. No one would argue that students profit by having high test scores or reading good books, but perhaps we need to rethink our approaches and broaden our goals to include some texts chosen specifically for students to enjoy and savor. My students tell me they began to find pleasure reading when they were able to read for themselves, selecting passages and ideas of importance to them. Once they became interested in the work, they also became more willing to listen to other people's ideas about the work. What turned them off was having to accept, automatically, one person's ideas as truth, of being made to feel as if they were too inexperienced to have concepts worth examining. If teachers can focus some class activity to create space and time for student- and teacher-centered exploration, students can become active participants rather than passive sufferers who endure the class period as something to just get through. Teachers who begin to work with a text by enabling students to enter into the imaginary world created by the author make possible subsequent exploration of reactions and responses to the work and to the ideas and feelings generated by the characters and events of the

Sourcework

.... 161

book. When processing ideas, exploring meaning, considering personal connection, I always use the text to explore the passages, helping students to connect their ideas and feelings. I encourage them to select excerpts that trigger and exemplify what it is they take with them after reading the work.

In this book, when I write about approaches to teaching poetry and short stories, I can easily include the full text—but not when the literary text is a full-length play or a novel. When choosing a dramatic work to use in this book, I was able to select *Romeo and Juliet,* a well-known play and potentially of great interest to students. But selecting a novel or novels posed a complex challenge. I couldn't print a complete text nor could I find a novel that pleased every teacher with whom I talked. Additionally, some said they didn't want to read about a novel they hadn't read, didn't remember, or might not have in their own libraries. Others named a variety of novels I might use, but no one suggested the same novel. So, I decided to choose two (a workable number) well-written novels that I liked, containing characters whom I found engrossing and presenting issues I could use to explore a variety of approaches to teaching literature. The two novels I selected are readily available and contain material of interest to students. When devising activities, my primary focus is on helping students enjoy reading and to encourage their active participation in a variety of class activities.

The first novel, *The Joy Luck Club* by Amy Tan, draws readers into a world of four Chinese mothers and their four daughters born in the United States. As readers, we look at issues and events through the eyes of both mothers and daughters, often seeing one experience from two very different points of view. The novel is arranged so that the mothers speak first. Although the daughters speak next, because the first mother is dead when the novel starts, her story is told by her daughter. This complicated arrangement can cause difficulties for some students so I include imaginative ways to help students keep the cast of characters clear. I also focus on ways to explore what it might be like to live in a culture based on Chinese customs, and to be the native-born daughter of a foreign-born mother whose understanding of the way the world works may vary considerably from that of her child.

The second novel I chose to include, *When the Legends Die* by Hal Borland, is about a young Native American boy whose life changes radically, many times, for reasons not of his choosing. As the boy enters each new stage of life he is given a new name. I thought this would provide an interesting point of departure for exploration.

Although the issues I chose to deal with can be found in other texts, what I hope to provide in using these two books is an approach to teaching literature that encourages teachers to design interesting and pleasurable ways for them and their students to study a particular novel.

When working with a long and complicated text such as a full-length play or a novel, imagemaking is one technique that helps students to keep track of the characters, the experiences they undergo, the effects of these events, and subsequent consequences. When students consider what happens in the opening pages of a play or novel and paint an image of the environment and sculpt characters in relationship to each other, they learn to explore and illuminate the underlying foundation of the world created by the playwright or novelist. Sharing images at the beginning, when students may not know how to articulate what they think or how they feel, encourages discussion that focuses on description rather than judgment. When I teach students to notice what is set up by the first paragraphs or pages I aim to gently ease them into exploration and examination. As Jing-Mei Woo, a character in Amy Tan's novel *The Joy Luck Club* says, "I can never remember things I didn't understand in the first place" (Tan, p. 19).

As I have explored ways to interest my students in reading, I have found enormous pleasure, as well as new ideas and questions, by sharing ideas, thoughts, and feelings about books with colleagues. These exchanges are a rich and continuing source of theory, practice, and practical advice. I encourage teachers who are considering the possibility of working in new ways to try these ideas with supportive colleagues.

The activities that follow are intended to help students to enjoy a novel that unfolds in a way that may seem strange to readers accustomed to more conventionally chronological material. This, coupled with unfamiliar Chinese names, places, and philosophy, might make it difficult for students to enjoy the book, yet this does not have to be the case. When I help readers to overcome initial resistance or discomfort, acknowledge the difficulties they may be having as they read, and provide techniques and experiences to improve skills, I increase student willingness to be engaged by the work.

The first activity is designed for students to do as they read the book and is not necessarily a class activity, unless the novel is read out loud in class. I encourage students to refer to the beginning of *The Joy Luck Club* where the author lists the names and relationships of

Sourcework

.... 163

the main cast of characters—the four mothers born in China and their four daughters born in the United States.

SUGGESTION FOR EXPLORATION

Text: *The Joy Luck Club.*

Task: To differentiate and identify the four mothers and their daughters as you read about the characters in the first two sections.

Paint: An image of Suyuan Woo on the left side of the paper. Title your image with the name of Suyuan Woo. On right side of paper paint an image of her daughter, Jing-mei "June" Woo. Title image with her name. Leave space in middle between images to make notes on each character as you learn more about them.

Consider: Suyuan Woo dies two months before the novel begins. Do we need to differentiate the relationships between the dead mother and her daughter and those between the living mothers and their daughters? If so, how? If not, why not?

Write: Words that describe daughter and mother as we initially read about them.

Repeat: Using a separate piece of paper for each pair of mothers and daughters, title and paint images of An-mei Hsu and her daughter Rose Hsu Jordan, Lindo Jong and her daughter Waverly Jong, and Ying-ying St. Clair and her daughter Lena St. Clair.

Write: The major events in each mother's life that caused her to emigrate to the United States.

Each section begins with a tale or a story involving a Chinese mother and her daughter who is born in the United States. The first tale, which precedes the first section, "Feathers From A Thousand Li Away," sets the tone for *The Joy Luck Club*.

The old woman remembered a swan she had bought many years ago in Shanghai for a foolish sum. This bird, boasted the market vendor, was once a duck that stretched its neck in hopes of becoming a goose, and now look!—it is too beautiful to eat.

Then the woman and the swan sailed across an ocean many thousands of li wide, stretching their necks toward America. On her journey she cooed to the swan:"In America I will have a daughter just like me. But over there nobody will say her worth is measured by the loudness of her husband's belch. Over there nobody will look down on her, because I will make her speak only perfect American English. And over there she will always be too full to swallow any sorrow! She will know my meaning, because I will give her this swan—a creature that became more than what was hoped for."

But when she arrived in the new country, the immigration officials pulled her swan away from her, leaving the woman fluttering her arms and with only one swan feather for a memory. And then she had to fill out so many forms she forgot why she had come and what she had left behind.

Now the woman was old. And she had a daughter who grew up speaking only English and swallowing more Coca-Cola than sorrow. For a long time now the woman had wanted to give her daughter the single swan feather and tell her, "This feather may look worthless, but it comes from afar and carries with it all my good intentions." And she waited, year after year, for the day she could tell her daughter this in perfect American English. (Tan, p.17)

SUGGESTION FOR EXPLORATION

Time:	45 minutes
Text:	"Feathers From A Thousand Li Away" from *The Joy Luck Club*
Focus:	A single feather
Read:	The prologue to "Feathers From A Thousand Li Away" out loud.
Paint:	An image of a telling moment in this tale.

Sourcework

.... 165

Share: Telling moments and talk about why the moment matters to you.

Reflect: On what kind of power a single feather could have. Consider the mother's intentions when she decided to come to America. Were these intentions affected by her emigration experience? If so, how? If not why not? What is the basis for your ideas?

The narrator, Jing-mei "June" Woo, is asked to take the place of her dead mother at the weekly meeting of the Joy Luck Club. Jing-mei talks about how her mother started the San Francisco version and the activities that drew the four Chinese women together.

> This is how my parents met the Hsus, the Jongs, and the St. Clairs. My mother could sense that the women of these families also had unspeakable tragedies they had left behind in China and hopes they couldn't begin to express in their fragile English. Or at least, my mother recognized the numbness in these women's faces. And she saw how quickly their eyes moved when she told them her idea for the Joy Luck Club. (Tan, p.20)

SUGGESTION FOR EXPLORATION

Time: 45 minutes

Text: Excerpt of "The Joy Luck Club" from *The Joy Luck Club*

Focus: Leaving the old life

Sculpt: An image of one of the mothers.

Share: Sculpture. Talk about why you chose her. Share a passage from the first section, "Feathers From a Thousand Li Away," which you choose to give a sense of who she is, what matters to her, and what issues affect her relationship with her daughter.

Reflect: On each woman's story. Think about what each woman had to leave behind in order to emigrate from China. Consider: Have you ever been in a situation where you had to leave all that was familiar to you to go to a new place? How did you decide what to take and what to leave behind? How did you feel leaving your old home and moving to a new place? Did you ever try to maintain contact with those you left behind? What was this like for you?

Jing-mei tells about visits to her Auntie An-mei where she, as the eldest, was expected to take care of the younger children of the four mothers. She looks at the clothes of her mother and aunt:

These clothes were too fancy for real Chinese people, I thought, and too strange for American parties. In those days, before my mother told me her Kweilin story, I imagined Joy Luck was a shameful Chinese custom, like the secret gathering of the Ku Klux Klan or the tom-tom dances of TV Indians preparing for war. (Tan, p.28)

Later she writes:

My mother and I never really understood one another. We translated each other's meanings and I seemed to hear less than what was said, while my mother heard more. (Tan, p.37)

SUGGESTION FOR EXPLORATION

Time: 45 minutes

Text: Excerpts of "The Joy Luck Club" from *The Joy Luck Club*

Focus: Native daughter, foreign mother

Sculpt: An image of one of the daughters.

Share: Sculpture. Talk about why you chose her. Share a passage from the second section, "The Twenty-Six

Sourcework

.... 167

Malignant Gates," which you choose to give a sense of who she is, what matters to her, and what issues affect her relationship with her mother.

Reflect: How the daughters' lives differ from their mothers'. In what way, if any, are they similar? Have you experienced a situation where your responses are different from your parents or other family members? What were the issues? Were the differences resolved? Is so, how? If not, why not? How does it feel to be different from people you expect to be familiar? What might it be like to have no culture in common with your parents or other family members, where you speak two different languages? (These questions are meant to suggest possible areas of discussion.)

Jing-mei learns that her mother, caught in war, left behind two babies who are now grown women. The three women of the Joy Luck Club give Jing-mei a check for $1200 so that she can go to China and meet her sisters. When the women suggest what Jing-mei should tell them about their dead mother she is overwhelmed.

And then it occurs to me. They are frightened. In me, they see their own daughters, just as ignorant, just as unmindful of all the truths and hopes they have brought to America. They see daughters who grow impatient when their mothers talk in Chinese, who think they are stupid when they explain things in fractured English. They see that joy and luck do not mean the same to their daughters, that to these closed American-born minds "joy luck" is not a word, it does not exist. They see daughters who will bear grandchildren born without any connecting hope passed from generation to generation. (Tan, pp.40–41)

SUGGESTION FOR EXPLORATION

Time: 45 minutes

Text: Excerpt of "The Joy Luck Club" from *The Joy Luck Club*

Focus: The generation gap

In pairs: Select a passage in the first section that deals with the experience of one of the mothers. One person chooses the role of mother, the other, her daughter.

Read: The passage out loud to each other.

Create: A short dialogue where the daughter questions the mother about the incident and the mother tries to explain her history. Decide what the mother and daughter want from the dialogue. Is each agenda different? If so, how? Why?

Share: Essence of dialogue with class.

Reflect: What it might be like for a Chinese mother who has suffered unspeakable loss to communicate with her American-born daughter who "drinks more Coca-Colas than sorrows."

The second tale, which precedes the second section, *The Twenty-Six Malignant Gates* reflects the complexity of mother–daughter relationships.

"Do not ride your bicycle around the corner," the mother had told the daughter when she was seven.

"Why not!" protested the girl.

"Because then I cannot see you and you will fall down and cry and I will not hear you."

"How do you know I'll fall?" whined the girl.

"It is in a book, *The Twenty-Six Malignant Gates,* all the bad things that can happen to you outside the protection of this house."

"I don't believe you. Let me see the book."

"It is written in Chinese. You cannot understand it. That is why you must listen to me."

"What are they, then?" the girl demanded. "Tell me the twenty-six bad things."

But the mother sat knitting in silence.

"What twenty-six!" shouted the girl.

The mother still did not answer her.

Sourcework

.... 169

"You can't tell me because you don't know! You don't know anything!" And the girl ran outside, jumped on her bicycle, and in her hurry to get away, she fell before she even reached the corner. (Tan, p.87)

SUGGESTION FOR EXPLORATION

Time:	45 minutes
Text:	"The Twenty-Six Malignant Gates" from *The Joy Luck Club*
Focus:	Finding a path
Read aloud:	The above tale using two readers—a mother and a daughter.
Write:	Diary entry for mother after daughter's fall.
Put:	Diary entries into a box, and have each class member select one.
Write:	Comment on diary entry as if you were the daughter.
Share:	Diary entries and comments with class.
Reflect:	On what it might be like to be a foreign-born mother trying to protect her daughter from harm (issues and events that the mother considers to be dangerous or problematical). What it might be like to be an American-born daughter trying to be "like everyone else." Consider your own experience growing up.

The third section, "American Translation" is introduced by this tale.

"Wah!" cried the mother upon seeing the mirrored armoire in the master suite of her daughter's new condominium. "You cannot put mirrors at the foot of the bed. All your marriage happiness will bounce back and turn the opposite way."

"Well, that's the only place it fits, so that's where it stays," said the daughter, irritated that her mother saw bad omens in everything. She had heard these warnings all her life.

The mother frowned, reaching into her twice-used Macy's bag. "Hunh, lucky I can fix it for you, then." And she pulled out the gilt-edged mirror she had bought at the Price Club last week. It was her housewarming present. She leaned it against the headboard, on top of the two pillows.

"You hang it here," said the mother, pointing to the wall above. "This mirror sees that mirror—haule!—multiply your peach-blossom luck."

"What is peach-blossom luck?"

The mother smiled, mischief in her eyes. "It is in here," she said, pointing to the mirror. "Look inside. Tell me, am I not right? In this mirror is my future grandchild, already sitting on my lap next spring."

And the daughter looked—and haule! There it was: her own reflection looking back at her. (Tan, p.147)

SUGGESTION FOR EXPLORATION

Time:	45 minutes
Text:	"American Translation" from *The Joy Luck Club*
Focus:	The presence of the past in the present
Read aloud:	The tale using two people in the roles of mother and daughter.
Sculpt:	Image of mother in her world.
Share:	Sculptures of mother.
Sculpt:	Image of daughter in her world.
Share:	Sculptures of daughter.
Place:	Your sculptures of the mother and daughter in relationship to one another. Consider your choices, why and how you chose.

Sourcework

.... 171

Reflect: On how a parent's wisdom generated by past experience and culture affects a child who wants to make her or his own way. How is it for you, in your family?

The last section, "Queen Mother of the Western Skies," is introduced with this tale. Teachers may want to share some Buddhist concepts of life and death before working with this section.

"O! Hwai dungsyi"—You bad little thing—said the woman, teasing her baby granddaughter. "Is Buddha teaching you to laugh for no reason?" As the baby continued to gurgle, the woman felt a deep wish stirring in her heart.

"Even if I could live forever," she said to the baby, "I still don't know which way I would teach you. I was once so free and innocent. I too laughed for no reason.

"But later I threw away my foolish innocence to protect myself. And then I taught my daughter, your mother, to shed her innocence so she would not be hurt as well."

"Hwai dungsyi, was this kind of thinking wrong? If I now recognize evil in other people, is it not because I have become evil too? If I see someone has a suspicious nose, have I not smelled the same bad things?"

The baby laughed, listening to her grandmother's laments.

"O! O! You say you are laughing because you have already lived forever, over and over again? You say you are Syi Wang Mu, Queen Mother of the Western Skies, now come back to give me the answer! Good, good, I am listening . . .

"Thank you Little Queen. Then you must teach my daughter this same lesson. How to lose your innocence but not your hope. How to laugh forever." (Tan, p.213)

SUGGESTION FOR EXPLORATION

Time: 45 minutes

Text: "Queen Mother of the Western Skies" from *The Joy Luck Club*

Focus: The power of hope and the power of laughter

Read aloud: The story using two readers to play the mother and the daughter.

Paint: An image of hope and an image of laughter.

Write: The lessons: how to lose your innocence but not your hope; how to laugh forever.

Share: Images and lessons.

Reflect: On the transmission of knowledge, care, and love from one generation to another. Consider your experience growing up and separating from your parents. What do you bring with you as you become more independent? What do you choose to leave behind? How are your choices manifested?

In the final section An-mei Hsu says:

> Yesterday my daughter said to me, "My marriage is falling apart."
>
> And now all she can do is watch it falling. She lies down on a psychiatrist couch, squeezing tears out about this shame. And, I think, she will lie there until there is nothing more to fall, nothing left to cry about, everything dry.
>
> She cried, "No choice! No choice!" She doesn't know. If she doesn't speak, she is making a choice. If she doesn't try, she can lose her way forever.
>
> I know this because I was raised the Chinese way: I was taught to desire nothing, to swallow other people's misery, to eat my own bitterness.
>
> And even though I taught my daughter the opposite, still she came out the same way! Maybe it is because she was born to me and she was born a girl. And I was born to my mother and I was born a girl. All of us are like stairs, one step after another, going up and down, but all going the same way.
>
> I know how it is to be quiet, to listen and to watch, as if your life were a dream. You can close your eyes when you no longer want to watch. But when you no longer want to listen, what can you do? I can still hear what happened more than sixty years ago. (Tan, p.215)

Sourcework

.... 173

SUGGESTION FOR EXPLORATION

Time: 45 minutes

Text: Excerpts of "Magpies" from *The Joy Luck Club*

Focus: The worth of a life

Read aloud: This monologue.

In pairs: One person takes on role of mother, other person takes on role of person of his or her choice (daughter, son, husband, friend, whoever).

Create: A dialogue around the idea of choice. What is a choice? How is choosing not to choose a choice? Consider what it might take to comfort An-mei Hsu.

Reflect: What choices are you facing? What ideas, experiences, feelings, inheritance do you use to make your decision? Consider An-mei Hsu's words later on: "My mother, she suffered. She lost her face and tried to hide it. She found only greater misery and finally could not hide that. There is nothing more to understand . . ." (Tan, p.241)

After reading this book students might ask questions about life in China at the time the mothers left and life in China now. Perhaps class members with foreign-born parents might share some of their experiences as family members of two generations sort out two very different cultural experiences. Put on the board questions generated by the reading of *The Joy Luck Club.* Encourage students to share what they take away from their reading of this novel.

In the novel *When The Legends Die,* author Hal Borland explores the life of a young child caught between two cultures and examines what happens when the boy tries to live according to traditional Native American ways after his parents die. Despite his considerable life and creative skills, Little Black Bull is forced to attend a boarding school for Indians with no understanding of the English language or the ways of the white people. In the course of the novel Little Black Bull is given many names, which act as emblems of his life. One way to explore this novel is to look at the names and to consider how these names are given to him, by whom, and for what reason. At the end of the book he gives himself the name by which he will be called from now on. It is the name by which he has come to know himself.

SUGGESTIONS FOR EXPLORATION

1	**Time:**	45 minutes
	Text:	*When the Legends Die*
	Focus:	Names and naming
	Paint:	An image of Little Black Bull with his mother and father.
	Write:	A brief description of his life with them. Consider his birthright, his connection to the earth, his relationship with his parents.
	Share:	Images and words.
	Reflect:	The first name change comes when Blue Elk forces the parents to have the boy baptized and he is given a new name, Thomas Black Bull, even though his mother says, "He is Little Black Bull. He will choose when he needs another name." (Borland, p.10) What might it mean to be given another name despite your parents' wishes or agreement? What could this portend? Consider the meaning of names. Look at your own name and think about where it comes from and why it was given to you.

2	**Time:**	45 minutes
	Text:	*When the Legends Die*
	Focus:	The life of Bear's Brother

Paint: An image of Bear's Brother.

Create: A short monologue talking about how Little Black Bull became Bear's Brother. Decide to whom you are talking and why.

Share: Monologues and the name of the person to whom you are talking.

Reflect: On the significance of this name change and what happens to him when he is forced to change his name to Thomas Black Bull and is compelled to attend the boarding school.

Time: 45 minutes   3

Text: *When the Legends Die*

Focus: Thomas Black Bull

Paint: An image of Thomas Black Bull in the school.

Write: A diary entry at a particular point in his life at the school.

Share: Diary entries and why you selected this particular moment.

Reflect: On what is happening to him, especially after he escapes from the school, discovers someone has burnt his mountain home and stolen all his possessions, and returns to the school. Consider his school experience and yours. Explore the nature of his education, and compare it to your own.

Time: 45 minutes   4

Text: *When the Legends Die*

Focus:		Tom Black to Killer Tom Black to Devil Tom Black to Black Death
Design:		A logo for Tom Black, Killer Tom Black, Devil Tom Black, and Black Death. Decide where and how the logo will be used.
Create:		An advertising slogan for each of the above.
Share:		Logos and advertising slogans.
Reflect:		On how the different names reflect Tom's life in the world and within himself.

5

Time: 45 minutes

Text: *When the Legends Die*

Focus: Tom Black Bull

Sculpt: Images of all the names Tom Black Bull has called himself or been called. Put them into a meaningful relationship.

Divide: Into small groups. Each person takes on one role Tom Black Bull has played and the name by which he was known at that time in his life. Each person, in role, argues for the name by which Tom Black Bull calls himself.

Create: A ceremony for Tom Black Bull to incorporate all his former selves into his present self. Devise a chant to help him on his new path.

Reflect: On the life of Tom Black Bull. Consider:

It had been a long journey, he thought, the long and lonely journey a man must make when he is lost and searching for himself, particularly one who denies his own past, refuses to face his own identity. There was no question now of who he was. The All-Mother's words in the vision stated it beyond denial: "He is my son." He was a Ute, an Indian, a man of his own beginnings, and nothing would ever change that. He had tried to change it, following Blue Elk's way; and he had tried, following Red Dillon's way. He had tried, following the way of Tom Black. And still he had to find the way back to himself, to learn that none of their ways could erase the simple truth of the chipmunk's stripes, the ties that bind a man to the truth of his own being, his small part of the enduring roundness. (Borland, p. 215)

In time, he would go down to Pagosa, talk with Jim Thatcher, if he was still alive. Learn what happened to Blue Elk, try to understand why he sold his own people as he did. He would go to the reservation, eventually to the school, and see what was happening there now, try to understand that too. But never again would he go back to the arena. He had ridden his broncs, fought and killed his hatreds, and his hurts. He was no longer Tom Black. He was Tom Black Bull, a man who knew and was proud of his own inheritance, who had come to the end of his long hunt. (Borland, p.215–216)

What questions, ideas, feelings, thoughts, memories, experiences are evoked for you, if any, by this passage? Are there other excerpts from the book that you have noticed and wish to share? If you had been Tom Black Bull, what might have kept you going through the years of pain and heartbreak? Can you connect his experience to yours? If so, how? If not, what might account for this?

Working with Autobiography

While teaching "To Walk in Someone's Shoes," a course dealing with autobiography, I discovered that even though students took the course because it fit their schedule or because they were curious about the topic, most of my students had never read an autobiography, either as a required book in an English course or for their own pleasure. Initially, some students questioned my assumption that reading about someone else's life could encourage them to learn something about their own lives. The students' objections ranged from: "Who cares about what he went through? It's not an issue in my life," to "I'm not Vietnamese, what can reading about her life during the Vietnamese war say to me?" Their assessment, based on their previous reading experience (or lack thereof), led them to believe that reading about someone else's life was a waste of time.

Only after they had read a few autobiographies were they willing to consider: Reading autobiographical material may allow us to rediscover ourselves through reflection about the reading experience, reconsider issues and events in our lives through connections we make with the text, and reconnect ourselves to ourselves because of new understandings of ourselves and others. As part of my teaching autobiography I generally ask students to write their own autobiographies, to give them time and space to put their thoughts into words, to give concrete form to ephemeral existence. In the process, notions of self emerge. Questions arise: Are we who we thought we were? Is the creation of self a life-long process? What do we mean by "self"? Do we have a public and a private self? If so, what does this mean? Are they different? If so, how? If not, how do we protect ourselves?

An early issue for the class was the difference, if any, between the terms autobiography and memoir. We defined autobiography as the life story and memoir as an aspect of one's life story, where the writer focused on a particular time or issue. For the purposes of this book, I will use the term autobiography to include memoir. Richard Rodriguez talks about writing autobiography, and Nancy Mairs discusses writing a memoir, yet both are aware of the benefits and the dangers when writing about one's self.

Richard Rodriguez focuses on the benefits to the knowledge of one's self in *Hunger of Memory* when he talks about why he writes autobiography. "Such is the benefit of language: By finding public words to describe one's feelings, one can describe oneself to oneself. One names what was previously only darkly felt." (Rodriguez, p. 187)

Writing an autobiography or a memoir is a daunting task, no matter how old we are. Writers of autobiography generally want to tell the truth yet what does this mean? Nancy Mairs writes in *Remembering the Bone House:*

> In writing a memoir I have found, the temptation to censor material can grow enormous. Sometimes I have put pressure on myself to omit or prettify details in order to disguise truths about myself I didn't want to face up to or speak aloud. I've been drilled in the rules of polite discourse. . . .
>
> When it comes to censorship on behalf of others, the issues are different. It is one thing to expose one's life, taking responsibility for the shock and ridicule such an act may excite, and quite

Sourcework

··· 179

> another to submit people one loves to the same dangers. I can't
> resolve this dilemma to anyone's full satisfaction. But I have tried
> to keep my focus tight, speaking only for myself. The others all
> have stories of their own. . . . (Mairs, p.xi)

Choosing the issues on which to focus, selecting the episodes to illuminate one's point of view, even deciding how much of one's childhood experience to include, all depend on how one views one's life. For example, writing about childhood abuse from the comfort of successful adulthood is quite different from writing about this same abuse while sorting out the damaged fragments of one's life. Although there are facts, the date and place of one's birth, there is no one true way to write about one's life. The best the writer can do is to acknowledge one's biases, trust one's questions, and consider the process of writing as a search for one's truth. I generally ask students to use the autobiographies they read for class as a springboard to help them to name personal issues, ideas, feelings, attitudes, and formative experiences that go into the making of their selves. Reading about other people's experience helps students to begin wondering about their own lives.

Sometimes a teacher can interest students in autobiography by getting them to consider someone else's experience with books. It's a complicated process as the following example demonstrates, yet even though the passage describes being asked to read a novel, the incident is embedded in an autobiographical account.

In *The Call of Stories*, Robert Coles writes,

> When I was a high schooler of sixteen and inclined to be
> moody and troublesome at home, my mother bought me a copy
> of *War and Peace* and asked me earnestly, pleadingly, to spend
> the summer reading it. I refused immediately, of course, asking
> why in the world she was pressing on me such a big book written
> almost a century earlier. She answered that I might obtain a
> modest amount of sorely needed "understanding" (a word she
> favored) with Tolstoy's help. (Coles, p. xiv)

When I read this to my students they hooted with amusement.
"Whose mother would do such a thing?"
"What person in their right mind would spend summer vacation reading such a long book?"
"What about working?"
"And girlfriends?"
"And boyfriends?"

"All those words?" Their laughter grew stronger, fed by questions that reflected their amazement.

After the laughter began to wane, I asked, "Well, if reading about another person's life is such a waste of time, how come you all seemed to enjoy the passage I just read so much?"

"Oh!"

"So?"

"Well, that's different."

"How is it different?" I asked, and then added, "Different from what?"

There was silence. The few remaining fragments of laughter dried up, disturbing the easy agreement that had so recently pervaded. Taking advantage of their mental disarray I asked, "What assumptions do you make about this sixteen-year-old and his relationship with his mother?" Reluctantly, they answered.

"He's smart."

"He does good in school."

"She's smart—reads big books."

"Whatever trouble he gets into isn't big. Like he probably doesn't steal cars or do drugs or get his girlfriend pregnant."

"And what questions do you have?" I prodded.

"None. No one I know ever read that book."

"Well, what would it be like to have a problem and to have a parent say to you, 'Here, read this great book. It will make you feel better'?" Once again the laughter broke out but this time there was an edge.

"What's happening?" I asked.

One girl, noticeably pregnant, answered quietly, "I feel sad." There were murmurs from the group, as if she were a traitor in their midst. As I held up my hands to keep the group silent, she continued, "There's no books where I live. None. I wonder if my mom even knows how to read." Her answer worried me. Would her classmates tease her? Afterwards, would she feel bad for having talked so openly? One of the dangers of working with autobiography is that it can encourage students to reveal personal feelings in ways that require a tightly structured environment where students can feel safe. This is why I use passages from the book to continue the connection between self and text.

To cover the growing tension I shared a question raised by Robert Coles to his father, "Why do Mom and you read out loud to each other?" The answer his father gave him was, "Your mother and I feel rescued by these books. We read them gratefully." The class groaned, as if I were talking in a foreign language. I persisted and talked to them about how any of us could be affected by what we learn about peoples' lives when we read autobiography. I mentioned some books that had influenced me: *Black Ice* by Lorene Cary, which describes two years in the life of a young black Philadelphia woman who goes to a prestigious New England mostly male, mostly white boarding school as a scholarship student; *Asking for Trouble* by Donald Woods, which describes the perilous escape of a white journalist in South Africa whose fight for justice made him a banned person in his own country; *My Place* by Sally Morgan, the story of a young girl who is raised without knowing that she is the daughter of an aboriginal mother. I always carry a few books with me, with passages marked, so that I can read bits and pieces of writing that I hope will stimulate interest. With Rian Malan's book *My Traitor's Heart* in mind, I raised the issues of how we form relationships and the motives that may, unknowingly to us, influence our choices. One boy laughed and said, "I choose whatever girl chooses me. Love is what I care about. Ain't got nuthin' to do with books. No way!" He grinned salaciously, and everyone roared. I teasingly asked, "Shall we talk about love?" More laughter. Oh, they were having a fine time. Then I looked at the girl, too young to be carrying a child, whose face had become a mask.

I wanted to help her, help them all, help myself, to have a real conversation about issues of importance to us so I said, "Since you're so interested in love, I'd like to read you a passage from *My Traitor's Heart*. It's written by Rian Malan, a young South African white man who fled South Africa only to find that although he could leave his country, he could not erase the way the country existed within him. Unable to remain away from South Africa, he returned as a journalist, interviewing many people including a white couple who lived among the Zulu. The couple devised a variety of ways to help the Zulu improve their farming methods, develop water access and irrigation, and share resources so that productivity and incomes rose dramatically. Yet there were some who resented the influence of the white couple, and one day, the husband was ambushed. After the death of her husband, the wife chose to remain in the community despite terrorist attacks, drought, famine and loneliness. In the book, Malan asks her why she doesn't leave, that surely she has suffered enough.

> She just laughed, and pointed out something that I had misunderstood. "The path of love is not a path of comfort," she said. "It means going forward into the unknown, with no guarantees of safety, even though you're afraid. Trusting is dangerous, but

without trust there is no hope for love, and love is all we ever have
to hold against the dark." (Malan, p.423)

The pregnant girl nodded, her face once more animated,
"There's gonna be plenty of books where my kid grow up. Uh huh."
The class responded with what seemed to be a quiet approval until
one boy broke the silence.

"I still don't get it. So it sounds good, but what's the point of
reading books? They don't change nuthin' in your life. Still got to
watch out for the drugs and the guns and the drunks. What book's
gonna do somethin' about people being killed or folks starving to
death?"

The pregnant girl looked him in the eye and said, "Books help
you think about things 'stead of just doing what everyone else is
doing. Think about that lady . . . her husband was killed and she's got
hardly any food or water, and what does she do? She talks about love.
Real love. That just makes me feel like I got a lot of thinking to do
about my life."

Why does the bell always ring just when the talking gets going?
Still, I sensed a difference in the group from the way they looked
coming in to the room and the way they looked as they left. Who
knows when a seed is planted? Who knows how flowers bloom? I
bring with me to each class a variety of books from which I can read
to demonstrate my involvement with the kind of books I am asking the
class to read. Occasionally, someone is curious enough to ask to look
at the book during class. It has even happened that a student will ask
to borrow the book. While I don't make a practice of lending my
books, I balance out the cost of a paperback with the reward of
nourishing a student.

The next class began with a question from the boy who had
spoken so bitterly, "And what about them Zulus? Didn't they do
nuthin' if this guy was so great?"

"Yes, they did something."

"What?"

I was grateful I had remembered to bring *My Traitor's Heart* with
me. I asked, "Would you like me to read some more of *My Traitor's
Heart*?" He nodded and the class listened raptly.

Early one morning in the winter of 1988, two aging Zulu men
who'd loved and honored Neil climbed into a pickup and drove
to the bend in the road where he was killed. What they were about
to do had never been done before, and there were those Zulu

traditionalists who thought it should not be done at all. They asked, "How can you do this thing?" and the two men answered, "Because Neil, he was same like a black man. The skin was white, but the heart it was same like a black." (Malan, p.423)

"Yeah, but what did they do?" asked the student, demanding to know. I continued to read.

They stood over the spot where their white brother was slain, and invited his spirit to enter their sacred stick. "Numzaan," they said, "we come to fetch you. Come, let us go home." Then they placed the stick in a plastic bag and returned in solemn silence to the mud house by the river, bringing Neil's spirit back home. (Malan, p.424)

He was listening with such intent I gave him the book and suggested he read the rest of the story about how the Zulu community celebrated the life of the dead man who had lived and worked among them out of conviction and love. Slowly, he read for a few minutes. Even though the student occasionally stumbled as he read, the class listened attentively. The mood of the class had changed. They were involved.

I challenged them, "Let's think about what we mean when we use the word love. How does it play out in our lives? I'd like you to take a few minutes to write a paragraph about one experience you've had with love." Groans. Moans. Self-conscious laughter. Looks that said, "You can't be serious."

As the students were getting out pencils and paper, one young woman asked, "What if love is just the word someone used when they was doing bad things to you? What makes love, love?"

I answered carefully, "Perhaps you might begin by writing about what you mean when you use the word love."

"Then what?"

"This is your story, not mine. Just write about what you know, what you feel. Let your writing clarify your thinking. You don't need to know where you're going. You only need to know how to start." It took a long time—time for her to trust herself, time for her to trust me. Yet, by the end of the semester, she had written twenty pages about the way her brother and father used her sexually, always in the name of love. Her last sentence was, "I will never again let people treat me bad just cause they use a good word like love—I'm saving love for the good times."

Both novels and autobiographies make it possible for readers to examine their connections to issues and ideas that emerge from the reading. I look at novels as works of imagination filtered through the author's being and at autobiographies as the author's sense of reality filtered through the writer's imagination—the figure–ground relationship is different. What is similar for both genres is that the passages and ideas I choose to explore emerge from the intersection between what is written and who I am. To provide students with a chance to work with the passages and ideas of importance to them, I structure opportunities for them to select the telling moment or the vivid passage of any text we study. Occasionally a student will read an autobiography containing a troubling image that continues to prove bothersome. One good way to help students for whom this is happening is to encourage them to write about incidents from their own lives that are triggered by their reading. Such writing can provide the structure by which students begin to examine their own lives and the meaning they make from their own experience.

Rather than work with one or two books as I have in previous sections, I thought it would be useful to look at a variety of books to which my students responded, exploring passages they found particularly meaningful. I use their recommendations as the basis for selected texts, passages, and suggestions. I include one or two assignments per autobiography to keep this section to manageable length. In class I spend equal time on autobiography and novels.

Exploring Autobiography in the Classroom

When students have little or no experience reading autobiography it is helpful to select a text that explores growing up. Even when the author comes from another culture, such as Mark Mathabane in *Kaffir Boy,* the similarities in life and living help the reader to understand the differences. Familiar occurrences can take on new meaning as when Mathabane, growing up in South Africa, writes:

> The turning point came when one day in my eleventh year I accompanied my grandmother to her gardening job and met a white family that did not fit the stereotypes I had grown up with. Most blacks, exposed daily to virulent racism and dehumanized and embittered by it, do not believe such whites exist. From this family I started receiving "illegal books" like *Treasure Island* and *David Copperfield,* which revealed a different reality and marked the beginning of my revolt against Bantu education's attempt to proscribe the limits of my aspirations and determine my place in South African life. (Mathabane, pp.x–xi)

SUGGESTION FOR EXPLORATION

Time:	45 minutes
Text:	*Kaffir Boy*
Focus:	The same age in a different age
Paint:	An image of you in relationship to your world when you were eleven.
Write:	About what mattered most to you at this age.
Paint:	An image of Mark Mathabane at eleven in relationship to his world.
Write:	About what mattered most to him at this age.
Share:	Images and writing.
Reflect:	On how politics and culture affect (inhibit, shape, support, color, determine, and so on) our growing up.

Teenagers are generally very concerned about fitting in, being one of the group. When one is an outsider, life can be full of pain and inadvertent transgressions. When one is torn from the known and plunked down into the unknown there is a great sense of dislocation. This sense of loss is beautifully detailed in Eva Hoffman's autobiography, *Lost in Translation*. At thirteen, Eva Hoffman left Poland with her family because the continuing rise of anti-Semitism made their lives increasingly unbearable. Forced to leave her friends, language, landscape, and culture, she writes in her autobiography:

> No, there's no returning to the point of origin, no regaining of childhood unity. Experience creates style, and style, in turn, creates a new woman. (Hoffman, p. 273)

To a large extent, we're the keepers of each other's stories, and the shape of these stories has unfolded in part from our

STORYMAKING AND DRAMA

186 ···

interwoven accounts. Human beings don't only search for meanings, they are themselves units of meanings but we can mean something only within the fabric of larger significations. (Hoffman, p. 279)

SUGGESTION FOR EXPLORATION

Time:	45 minutes
Text:	*Lost in Translation*
Focus:	Hidden stories
Sculpt:	An image of yourself in relation to what matters most to you.
Share:	Sculptures.
Write:	A letter to an unborn grandchild in which you tell this child-to-be an experience, story, understanding, or memory you would like to preserve by sharing. Consider your reasons for sharing this particular bit of your life.
Share:	Letters.
Reflect:	On how we make and assign meaning to the events, experiences, and memories that make up our lives. Consider your life in relationship to Eva Hoffman's. For her, leaving Poland at age thirteen radically transformed her. What event in your life might have potent significance? What makes an event traumatic? How might the passage of time affect memory?

Many of my students are concerned about religious issues: What does it mean to be a member of a particular religion? How can I be who I am and still accept the notions of my religious community? How do I want to practice religion (or not being religious)? In his autobiography *Lovesong*, Julius Lester writes with power and passion

Sourcework

.... 187

about his changing relationships as he leaves the religion of his father, an African-American Methodist minister. Drawn to Judaism, Lester decides to become a Jew and soon realizes this also means he must confront his and other peoples' notions of what it means to be an African-American person in the United States. Julius Lester writes:

> I am tired of people trying to impose their idea of me on me. I am not an idea, dammit! Whatever someone says about me is not true, and I refuse to be pinned by anyone's words, even my own. (Lester, p.84)

SUGGESTION FOR EXPLORATION

Time: 45 minutes

Text: *Lovesong*

Focus: Me being me

Paint: A collage of images as you think significant people in your life see you. Label the source of the image ("my dad's view" or whatever).

Paint: An image of you as you see yourself.

Write: A journal entry describing yourself to yourself as the result of a particular experience.

Share: A significant observation about your images and writing. If you wish, share your images and entry.

Reflect: Explore your meaning of the sentence, "I am not an idea."

Students are often concerned about their relationship with their parents, especially as they move toward independence and make significant life choices. Many young men in the class found that reading about Julius Lester's struggles with his father and his own son helped them to begin thinking about their relationship with their fathers.

STORYMAKING AND DRAMA

188 ···

Ah, my son! I call him my son, but that word reveals only his relationship to me. I call him my son but I do not know who he is or how he came to be him. (Lester, p.212)

SUGGESTION FOR EXPLORATION

Time:	45 minutes
Text:	*Lovesong*
Focus:	Who is this child who calls me father?
Sculpt:	An image of yourself in relationship to your father or a significant male in your life.
Share:	Sculptures.
Consider:	If you could safely tell this person anything about you, what might it be?
Create:	A poem, chant, or word collage that expresses the essence of what makes you you from your point of view.
Reflect:	Have you ever talked with this person about who you are, what you want, how you feel? If so, how did the experience affect you? If not, why not? What does it mean to you to be known (or not known) by an important person in your life?

There comes a point in a daughter's life when she begins to look at her mother's life, not merely as daughter, but as part of her search for her own identity as a woman, adult and possible mother. Mother–daughter issues are complicated and often prove difficult to sort out. Many students (female and male) were interested in and fascinated by *The Road from Coorain,* written by Jill Ker Conway, formerly president of Smith College. She writes movingly about her early life when she lived and worked on an isolated Australian sheep station, experiencing

Sourcework

.... 189

an eight-year drought and having to school herself by reading available books, magazines, and printed matter. After the death of her father, she and her family moved to Sydney where Conway made her way despite male chauvinism and provincial ideas about scholarship. Yet it is her description of her struggles with her mother that most moved my students, especially the following two passages:

> I knew that my mother's gifts came at a considerable price. They might seem to be freely given, but there would come a time afterwards when they had to be earned. (Conway, p. 135)

> Thoughts of escape were unrealistic. Daughters in Australia were supposed to be the prop and stay of their parents. Would I ever get away? How on earth could I set about doing it? How could I tell this woman who lived for me that I did not want to live for her? . . . I often watched the Southern Cross in the night sky, but it was not just a compass bearing I needed now, it was a judgment about what would be the moral path to choose. (Conway, p.151)

SUGGESTION FOR EXPLORATION

Time: 45 minutes

Text: *The Road From Coorain*

Focus: My mother, myself

Paint: An image of you in relationship to your mother.

Write: Words that come to mind when you think about you and your mother.

Share: Images and words.

Select: The word or idea you have written that seems most important to you.

Write: A memory, episode, experience, or feeling that comes to mind when you think about you and your mother.

Reflect: On Conway's words. Think about what, if anything,
they have to do with your relationship to your mother.
If your mother is dead or died before you knew her,
how does this affect your current choices?

Many of my students consider themselves to have difficult lives.
They worry about important life issues like how they're going to earn
a living, whether they'll find someone to love, if they can earn the
money they need to buy and do what pleases them. Yet when they
read about Phung Thi Le Ly Hayslip, who was twelve years old when
the war between the Viet Cong and the South Vietnamese began,
many begin to reconsider their earlier perspectives. In *When Heaven
and Earth Changed Places,* Phung Le Ly Hayslip describes the
changes that took place in her life and within herself after three years
of war where no one and no place were safe:

> Either I would be raped again, or I would not. I might be
> arrested again by the Viet Cong, or perhaps by the Republicans—
> but what did it matter? The bullets of one would just save bullets
> for the other. I no longer cared even for vengeance. Both sides in
> this terrible, endless, *stupid* war had finally found the perfect
> enemy: a terrified peasant girl who would endlessly and stupidly
> consent to be their victim—as all Vietnam's peasants had con-
> sented to be victims, from creation to the end of time! From now
> on, I promised myself I would only flow with the strongest current
> and drift with the steadiest wind—and not resist. To resist, you
> have to believe in something. (Hayslip, p.97)

SUGGESTION FOR EXPLORATION

Time: 45 minutes

Text: *When Heaven and Earth Changed Places*

Focus: Belief and believing

Paint: An image of belief.

Write: A brief paragraph stating your most firmly and deeply
held beliefs.

Sourcework

.... 191

Consider: How did you come to have these beliefs? Have they ever been tested? Under what circumstances? Have you ever stopped believing in something that was once very important to you? What, if anything, took its place? How did the loss affect you? Are there long-term consequences?

Share: A belief that is important to you.

Reflect: On what it means to believe in something. Think about Le Ly Hayslip's life and the way the war affected her beliefs. What sustained her enough to keep her from committing suicide? What sustains you when you find life difficult? What connects you to life and living?

Moving From the Reading to the Writing

As we read an autobiography, students often write short pieces—a memory, a description of a significant person in their lives, a particular event that proves to be a turning point. These pieces are shared with the class as students choose or time permits. No one ever has to read. The class responds to each reading according to the writer's focus: "I'm trying to remember when I tripped and smashed into my mother who was pouring hot coffee into my father's cup." "I want to describe my feelings when I saw the sign, 'Whites only.'" "I'm the first person in my family to go to college. I want to talk about what it's like to love math when everyone else loves sitcoms."

These short pieces help students to discover a time of their life or an issue in their life on which to focus. In the beginning, many students think their lives are so ordinary that there is nothing of interest to write about. Reading a variety of autobiographies enables students to understand how differing perspectives and points of view can make even mundane experience potentially interesting. As classmates question each other, wanting to know more about each others' lives, a change begins to happen. Students look at their own lives from their own points of view. They learn to value their ability to tell the stories of their lives for their own reasons.

Working with short pieces keeps the risk level to a minimum, helping the class, both as individuals and as a group, to define parameters and boundaries of issues and comments. Usually students avoid reading extremely emotional material out loud. Yet occasionally someone's writing strikes a raw nerve. One such incident took place while we were reading *The Road from Coorain.* At issue was the responsibility the author felt toward her mother and brother who remained in Australia. One student wrote a short piece, caught by the following passage:

> Now I realized, in what amounted to a conversion experience, that I was going to violate the code of my forefathers. I wouldn't tell myself anymore I was tough enough for any hazard, could endure anything because, as my father's old friend has said, "she was born in the right country." I wasn't nearly tough enough to stay around in an emotional climate more desolate than any drought I'd ever seen. I wasn't going to fight anymore. I was going to admit defeat; turn tail; run for cover . . . I was going to be different. I was going to be life-affirming from now on, grateful to have been born . . . (Conway, p.232)

The words leaped out at her, triggering the misery she tried to hide. She wrote about her brother's increasingly severe mental illness while she was applying for college. Her piece, four paragraphs long, described her anguish: "Do I have the right to leave my parents and my brother? How can I go off to school and live a happy life when they're so unhappy?" She read the passage that triggered her writing, and began to cry just as she began to read her own work. Probably because the student was writing in relationship to another writer's work, the first student to respond focused on the author of the original passage.

"I bet Jill Ker Conway felt pretty terrible having to choose between her mother and her self. I bet lots of people tried to tell her it was her duty to stay and take care of her mother."

Another student added, "My mom told me her father used to pretend to have heart attacks every time she said something about leaving home. It took her a long time to find the courage to leave—she was over thirty."

"Maybe that's why Conway wrote the book," suggested a third student. "Maybe she wanted people like us to know it's okay to say 'yes' to ourselves." By this time the student writer had gained enough control to finish reading her piece. When a student reads personal writing I ask the author to tell us what kind of writing suggestions are wanted. Given the power of her writing we were surprised when she said, "How's my grammar?" We all burst into laughter—a little bit of comic relief is always welcome.

Just to make sure she understood our position one boy explained, "How can I think about grammar when all I'm wondering about is how you're gonna find the courage to do what you need to do?" I reminded the class that there is a need to correct grammar, but it does not necessarily have to be the first issue.

After we have read several autobiographies, I ask my students to select a passage from one of the books we have read to use as the springboard for their own writing. Although most of this writing is done out of class, periodically students exchange passages or bits of their stories they find problematical or satisfying. Classmates ask questions of each other as they attempt to deepen and clarify their understanding of the issues in their lives. Some resent these exchanges of stories, calling them a waste of time. Others eagerly participate. But gradually, as patterns emerge, student attitudes change. One student wrote: "I really did not see how these books related to my life. This all changed December 5. This is the day I learned the true meaning of stories. I thought that I did not relate to these stories, but I was wrong. I just did not realize how much these stories changed me. When I heard my fellow classmates recite parts of their papers, I realized the impact of these stories on my life."

What goes on in this autobiographical exploration is not "true confessions" but rather a focused and disciplined writing assignment encouraging students to explore self in relationship to an issue successfully negotiated by the author. The text acts as container and point of reference. Students are free to choose the issue(s) in their lives to write about, as well as the depth to which they are initially prepared to go. Many begin with what seems most accessible—a favorite memory, a funny experience, a fight with a family member or friend. However, as they write, their relationship to these issues changes. What seemed funny then appears more telling now. What began as a superficial exploration begins to resemble a deep-sea-diving expedition. As students improve their ability to share their responses to the autobiographies (both their own and published), they learn to trust their own voices. Almost without noticing, they begin to connect their own experiences to those of the people in the books we have been reading. The students are affirmed as persons of worth, of people with stories to tell and knowledge to share.

Evaluation

It was my first teaching job—a junior counselor, working wherever I was needed. This morning I was directing a puppet project for ten-year-olds who were preparing for a puppet show. The regular counselor in charge of the program had suddenly left camp, too ill to continue. There was no one to ask "if I was doing it right," and probably no one I would ask even if there had been someone. The pigtailed little girl brought me her puppet, which still needed clothes and hair. "What do you think?" she asked.

More wise-alec than pedagogue I turned her question back to her, "What do *you* think?" She looked at me, a bit startled, then stared intently at her puppet. She was hard at work, thinking.

"Well . . . Maybe I need to put more clay on his cheeks before I put the final layer of paper on his face. He's the king. People who look at him have to be impressed, 'Yes, your majesty. No, your majesty.' " Running off she yelled, "Thanks for your help."

Now I was the one who was startled. Without my saying a word, she now knew what her puppet needed and was off to make adjustments. For the rest of the summer I tried to turn all questions of judgment back to the questioner. It was one of the best summers of my life. But I went to college, learned to be a teacher, and forgot what I knew from experience.

More than five years later I was sitting at the back of a classroom watching a group of fifteen-year-olds show a bit of a play they were making. As soon as they finished everyone looked at me. I didn't hesitate to tell the students what I thought of their work—their words were hard to hear, the action was impossible to understand. Sullenly, the group sat down, and the next group took their place. I could see the effect my words had on them as they dispiritedly returned to their seats. The contrast between the energy and excitement with which they began and the spiritless way they ended made me feel as if I had smashed their creative spirit. I pushed away the nagging doubts about

195

my role in their learning. After all, I was the teacher, wasn't I? It was my job to correct students, wasn't it? Why was I feeling so bad?

With time I became more experienced, a little kinder perhaps, but I came to hate the moment when a group finished and all eyes focused on me, waiting for my words to condemn or validate their work. I grew desperate to find a more productive way to help students learn. Although I recognized that students need and want to do good work, I so resented the high price we paid that for a time I refused to make any comments at all. This helped no one, increased everyone's frustration, and left me totally unprepared when it was time to grade students' work. There had to be a better way, but I didn't have a clue. Nothing solved the problem—helping students learn how to make productive choices about their own work without crushing their creativity.

I continued to muddle and mumble when it came time to make judgments, growing more uneasy and uncertain—a horrible state for someone with strong opinions. I began to get stomachaches and headaches. I thought about leaving teaching. I'd become a baker— yeast knows what to do as long as you give it warm water, a bit of salt, and some sugar to get it going.

I'm not sure how long I continued in this state of limbo, but I am forever grateful to the students in one class who looked at me after showing their work and demanded to know, "What's good?" I laughed and without thinking said, "You tell me!" They did. But, what followed made me remember my young puppet maker. After their initial exuberance came a period of reflection, some questions for the audience, and a rising sense of relief within me. The Quakers have a saying, "The way will come," and it certainly did that afternoon. After so much misery I finally understood that evaluation—grading, grades, and comments on papers and projects—did not have to automatically leave people feeling heartbroken, or stupid, or incompetent. The clouds that had hung over me for so long gave way to glorious sunshine and hope. I happily gave up thoughts about leaving teaching.

In the years that followed I observed the process by which performance is judged, whether it was my thoughts about my own work, students' comments about their classwork, or colleagues' responses to letters of rejection or acceptance. Ideas emerged and evolved, transforming evaluation from an immediate authoritarian judgment to collaborative questioning and reflection. These procedures became an integral part of the total learning experience that I structure for my students.

Some Ideas About Evaluation

- Learners often know what's wrong as well as what's right about their work. Telling them what they already know is a waste of everyone's time and energy.
- Dependence upon the teacher as the sole arbiter of good and bad or right and wrong disempowers students and prevents teachers from learning what students know.
- Asking questions about work opens up exploration and discovery. Merely stating opinions closes off possibility and increases discouragement. If students don't know how to phrase a question I tell them to state their idea of the problem (using "I") so the class can help the person to frame a personally satisfying question that the student then poses to the group showing their work. The process of asking questions is effective whether the work in question is a paper, a project, or a performance.
- Students respond most favorably when they believe the grading system is fair. Asking students to participate in the establishment of a fair grading system acts to empower them, especially when they trust the teacher to take their suggestions seriously. I have discovered this also improves student engagement in class activity.
- Although as a teacher I am responsible for giving students grades, I involve them in the grading process by asking class members to develop the criteria by which they choose to be graded. This is handed in with their midterm evaluation and serves as preparation for the final evaluation and criteria, which by then have been fine tuned. Even when students disagree with me, the discussion about grades invariably includes talk about values, standards, expectations, and notions of self-esteem, which prove enormously helpful as part of the means by which I establish classroom dialogue.
- Although this is not an option for many teachers, I give no grades until the end of the semester. I respond to student papers and projects with detailed questions and a few comments, and I am available for student conferences when students have questions about their work and progress. Although this process comes as a shock to most students initially, it generally serves to free them from the tyranny of grades, encouraging them to engage more openly in their learning. Teachers who are required to give grades on a

regular basis can still invent ways to include the participation of their students in the development of grading systems. I believe there are real differences between acquiring and learning to use tools, which is what I think happens in the first part of a semester, and putting these tools to increasingly more effective use. Grading beginning efforts tends to stifle imagination, creativity, participation in class activity, and openness about one's need for help and attention.

- Evaluation is most effective when it is a continuing process where students can defend their ideas and work without fear of retribution. Teachers can use this debate more effectively when they focus on the establishment of criteria rather than on issues surrounding a particular grade. The time to begin this discussion is before any grades have been assigned.

- I have found it useful to share my discomfort about grading with my students. Apparently it never occurs to them that as a teacher I might hate to give grades as much as they hate to get them. In disclosing my dislike I open up discussion about ways to improve the grading process so that it becomes more equitable.

- There is no such thing as an objective grade. Even in classes where grades are established by simply adding up test scores and dividing the results by the number of tests, teachers still decide what will be on tests and the relative importance of each question and test.

- Student work can and does improve without judgmental comments from other classmates or teachers. What students do require is articulate feedback, which helps them to make their work as good as possible according to the students' vision of their own work.

- Students often respond enthusiastically to teachers who make it clear they value their students and expect them to do their very best. Recent movies such as *Stand and Deliver* demonstrate the power a teacher can have on students accustomed to not being valued or cared about or expected to achieve. All of us are more capable than we know. It is the teachers' job to acquaint students with unexplored or unknown talent, knowledge, ability, or useful qualities such as perseverance and curiosity. Student ingenuity, demonstrated by the way they meet life's demands, can be incorporated into useful classroom attitudes and behaviors. The classroom can be an important place where inside and outside life are connected and examined.

Collaborative Learning: An Effective Climate for Evaluation

I find it useful and necessary to confront the issue of evaluation on the first day of class when students have the least fixed notion of who I am, how I teach, how I grade, and what I expect. How I initially act and react to students on the first day affects their attitudes, expectations, hopes, fears, and our ability to work together effectively. A bad start creates an ineffective climate and, once initiated, is hard to correct or change. Because most students are concerned about grades, the subject of grading is loaded, especially when a teacher talks about grades in ways that may be new to students. The first step is to get everyone's attention, using a calm and friendly tone of voice. The second step requires that you state your case clearly and without defensiveness. I find it useful to include my grading policies on the syllabus so that students can refer to it as they choose. The third step involves connecting grades and grading to the total course experience and my philosophy of teaching. The fourth step I take is to reinforce the idea that all my policies on evaluation, grades, and grading are designed to help students learn effectively with as little reference to grades as possible. The fifth step consists of actions that I take and techniques that I use to build trust and responsibility, which includes creating an educational community, collaborative learning, the importance of exploring alternatives before making decisions, and the availability of the class as a resource for any individual or group.

I find it necessary to differentiate judgment after work is finished or a solid draft has been made, from judgment that is premature because the work is still at the beginning stages. When students submit a piece of work I always ask them to tell me about their focus and the kind of informative response they want from me just as I do with my own work and that of my colleagues. For example, when I ask a colleague to look at a first draft of a chapter I'm writing, I don't worry much about grammar and punctuation. What I primarily want to know is whether I have a clear and consistent focus, if I have articulated my ideas so they are understandable to a reader, and if my material is interesting. In the beginning I center on large issues such as defining ideas, articulating supporting information, and giving interesting examples. Only when I am close to the final draft do I focus the criticism on fine points such as grammar, spelling, and punctuation.

When students present material I use the same system. Before sharing their work I ask the group to tell the class their intentions, their issues, and any problems they have identified or areas they know need help. After the work has been shared, one member of the group is designated secretary, and this person writes down all the questions the class asks. At this time no questions are answered by the group sharing their work nor are they permitted to defend or explain their choices. The reason I do not let the group answer questions or defend choices is that I have found it interferes with the learning process. By not being able to defend, answer, or explain, students find it easier to listen to the questions and to understand the issues and concerns of those watching. After the class has asked their questions the next group shares their work. When every group has worked, the groups examine their questions and explore the ideas and issues suggested by the questions. Each group decides which questions to deal with as well as ways to respond. They are also free to ignore all the questions though this seldom happens. Because all students have been involved both in the sharing of work and the process of questioning as individual members of an audience, there tends to be good interaction within group members.

Yet, there are times, despite all the questions, that a group gets stuck. The more they try to untangle themselves the more muddled they become. When this happens students tend to become embarrassed and self-conscious. How a teacher handles this situation speaks volumes to the class about trust, caring, and a genuine desire to facilitate learning. With no condescension I begin by thanking them for creating a good learning situation for the class and ask if they are willing to have the class help them. Even when the eyes roll and the cynics laugh, I hold to my question. Usually the group agrees, but if they seem uncertain or unwilling I reinforce the power of this particular learning opportunity. Very gently I ask the troubled group about their perception of the problem. If they know what it is we help them to sort out the source of the muddle. Most often however, they don't know what's wrong except to say, "Nothing's working."

For example, one group had been working with an idea about how an enraged passerby affects three friends who are having trouble talking about their feelings, but the group was unable to make the disparate parts come together in any way that made sense to them. The class and I first questioned the enraged passerby. Some of the questions he wrote down were: How old are you? With whom do you live? Where are your coming from? Where are you going? Why are you so angry? Why do you bother noticing the three friends? He looked as if he had more than enough to consider so we switched our attention to the three friends. They wrote down the following questions: How do we as an audience know how you feel about each other? What is happening among you? Why does the passerby have such an effect? Why do the three of you react as one rather than individually? How old are each of you? What have you been doing before the beginning of the scene? How often do you see each other? Is your meeting now an accident? If it was planned, what was the reason for getting together? Drama requires action—what is your action? Soon the three friends held up their hands. They had enough questions. Each individual was asked to answer as many questions as possible before the group explored their common action.

The second sharing was much clearer in that we could understand why the passerby was enraged, but the three friends remained stuck. I asked each of them to create a one-minute monologue to tell us what each person was thinking about the other two. Their spontaneous monologues resulted in some laughter and some ideas. The third sharing resulted in a fight among the three friends, which totally left out the passerby. The group felt discouraged and asked to stop, "We're taking too much of the class's time. At least we tried."

I asked the group, "Do you agree?"

"No! Keep going." was the response. To ease the working group's discomfort I asked them to look at the class. "Do they look angry? Bored? Resentful?" Each question was answered by a shake of their heads.

"So, let's keep going. You're almost there. Anyone have any questions for them?"

"What if the angry passerby comes upon the three friends fighting—like he almost crashes into them because he's not paying attention, and they're not paying attention?"

"Yeah, what if the conflict isn't about the angry passerby or the three friends fighting? What if it's really about feeling as if nobody cares about you?" More ideas and questions flew about the room at such a rate the group couldn't write fast enough. I asked them to take a minute to look at all the questions and, without discussion, play the scene again. With the class watching intently, the group created a focused scene where the angry passerby trips and falls into the three friends arguing.

One of the friends asks, "Why don't you watch where you're going?"

The passerby retorts, "What's it to you? What difference does it make?" One of the friends notices that he looks as if he's been beaten

STORYMAKING AND DRAMA

202 ···

and uses her handkerchief to stop some bleeding from an injured eye. The scene continued with the passerby telling the three friends about being thrown out of his house for cursing his father. Each of them responded to his predicament as individuals.

When one of the friends said, "You sure are in a mess. I wish we could help," there was a silence and a sense of closure, at least about the initial issues raised. They had found a stopping place. The scene might not be finished but the group felt clear about the situation they had set up and the characterization they had created and had ideas about strategies for resolution. The whole class responded appreciatively to the work both they and the small group had done. Everyone looked satisfied as we discussed what had and had not worked, the direction in which they might continue, possible endings, and what class members had learned. They all agreed that helping the group become unstuck was a satisfying use of forty minutes of class time and a clear demonstration of the power of collaborative learning.

It takes time and experience before a group trusts the teacher and other class members. One way to build this trust is to establish a format for responding to other people's ideas whether these are written, acted, moved, painted, or sculpted. I strongly encourage a bit of silence between the time a person or group has finished and the moment when someone comments or questions. Students tell me this active, personal consideration is eminently satisfying, a time when their ideas are given serious and focused attention.

Another way to help build an effective working environment is to include myself as teacher in the process. In the past I have asked the permission of a class to hear a paper I was presenting at a professional conference, to read parts of a play I was writing, to consider an outline of a book I was planning. In every case they responded with genuinely helpful remarks and questions. Occasionally I have been able to share enough work in progress that I could mirror the process they were experiencing in class. Students are often initially surprised and/or annoyed when they discover they have to write two or three drafts of a paper, so when I describe my reactions to writing a tenth draft they are astonished and comforted. What's good for them is also good for the teacher.

Grades and Grading

If I had to reduce my philosophy of teaching into one word that word would be *dialogue.* Given a second word I would choose *empowerment.* Provided with a whole sentence, I would say that students must have a chance to explore and share their ideas and feelings about classroom issues that affect them. Perhaps no issue affects students as powerfully as grading, yet few students have any meaningful input into grades and grading policy. They are only free to resent, approve, distrust, dislike, or hate the way teachers grade. This strikes me as counterproductive and an unnecessary waste of energy.

Although the majority of teachers from first grade through university have to assign grades, how they do this is mostly a matter of individual design and school policy. There is usually no law that says students cannot participate in the design of the processes by which they are graded. Faced with "being done to" or "participating in the doing" many students come to appreciate the chance to design the criteria on which they are graded and to construct the means by which grades are given.

When students have to use their own criteria to defend their grade and to give examples of their work and participation in support of their chosen grade, I find that 85 to 90 percent of my students give themselves the grade I have given them. The rest are equally divided between grades that are too low and too high. Although I always use student criteria and evaluation as part of the information I use to give final grades, the final grade each student gets is my decision. As the result of many years of experience, I've learned that students find it helpful for me to give them C criteria. They then differentiate between A, B, and D, F. For my students C criteria look like this:

- Attend all classes.
- Participate in all class activity.
- Hand in all papers and projects on time and fully complete.

As you may notice, these are all behavioral objectives. Students know whether they have satisfied them or not. Initially they ask, "Why is this a C and not a higher grade?" I point out to them that these standards are minimal and do not include student initiative, quality of work, or contribution to class.

My policy, which students often initially resent, requires that they develop the criteria by which they would like to be graded as part of their midterm evaluation. In the midterm evaluation they supply substantive evidence of what they have learned, how they know they have learned this, and their contribution to the class's learning. Evidence can be in the form of anecdotes, papers, projects, or extra work. The more details with which students write, the more persuasive their arguments tend to be. I return the midterm evaluation and

criteria with comments and questions. Usually students fail to men-
tion evidence of quality or scholarship and may need help deciding
how one knows what quality work means. As part of the class
midterm discussion we discuss both personal and general issues of
documentation, grading, and evaluation. At the same time, I keep
notes on the quality of their class participation, homework assignments, and in-class writing and speaking assignments. I note when
students provide important collaborative help and when they actively
block the learning of others. My goal is to track individual student
progress so I have the necessary data to use in grading.

Most of my students have never before had the opportunity to
design the means by which they are graded, and not all of them welcome the chance to do so. Comments include: "You're the teacher,
why ask me to do your job?" "What's the point? You'll give me the
grade you want to give me no matter what I say." "This is a mindless
exercise that merely demonstrates teacher incompetency." "Why ask
me? You're the expert!" One or two say, "This is neat!" "I never realized
how hard it is to decide how to grade, let alone what grade to give."

In the beginning, when students are most unsure of "what I
want," their ability, and the course material, I refuse to allow grades
to be a reference point; but as students gain experience they begin to
analyze their work and learn to look at the clarity of their objectives,
how well they met their own goals, the extent to which they took a
risk, and how or if they responded imaginatively or creatively. By
bringing issues of grades and grading into the open as an important
topic for discussion, students are empowered. They learn to articulate
what it means to assign a grade and the role they play in the grades
they eventually receive. Even after a grade has been given, students
are free to discuss their grade and to make a case for a different
(usually higher) grade. At the very least, this procedure encourages
students to think about the meaning and makeup of a grade, but when
the system works best, students actively participate in grading and
use the experience to enhance their own learning.

5

Storymaking and Drama in the Teaching of English as a Second Language

While teaching in Hungary I was asked to explore the use of storymaking and drama with two groups of students who were studying English as a foreign language. Their teacher regularly read them old and new stories, explaining all new vocabulary words before reading the story, using visual aids to improve comprehension as she read. I proposed to tell old stories with which they were unfamiliar, use no pictures, and explain no words beforehand. I planned to use stories that I liked, without tailoring my vocabulary or the contents to the students' supposed level of proficiency. I based this approach on my previous experiences when teaching in Sweden and Denmark, where I discovered that when I told myths and tales to my students they listened with rapt attention. Even when they didn't understand every word, they understood enough of the story to maintain interest and were able to ask questions about words they didn't understand after I had finished telling the story. Although I was teaching drama rather than English as a Foreign Language, many of the students commented that their English improved, almost without their noticing.

Like the Swedish and Danish students, the Hungarian students listened to the story avidly, occasionally asking me or their regular teacher for the meaning of a word. What was particularly impressive was the way storymaking and drama techniques fostered language development and usage in surprising ways. For example, after telling a Laotian story, "A Community of Knowing" (see page 26), I asked students, in pairs, to write a letter to a public official in Hungary, commenting on an issue important to the writers. One duo wrote a letter to the Minister of Education complaining that they had too much academic work and not enough time for sport in their regular school day. The two students signed their letter "on behalf of one million Hungarian school children." After they shared their letter with the class I commented that what they had written was a class-action letter. The two writers were fascinated by the idea and preened

205

as I explained about class action, as best I could. (I never know how much I don't know until I'm asked questions by my students.) As my work with the students was ending, and we were reflecting on the value and worth of the storymaking and drama work we had explored, one boy who had not written the letter about too much academic work said, "I really liked the stories and the words that came out of the stories, like—class action." Many students nodded in agreement.

Using old stories such as myths, tales, and legends has several advantages. There are many stories that can be told in three or four minutes, have simple plots, vivid imagery, and relatively few characters. Most often there is little direct dialogue, leaving lots of room for listeners to jump into a story and to make it their own. I think myths and tales hold interest because they tend to be essential stories containing little description of place, character, or motivation. Even though there are notable exceptions (such as Eastern European stories, which can be long and complex), it is relatively easy to find short tales that are powerful and intriguing enough to encourage listeners with limited vocabulary to stay involved and to care about the story.

Telling stories from a variety of cultures also enables students to become more appreciative of unfamiliar ways of living. Occasionally, I will tell a story from one culture and have listeners tell me a similar story from another culture noting their appreciation for the similarities and the differences. These experiences help to reinforce the idea that what is familiar and comfortable is not necessarily the only or right way to behave.

In this section I retell one story and explore a variety of ways to use it when teaching English as a Second or Foreign Language. Common to all the suggested techniques are the ideas that: Stories beget new stories just as words evoke new words; working as a class as well as in small groups helps to create a collaborative learning environment where it is perfectly acceptable to not know an answer; the use of storymaking and drama helps us to connect our inner knowing with our outer expression.

I recognize that students have to have some working knowledge of English before these techniques are appropriate, yet my experience confirms that once students have some vocabulary, hearing old stories (myths and tales) seems to be a powerful catalyst for language development. Part of the effectiveness of using storymaking and drama comes from the great difference in being read a story and being told the same story. In part it has to do with the process— when we read a story to a group we read the story using someone else's words, constructs, and contents. When we tell this same story as the story-

Storymaking and Drama in the Teaching of English as a Second Language

.... 207

teller, we must use our own words and are more dependent on the listening audience. We have more eye contact, a deeper awareness of response (or lack thereof), and a greater sense of community. It is difficult to continue telling a story when no one wants to listen.

When exploring a myth or tale with a group of students who are unaccustomed to being allowed to think about a story in their own way, it is particularly crucial that the teacher word each task carefully to encourage diversity in the answers. I have been in situations where students copy the first presenter, expecting to meet with my approval. I have learned that the best response is some version of: "We seem to have one prevalent idea. How else can we think about this story?" If no one responds I have to give them more help. Let us use "Little Red Riding Hood" as an example. I asked students to create a monologue as a character in the story. Most chose to be the mother blaming Little Red Riding Hood for her troubles. I tried to get them to take on another role, but they stonily refused. I could see they had decided that this was the right response. Finally I said, "You have all commented that Little Red Riding Hood got into trouble because she didn't listen to her mother. But what about Little Red Riding Hood? Might she not have been curious? Couldn't she have been so interested in what she was seeing in the forest that she forgot to pay attention to where she was going? Isn't it possible that she was so intrigued by the wolf she forgot how dangerous wolves can be?" It can be very difficult and tedious work to get students to let go of the notion, based on their experience, that there is ultimately only one right answer, and that their problem is to figure out what the teacher thinks is right. I have found this to be particularly true when students are being asked to respond in a language that is not their native tongue. Still, it is possible for students to value their own responses when the teacher remains firmly committed to active, open exploration. Patience helps. Lots and lots and lots of patience!

I will suggest ways to use the Chinese story of Li Chi to exemplify my storymaking and drama approach to teaching English as a Second or Foreign Language, because it has proven to be one of the most popular stories with which I have worked, regardless of the age or experience of listeners. It is also one of the few stories where a young heroine succeeds after others, older and supposedly wiser, have failed.

The Story of Li Chi

Many years ago, in the Yung Ling mountains of China, there lived a huge serpent, ten stories high and forty lengths long, who was always very hungry though it ate whatever it could find—sheep, cows, pigs, ducks, dogs—even people.

The frightened villagers went to the village magistrate and complained, "It is your job to protect us against this dangerous serpent. If you do not help us we will lose all our animals."

The magistrate had no idea what to do so he consulted a sorcerer who advised him, "Tell the villagers to meet in the village square on the first day of each month with a small animal who will be brought to the serpent on the mountain by different villagers each month."

The villagers agreed to the plan, yet on the first day of the next month, no one appeared in the village square. More animals disappeared. The villagers went to the magistrate and demanded that he do something.

The magistrate returned to the sorcerer who said, "Each year, in the ninth month, a fourteen-year-old girl must be brought to the cave of the serpent." When the magistrate objected the sorcerer retorted, "Surely the sacrifice of one small girl is worth the safety of the villagers and their animals." Reluctantly, everyone agreed to the plan.

For nine years, despite the pleas of families who did not want to lose their daughters, nine young girls were forced to sacrifice their lives in order to keep the village safe.

In the tenth year, Li Chi, a fourteen-year-old girl, the oldest of six girls in a very poor family, decided to volunteer to go up the mountain if the magistrate would promise to take care of her parents in their old age. Li Chi knew that her sisters would go to live in the homes of their husbands, and she did not want her parents to die in poverty. Though her parents and her sisters begged her not to go, Li Chi refused to change her mind.

Early one morning, she went to the magistrate and said, "I will volunteer to go up the mountain to the cave of the serpent if you will grant me my conditions." The magistrate was relieved that this year he would not have to search for a young girl. But Li Chi told him, "I want you to take care of my parents as they age so that they will not die in poverty. And you must give me what I need if I am to go up the mountain. I want some food, a flint, a dog, and a sword."

"A sword? Who ever heard of giving a sword to a young girl?"

"If I am eaten by the serpent who will know?"

"Very well. I grant you your request."

Slowly, following the terrible stench of the serpent, Li Chi and the dog made their way up the mountain. Li Chi used the flint to build a fire in front of the mouth of the serpent's cave. Soon the serpent was lured out of its cave by the delicious smells of the cooking food. When she saw the serpent's head was fully out of the cave, Li Chi signalled the dog to jump on to the serpent's face and claw out its eyes. Then, Li Chi stabbed the sword into the serpent until it died.

The dog started to run toward the village, but Li Chi called him back. She walked into the cave and found the bones of the nine young girls who had been sacrificed to keep the village safe from the serpent. Tenderly and carefully, she wrapped their bones in her shawl and gently carried them back down the mountain.

When the magistrate saw Li Chi and the dog he was furious that she had broken her agreement. But Li Chi said, "These are the bones of the nine maidens sacrificed by the village. Surely they deserve to be treated with reverence and appreciation."

And so the villagers buried the bones of the nine girls and honored Li Chi for her courage and wisdom. Even today, if you go to the area near the Yung Ling mountains of China you can still hear the story of Li Chi, the serpent slayer.

SUGGESTIONS FOR EXPLORATION

Time:	45 minutes	1
Text:	The Story of Li Chi	
Focus:	Exploring ideas around unsafe and safe	
Paint:	On left side of paper, an image of "unsafe."	
Write:	Down some words that come to mind.	
Paint:	On right side of paper, an image of "safe."	
Write:	Down some words that come to mind.	
Share:	Images and words.	
Tell:	Class "The Story of Li Chi."	
List:	On paper three words to describe the serpent.	
List:	On paper three words to describe Li Chi.	

Share:	Words and list them on the blackboard. Ask for synonyms.
Reflect:	On experience and notions of unsafe and safe as these words relate to the story.

2

Time:	45 minutes
Text:	The Story of Li Chi
Focus:	Telling moments
Tell:	The Story of Li Chi
Paint:	An image of a telling moment (a point in the story which each student finds most vivid, interesting or important).
Title:	The image by naming the picture.
Divide:	Into groups of three.
Select:	Three moments of importance to each group.
Create:	"Still photographs" of three important moments. Students can change the roles they take on for each choice. They also need to plan transitions—how they will get from one pose to another with no extraneous movement—how they will know to move from one pose to the next without talking—how they will know when and how to end their work.
Share:	Still photographs.
Reflect:	On how choices were made regarding which moments to choose and how roles were selected.

When I did this exercise in Hungary some of the students complained that the story was too complete, that the choices for telling

Storymaking and Drama in the Teaching of English as a Second Language

.... 211

moments were too few and too obvious. Indeed, most students did choose the same moments. But instead of agreeing that the story was too complete, I challenged them: "What moments did you consider and discard?" Silence. I pushed some more: "What about the moment when Li Chi decides on the strategy she intends to use to kill the serpent and rescue the maidens' bones?" More silence. "What about a society that sacrifices fourteen-year-old girls?"

One student shrugged, "Well, if people are going to die anyway, what's one more death? Especially when it's a young girl who has no value?"

Suddenly the room was buzzing as several young women took umbrage. "What do you mean a young girl has no value? Who's going to have the kids if all the girls die?"

"All the girls aren't dying. Just one, once a year."

"But the whole point of the story is that men decided young girls were expendable. Li Chi did what no man thought to do."

I sat, happy to watch the fray. When the arguments became a jumbled confusion of voices I called the class to order and asked, "So where are these moments in your collection of three still photographs?" Silence.

"We didn't think you would let us be so political."

I reminded them that the assignment was to choose their moments in their groups of three and that I said nothing about which moments to chose. I suggested we look at the images they made of their telling moment. I finally commented, "No politics at work here either. So what's going on?" I looked at their faces—a jumble of embarrassment, anger, shame, frustration, and shock. No one was willing to put words to their thoughts or feelings. "Right," I said. "Let's repeat the assignment. This time make sure you respond as you choose. Don't censor yourselves. Anything goes."

Not every student believed that I meant what I said, but the choices they made as a group the second time were clearly coming from a different place inside them. Their initial choices, selected to please me, gave way to choosing that which pleased them. In the process they not only experienced the power of free choice, they also learned a lot of new vocabulary as they asked me for words and argued with each other in English and Hungarian. Just before class ended, I suggested they identify words they had learned or wanted to learn. I put all the new words on the board, and soon the whole blackboard was filled with words such as personal power, vulnerability, value, social compact, social contract, disproportion, and corruption. I noticed most students chose to write them in their notebooks.

In the days following our session, each time I met one of my students, they stopped to chat. They had words they wanted me to define.

SUGGESTIONS FOR EXPLORATION

1	**Time:**	45 minutes
	Text:	The Story of Li Chi
	Focus:	Creating a character
	Tell:	The Story of Li Chi
	Sculpt:	An image of one character of your choosing in relationship to another character in the story. Second character can be someone with a small voice like the mother, father, sisters, or relatives of the dead maidens, or a character with a large role like the magistrate.
	Share:	Sculptures. Using "I" as if you are your character, tell class something about who you are, what you're feeling, how you view what's going on in the village. Each monologue needs to be less than one minute.
	Class:	Listens to monologue and then class members ask questions of each character, in role. For example, suppose I have chosen to be Li Chi's mother, and I'm listening to a sorcerer's monologue. Depending on my view of myself I might challenge, placate, beg for mercy, or confront through the question(s) I ask. Each time a question is asked, the monologuist answers using, in role, "I."
	Reflect:	On how asking and answering in role helps to define character and deepen our understanding of the story.

2	**Time:**	45 minutes
	Text:	The Story of Li Chi

Focus: Exploring perspectives

Tell: The Story of Li Chi

In role: Imagine you are the editor of a magazine, newspaper, or journal. You have heard about Li Chi, and you want to interview her. Decide what kind of publication you are editing and why you want to do the interview.

Write: An editorial for your publication regarding Li Chi.

Share: Editorials.

Reflect: On what editors chose to focus on—how their point of view might affect their choices. Consider how differences in geography, experience, gender, and age might influence what is written.

Sometimes, especially when students feel limited by a lack of language experience, it's difficult for people to express themselves emotionally. I have often noticed the flatness of answers in English compared to the vitality of expression when students use their native language. This is particularly true of older students who have learned proper classroom behavior and tend to censor their strong feelings and ideas in order to please their teacher or the system. To encourage emotional language development I suggest students speak in their native language when they are emotionally involved in an activity such as drama, and then to ask me or the class for help in saying the equivalent in English. Turning individual deficiency into a group project deflects the spotlight on a particular student and focuses the class on ways to augment language acquisition. This process also helps to decrease anxiety when students can't find the word they want.

Culture also affects language learning. In Hungary, students had almost no experience with freewheeling classroom discussion, which required class members to think on their feet. They were used to listening to lectures, taking tests, and doing written translations. Many continually apologized for their use of the English language even when I thought and said their ideas and feelings were clearly expressed. I got so tired of assuring that I understood them I decided to change my tactics. The next time someone apologized I asked, "So what's wrong?" Bewildered, the student looked to his classmates who suddenly found the floor to be a fascinating place. I waited. He stammered more apologies. I waited. He got himself into an increasingly negative spiral before I rescued him. I suggested the problem was not their use of language, but rather, their confidence in their ability to find the words they wanted, particularly when they felt under pressure to come up with the right word or phrase.

To test out the idea we set up a series of improvisations designed by the group. In order to make this charged environment feel more safe, I suggested that we set aside one word that anyone could call out at any time to stop the improvisation and to get help. Each class chose their own word, often nonsensical, which wouldn't otherwise interfere in the drama as might using a word such as "help." The first situation called for a passenger to arrive at a train station late, not knowing where a particular train was leaving from and whether it was leaving on time. To increase the pressure several students began to imitate railroad announcements, which were muffled and muddied, impossible to understand. Students took turns playing roles until it seemed as if we had exhausted most possibilities. Those watching the dramas could clearly see how stress affected language availability and choice.

A second improvisation involved a person who is hit by a car, injured, and rescued by a team of paramedics who speak gibberish initially. Without designing this strategy in advance, the more clearly the injured person spoke, the more English the paramedics used. Later, when reflecting on this unexpected reaction, students playing the paramedics said their response was unplanned and a surprise to them as well as to the rest of the class. When we explored possible reasons for their response, students seemed to think that their reactions stemmed from their notion that anxiety gets in the way of understanding—when the anxiety level goes down, comprehension goes up.

All effective language learning, whether primary or secondary, requires the establishment of a specific context. When the context is merely one of memorizing lists of vocabulary words and grammatical usage, little learning is retained because there is seldom a meaningful connection between the language use and the individual. In order to retain language, speakers have to be able to make sense of what they are saying and to use it in ways that seem logical to them. We can see this principle at work when we teach vocabulary words and require that students use the new words in sentences. Even so, if the usage is not regularly repeated, most people will soon forget the new words.

Storymaking and drama activities always involve listening, imagining, creating, telling, and/or acting. Language use is always immediately connected to an idea, theme, plot, or purpose. Afterwards, the teacher can use the process of reflection to augment initial usage and reinforce the learning of new words, ideas, and expression. Teaching language through the use of collaborative learning techniques creates a wider, deeper base among students and promotes easy access to further language acquisition.

6

Drama in Performance

The five tenth-year students were all excited about the short story they had dramatized and performed for the rest of their class. It was as if they had created magic. Fueling their delight was the idea that they could present their work at a school assembly scheduled to take place in two weeks. The teacher, happy to see his students so enthusiastic, agreed to make the necessary arrangements. Everyone thought they could repeat what they had done in class with some attention to better costumes, a bit of makeup, a little scenery, and some lighting. The students and teacher worked diligently to improve the technical aspects of the drama, and the cast spent much time practicing their lines. Satisfied with their preparation, everyone looked forward to the assembly.

The drama was performed. The costumes were fine, the makeup looked nice, and the lighting enhanced the scenery and actors. Everyone remembered their lines. Yet there was no magic. No delight. No enthusiasm. The students left the stage feeling miserable. The teacher was baffled. What had gone wrong? What more could or should they have done? My heart ached for my colleague and the students who didn't know what they needed to know in order to incorporate the quality of their classroom drama into the larger space of the auditorium.

Students who are not professional actors are not likely to recreate the magic of their initial performance merely by improving the technical aspects of production, especially when the second performance will be taking place in a larger setting that requires more emotional, vocal, and physical projection than was necessary for the original performance. What is needed, in part, is the ability to transform a small production into one that fills a larger space, as well as the experience to create, rather than recreate, the magic of the initial performance.

217

Teachers with little or no theatre training or performance experience can still help their students to share a particularly meaningful presentation if they remember to focus on what matters most—helping students to continue learning and creating while using theatre as the learning medium. Although many books contain information on how to create theatre, the material in this section focuses on ideas to contemplate when teachers are considering moving from classroom drama to public performance. One good way to explore performance is to set up possibilities for learning that have clear parameters, deciding: what will be learned at each rehearsal; how each performer will be encouraged to find answers rather than merely told what to do and how to do it; how class members not in the performance can help and participate; how the performance can be structured to remain a learning experience rather than simply a chance to show off. I believe that many students can enjoy the benefits of performance if they have the opportunity to study the making of performance, step by step, with the support and ideas of their classmates, in the service of exploring a text (poem, short story, novel, or student-written scripts).

In this section I will focus on the heart of theatre—making a moment and its relationship to the total performance experience—so that teachers and students have some understanding of what is needed when rehearsing and performing in order to move successfully from drama to performance. I will then describe ways to explore the making of a moment as part of the regular classroom drama experience.

Making a Moment

When we watch a theatre performance we sometimes have the experience of feeling as though we are no longer members of an audience watching actors at work; instead, we are one with the actor or actors as they perform in role, almost as if we feel what they feel. When this happens, our whole being is involved, and the effect can linger long after the performance ends. In the theatre this experience is called "making a moment." Technically this is described as an accent in the beat structure. What this means is that the actors and directors design the performance dynamic so that all attention is focused on a particular point, when speaking, moving, feeling, staging, and lighting all combine to create a particular and powerful effect. Actors and directors use the rehearsal period to make this possible in performance, but everyone involved in theatre knows how difficult it can be. This is because theatre is a living experience happening in real time with

Drama in Performance

.... 219

actors who must invest a script with life and human interaction. Actors sometimes fail to make a moment for the same reasons human beings fail in life—poor timing, inadvertent changes of focus, external noises, and so on. If professional actors have difficulty making moments, is it possible for inexperienced students to do this? To make magic on command?

In my experience, when students think about sharing what they value rather than focusing on what they want to show, they are more likely to create a memorable theatrical event for an audience. Although this is not as easy as it sounds, and no technique can ever guarantee the making of a moment, it is possible to accomplish. Teachers and students must decide where the high points are in a script (oral or written) and then use the rehearsal period to select the elements of performance that support student actors' capacities to share the meaning of the script with the new and larger audience.

The text provides the words, but actors create life—in performance characters come alive with all their wants, needs, wishes, and experience. For every action on stage there has to be a focused reaction to the action that shows and tells the audience the importance of what is being said and done. There are many elements that affect performance and for purposes of clarity, I will define them as they are generally used on stage and in textbooks describing theatre terms and techniques.

Breathing Life into Script and Performance
Timing

Timing, the speed at which a character speaks, moves, and reacts, plays an important part in how a character's words and actions are perceived by the audience and consists of the elements of pace and dynamics. In a scene where royalty appears, do the courtiers respond to the arrival of the king or queen quickly or slowly? Does the timing of the actors' response feel consonant with the action? If so, how do we know? For example, if the king and queen have the reputation of being cruel and quick to take offense, and the actors move too slowly, the audience may be confused by the discrepancy between what they have been told and what they are seeing. If the actors scurry while maintaining deferential positions, then the audience can see and feel the power of the king and queen. Timing gives the audience the space/time to take in what is happening so they can react to it. In a stage fight, actors generally need to plan their moves so the fight doesn't happen too quickly for the audience to see it. Most of us can remember a point in a scene when the audience laughs and the character speaking goes right on speaking without stopping, making it impossible for the audience to hear what is said next. When we create theatre we work with illusion, but it always happens in real time and real space with real people. This means actors have to choose each aspect of performance deliberately rather than relying on habitual, personal response, which may not fit their particular character. For example, an actor may have been born in a city, accustomed to walking and talking very quickly. If the actor plays a character who is slow of thought, the actor's natural timing in speech, movement, and response will have to be considerably slowed down, a feat that can take considerable practice.

Pace

Pace allows an audience to get caught up, to catch their breaths, to change their level and intensity of participation. If the pace doesn't change, the audience will soon become restless. Too much of a good thing is still too much. The use of pace enables a director to create an emotional response in the audience by pushing, pulling, stopping, and slowing down speech and action. When the aforementioned king and queen enter, perhaps a nervous courtier speaks too quickly to be understood. The director can underscore the power of the king by having him speak slowly, forcing the courtiers to pay attention no matter how much time he takes to speak.

Dynamics

The dynamics of a scene occur when directors vary the pace to provide rises and falls in intensity that gives life and interest to a performance. Variety is always the key. Without clearly planned dynamics, it will be hard for an audience to stay involved. For example, if the king and queen always speak and move slowly, the audience will lose interest. If the courtiers are always scurrying about, the audience can become bored. The director orchestrates each scene to provide a climax, to keep the audience's interest. But the director also plots the dynamics of each scene within each act and each act with the entire play in mind, so that there is a rhythmic rise and fall in timing, pace, and dynamics that keep the audience attentive and involved.

Creating Believability

Nonverbal Communication

Nonverbal communication involves the way words are spoken, the way actors move (both bodily and in space), the ways they use props, and the nature of relationships that are established geographically. For example, if an actor playing royalty appears, part of the way we know the power of this king or queen is by the physical, emotional, and psychological reaction of those on stage. Do the characters bow? Are they obsequious? Do they flatter? Ignore? Conspire? Advise? And if so, how? On-stage reaction enables the audience to know the context of what is happening.

Focus

Focus enables the audience to know where to look. Part of the director's job involves setting up stage pictures that help the audience know where and when to look. For example, if it is important for the audience to know that the entering king and queen are important persons, the director might have all characters on stage bow and make a path for the king and queen to enter. The director might have the on-stage characters fan out to the front and sides so the entering king and queen are centered and central. The most powerful moment can be invisible to an audience whose attention is elsewhere. Therefore, during rehearsal, the director is always watching the actors, designing the way they move in space, both individually and as a group, so the stage picture tells the audience where to look and which character to watch. To observe the importance of focus, watch a television production, and notice how often the camera view changes.

Projection

Projection, a key factor for inexperienced actors and directors, involves the way characters speak, move, and feel so the audience can see, hear, and feel what is happening on stage. Most of us think that good projection is merely a matter of being heard by everyone in the audience, but in addition to vocal projection actors need to be concerned about emotional and physical projection. Can the audience see and feel characters act and react? Projection must be tailored to the size of the play and the playing space, which includes both performing and audience space. Generally, the less experience a group has, the smaller the playing space needs to be. Beginning actors tend to rely on their own natural ability to physicalize a character (such as the way a character moves in space or uses props), and in a small space, these natural reactions can be seen, heard, and felt by the audience and the other actors. But, when beginning actors move to a larger space, natural response often means the audience can't hear well enough, may not see character reactions, and may not feel the emotional life of characters because the actors don't know how to enlarge their sound and movement without looking and feeling artificial.

During rehearsal, as a director, I ask a few people to act as audience members. I want them to observe their own reactions as well as their responses to the play. Their comments give me some measure of whether my intentions as director are meaningful to the audience. When they tell me, "Oh, I got so caught up in what was happening I forgot to think about myself," then I know I'm on the right track. Once, when I was directing a play I had written for children, I invited some young members of a local gang to watch rehearsals. I knew I was making progress when they became so interested in the play they forgot to throw paper airplanes.

Before a teacher takes on the responsibility of helping students create performance it is important to understand the functions of everyone involved. It is the director's job to focus all the elements and to coordinate all the action. Actors must invest intention, importance, and physicality into their lines. Both actors and the director need to ask themselves: Where is the high point of this scene? What do we want the audience to think about? To remember? To feel? Once there is a common vision and point of view, the hard work of making a moment begins. It is, at the same time, a delicate, challenging, frustrating, and difficult experience, but when the characters create a moment, it is a glorious and powerful experience for actors and audience alike.

Making a Moment with Monologues

Creating Monologues

One way to begin exploring how to move drama from the classroom onto a stage is to start with small units such as monologues. When the teacher and students can successfully shape monologues to create believable characters, they are more likely to understand the necessary elements of performance. The experience of creating a monologue is also a good way for students to explore what it means to be

Drama in Performance

.... 223

a particular character at a specific time in the text. What may look improbable from the outside becomes more accessible when one enters into the text. Here is one way to begin.

SUGGESTION FOR EXPLORATION

Select: A text—a novel, short story, play, or poem that the class is studying.

Select: A character who interests you.

Select: A specific scene, action, or event to frame the work.

Sculpt: An image of your chosen character at a specific moment in your selected scene, action, or event. Think about what has just happened to your character (precipitating event). If another person (or persons) is (are) involved, sculpt your character in relation to the person (or persons).

Paint: An image of your character at this specific moment just after the precipitating event.

Create: A one-minute monologue to describe what is going on for you, using active, vivid language to explain why you have done what you have done, to justify your actions (to yourself or others), or to attack your tormentors in terms of your character's needs, wants, wishes, or dreams. Do not judge your character as yourself.

Response: After the monologue, students choose a character from the text and ask a question in role. Students can choose to be judgmental, sympathetic, bored, angry, or whatever, as long as they stay within the parameters of their chosen role.

   Sometimes, powerful exchanges in role create a highly charged environment that needs to be dealt with before students leave for their next class. I debrief the actors by clearly setting the new task. "Leave your role. Stand up, say hello to the person next to you, or take a moment to think about yourself. Remember what you had for breakfast, how you chose the clothes you are wearing . . . whatever it takes to return to yourself." As a class, students process their experiences (the monologue and asking questions in role) to focus on the process and their learning. If the experience has been particularly emotional I take extra time to make sure students are ready to go to their next class.

Suggestions for the Teacher When Working with Monologues

• Encourage students who ask and answer questions to stay in role, as the character, until the entire transaction is finished. Develop a signal to use with the class to stop the interaction if students venture into waters that are too deep. It occasionally happens that students lose their boundaries when doing monologues and become the character rather than acting as if they were the characters. Signs that this may be happening include inappropriate volume, size of movement, or extreme emotionality. If I am in doubt I act to help the student make the necessary transition from character to person without waiting for the monologue to be finished. One suggestion that works is to use the words, "Thank you very much [name of student]. Good work!" When the student has recovered the necessary composure I explain why I stopped the monologue and suggest ways for the student to do a monologue without losing the necessary boundaries.
• Make sure you limit the time of the monologue and stick to it. I have found that one minute is time enough for students to get emotionally involved in their material but not so much time that they drown.
• Insist that students select a specific precipitating incident from the text to evoke the monologue. Before beginning the monologue, I only allow students to tell us who they are and to describe briefly the precipitating incident. Anything else must be incorporated into the monologue.
• Students sometimes choose to use their sculpture or their image as part of their monologue or bring a small prop or

bit of costume to enhance their work. I tell my students, "Use whatever works for you in the minute you have."

- If students get stuck I ask defining questions and encourage their classmates to join in. For example, a student playing Robinson Crusoe wants to tell us how he feels when he realizes he is utterly alone but can't find the words. The class might ask the following questions to help him get unstuck. "What is it like to have to make all your own meals and to eat them by yourself?" "Do you ever talk to yourself? If so, when? Do you talk out loud?" "What do you miss most about your previous life?" Questions seem to unlock ideas and feelings even when left unanswered. Further, the questions students learn to ask each other in class teach them the kinds of questions they can ask themselves when they are preparing to work in role, doing monologues or scenes.

- Questions and answers bridge the gap between monologue and dialogue when they are done in role, especially when the whole class enters the process. A monologue is by definition one person talking. But most scripts require dialogue, actors talking to each other, giving and taking ideas and energy. Moving from monologue to dialogue is not necessarily an easy transition. Actors doing monologues have only themselves to think about. Actors speaking lines to each other, having to respond appropriately, is a more complex process. When students can learn to enlarge their areas of concern in small steps, at small risk of looking foolish or being embarrassed, such as moving from monologue to dialogue through questioning as characters in role, they enlarge their areas of concentration and better understand what it means to create a believable character in performance.

Processing the Work

Immediately after a monologue is shared, the class and I process what has happened during the monologue. We question the student, who then describes or explains choices as actor and as character. I point out ideas or issues that have been evoked, or I may frame unsettling exchanges that leave characters/students with unresolved feelings so we can both generalize and particularize issues. Let us consider three examples of students working with characters they selected as part of their work with the text *Floating in My Mother's Palm* by Ursula Hegi, a novel about a young girl, Hanna, who grows

STORYMAKING AND DRAMA

226 ....

up in Germany after World War II. Her mother, a painter, is the tallest woman in the town. Hanna describes herself as the second tallest in her class. Each chapter explores powerful events in Hanna's life from Hanna's point of view. When she hasn't actually witnessed an event, she imagines how it was.

Example 1: A student, working in role as Hanna, chose to talk about the time when she was seven and went to visit her friend Karin's grandfather, a bicycle-maker, who often told her stories. The precipitating circumstances for the monologue occurred when the grandfather asks her if she is a big girl. Hanna answers that she is, and the grandfather says, "We'll see." He puts his hands up under her dress and touches her panties with his fingers. Hanna is confused but senses something wrong is happening and runs out of his shop. Hanna tries to convince herself that nothing happened, but she is upset and confused.

After the monologue was over, another student took on the role of Karin, the granddaughter who is later impregnated by her grandfather. Karin questioned Hanna, "Why didn't you tell me what my grandfather did to you? Why did you just stop being my friend when we were seven years old? I didn't know what I did that was so terrible you stopped talking to me. Maybe if you had told me what my grandfather did to you, I wouldn't have had to face carrying his child." The class gasped.

Hanna curled herself into a tight ball saying, "I don't know."

Karin persisted, "I'm fourteen years old. I had a child and I had to give it up for adoption. You could have saved me." Hanna curled into a smaller ball. I was about to stop the questioning because Karin was talking about being pregnant, an experience that happened seven years after the time of the event in the monologue.

But Hanna remained in role and refused to leave her child character. She looked up at Karin and said, "I'm only seven years old."

Karin looked away and said, "Yeah. I forgot."

What happened was that Karin, in role, was caught up in her pain and wanted to blame it on someone. At this point I said, "Let's leave the characters and step out of role to look at what's happening and why."

The class decided that Hanna provided a good target for Karin to dump her anguish. Without knowing what she was doing, the student playing Hanna stayed in role, as the seven-year-old who is confused and upset, unaware of why the grandfather's actions have created such turmoil within her.

When I explained the changing points of view to the class, the student playing Karin asked, "Did I do something wrong?"

"No," I answered. "You, as Karin, are entitled to ask any question you choose to ask. Hanna, playing a seven-year-old, is expected to stay within the parameters she has chosen for her monologue. As a seven-year-old she didn't know what was going on until her mother told her that Karin's grandfather had not acted responsibly and that Hanna could no longer go to his shop. At seven, Hanna cannot know the subsequent consequences for Karin."

"So what's the point of our questions then?" asked a disgruntled student. "No sense asking questions someone can't answer."

I asked the rest of the class if they had any ideas about the value of the questions I was encouraging them to ask.

The girl playing Karin said, "When Hanna wouldn't answer my question I realized how angry I was at her for not telling me. I was even madder that she just stopped being my friend and I didn't know why or what I had done. The questions showed me the depth of Karin's pain and anguish even though she and Hanna eventually mend their friendship, years later, just before Karin gives birth to the child her grandfather sired." Our discussion helped Karin to process her anger both in and out of role. Just before the class ended, the student playing Karin said, "I think the reason I got so upset is that it reminded me of what happened to a friend of mine. I didn't know I was still thinking about her."

Example 2: A woman student chose to create the character of an alcoholic father. In the book, he holds his young son out the window, six stories above the ground, until his wife gives him the money she's been saving for their children's care. He takes the money, goes to his tavern, and buys drinks for everyone. The student chose as the precipitating event the time when the husband comes back home to find his children not in their beds and not in the house. His wife will not accept his apology. He threatens to hang himself, expecting his wife to stop him, but she sits at their kitchen table in stony silence, until he accidently hangs himself. The student doing the monologue chose to stand on a cushioned chair, which provided an unstable base. As she was playing the sniveling husband, I encouraged the class to ask questions in role, or to make comments without waiting for the husband to answer. The trickle of questions grew into a torrent and the atmosphere crackled with accusation and judgment. Suddenly, the student playing the husband looked at me and asked, "Can we stop now?" I nodded yes, and as she stepped down, the class gave her a thundering ovation.

As part of the processing, a student asked her, "Why did you choose to play such an awful man?"

Another asked, "Why didn't you pick a female role?"

The student looked at me and said, "You told us that doing a monologue was a good way to understand a character. So I picked Manfred's father. I couldn't imagine how a father could hold his son out the window just to get money to buy drinks. I mean the money he wanted was money the wife had saved to buy food for their kids. I also couldn't imagine how his wife could just sit there and watch him hang himself. So I thought," she said with a laugh, "since I have such a limited imagination I better play this man and see if doing the monologue helps me imagine his life."

We all asked the same question, "Did it?"

"Yes. When I was up there, on that chair, shaking, I felt like a child who is totally out of control. I want someone to stop me from hurting myself, but no one comes. I began to feel like he might have felt, lonely, ashamed, unable to face what he did. I imagine drinking makes him feel less lonely . . . less frantic. Maybe buying drinks for everyone makes him feel like he's not such a bad person, especially when they all cheer him as he pays for their drinks. But I also see how his wife stops caring about him when he threatens to hurt their son."

"How did you feel when you were up there and none of us would look at you? When we kept throwing questions and comments at you?" asked a classmate.

"Horrible. I asked to stop because I felt like I was becoming him, like my life was unmanageable. When I got down from the chair I was so relieved. When you all clapped I could feel myself becoming me again. In a million years I wouldn't want to be that guy. Not for anything."

"What did you learn?" I asked her and the class. There was a thoughtful silence before the student who asked about the value of questioning said, "I don't want to think of myself as a bad person. But when she was up there I began to see how easy it might be to get myself into a mess and not know how to get myself out. Much as I hate what he did, he's a real person to me now."

It's difficult for most of us to look at our shadow sides, yet as this incident illustrates, drama gives us a vicarious opportunity to explore this experience through involvement with characters who do what we may not even dare to contemplate.

Example 3: A third student chose to play Rolf, a boy conceived out of wedlock, whose father is a soldier from the United States stationed in

Germany just as World War II is ending. The student took as his precipitating event, the time Rolf finds a crinkled, worn, picture of a young man at the bottom of his mother's box of jewelry. She has told him many stories about his father but none of them answer his question, "Why did my father leave me?" When he finds the photo he knows it is his father. As Rolf, the student lashes out at some of the other children, angry that they call him bastard, furious at how they take for granted their fathers' presence in their lives.

During the questioning, one student, stung by Rolf's anger, spit out, "My father beats me. I'd rather have no father than have the one I have."

Rolf countered, "He doesn't always beat you. Besides, he goes to work. He gives your mother money to buy food. When you come home from school your mother is there. My mother has to work. When I come home from school my mother is at Hanna's house, taking care of Hanna. You don't know how lucky you are." I wondered how we would end this encounter. Passions were high and the class, as Rolf's classmates, were fully engaged in protecting themselves and attacking him.

Then, a student playing Hanna quietly interjected, "I'm sorry I called you a bastard, Rolf. You didn't do anything wrong but you get called the bad names. I'm really sorry for what I said." Many nodded and looked away.

The student playing Rolf said, "Thank you, Hanna."

Just as the passion had risen there was now a sudden emotional shift—a quiet calm. It took a bit of time before we could process the issues. The first question for the student playing Rolf was, "How did you know how to do it? I mean how could you be so angry?"

The student playing Rolf answered, "Me and my dad—we get along. He takes me fishing and we talk about things. He's always there for me. I tried to imagine what it would be like to have no father. To have a mother who keeps making up stories and never really answers my questions. The more I thought about it the angrier I got."

"But how could you be so angry . . . just like that? One minute you're sitting in your chair, the next minute you're up in front of the class. Where does the anger come from? How do you make it look so real?"

"It is real, but it's not my anger, it's Rolf's. All I have to do is to think what Rolf's life is like. His mother is ashamed. The neighbors know the truth but won't talk about it. The kids in his class call him bad names. No one's on his side. As soon as I picture him in my mind the anger is just there, in the first words that come out of my mouth."

Implications for Performance

Reflections on the Process

I describe these episodes in some detail because they illustrate the kind of intensity and commitment to role that students have to have in the classroom before the teacher considers the possibility of performance. What makes performance possible for students with no acting experience or training is the depth and degree to which they are able to enter into role as well as their ability to sustain themselves in role. A second consideration concerns how well they can sustain character action and interaction for a period of time. A third factor concerns the reasons for performance. Are students merely showing off? Are students so excited about their discoveries they can't bear not to share them? Has the teacher been asked to provide the entertainment for a school function? Does the teacher "just love theatre?"

Whatever the motivation for performance, the central question for the teacher needs to be, "Is performance good for my students?" If so, then the teacher might consider the following questions:

- What rehearsal and performance conditions will provide optimal learning experience? How do I define this, and how does it flow from or support good educational experience for the students?
- What do I want students to learn from the experience?
- How can I design rehearsal techniques and training to sustain students as they make the transition from sharing in the classroom to performing in a larger and/or less intimate space for people disconnected from the original experience and process?
- How do I help student performers continue to learn and grow, both in knowledge of human experience in action and in self-confidence during and after the performance experience?

Moving From Monologue to Dialogue

Each time we add tasks we complicate the process. After students memorize dialogue they often forget it as they incorporate physicalization and blocking (movement in space on stage and use of props) with their lines. This is inevitable. Once students and teachers understand this they can allow time in rehearsal for all the separate elements to come together. To help students succeed teachers need to make the learning steps small enough for students to understand what they have to do and how they can learn this. This is why I favor short performance pieces (monologues, short bits of two- or three-person dialogues, scenes, and short student-written plays) that evolve from classroom work as the initial performing experience for beginning students.

I move from monologues to dialogues by having students, in role, question characters from the text we are reading in class. When students are able to think and feel on their feet, think in role, act on their feelings in role, and articulate their ideas and emotions as a character, it is then possible to extend the parameters of the interaction tasks from one-character monologues to two- or more character dialogues. Students select a character they want to play and pick a classmate who is playing a character from the same text with whom they (in role) have unfinished business. Working in pairs, I ask them to establish where they are, the precipitating event that provides the context for the scene, the immediate reason for the meeting, and how they plan to make a moment. When these decisions have been made, the students script a page of dialogue.

The dialogues are initially read by the pairs, to the class. The class asks questions, which each pair writes down. The pairs, working in class, consider the issues raised by the questions and revise their scripts. The reworked scripts are read, and the pairs ask the class for suggestions (I encourage all comments to be asked as questions), which each pair again writes down. The third time the pairs share their scripts, they act rather than read their work. At this point the class and I help them to focus on character development; action and reaction; the scene's pace, timing, and dynamics; and how or if the pair created a moment. As the class and I help the pairs to shape their scenes, students learn how to move from drama to performance keeping the risk small while the opportunities for learning are great.

Post-performance Reflection

It's all over and students want to know, "How did I do? What did you think? Weren't we great? Weren't we terrible?" If the performance went well, it's easy to comment, but what if everything fell apart? What if some of the students feel they did a bad job? How do we comment in ways which continue the learning process of students? Not easy!

I have worked out ways of responding that help me to do so with a fair amount of honesty and integrity without destroying or demoralizing a student's sense of self. I am reminded of the exchange between Hermes and Zeus. Zeus tells Hermes, "I want you to be my messenger."

Hermes answers, "Father, I will do as you desire."

Then Zeus demands, "And you must promise you will always tell me the truth."

Hermes doesn't miss a beat, "I promise you to tell you the truth as long as you do not require me to tell you the whole truth."

My first step in post-performance reflection is to gather all the members of the class—actors, technicians, and any others who have contributed to the performance. We sit in a circle, and each person has the opportunity to speak about anything connected with the rehearsal or performance experience. Each person must use "I," and everyone is strongly encouraged to focus on observation rather than judgment.

When everyone who wants to speak has spoken, I generally ask the group, "What has been your most powerful or important learning experience?" Again, the focus is on observation and description. I also ask each person to speak only once and to refrain from commenting on anyone else's comments.

The next step involves students raising questions about the rehearsal and performance experience, which one student writes on the blackboard. The class and I look at the list of questions before proceeding further. When there has been some time to contemplate, one person writes on the blackboard suggestions and/or recommendations regarding any aspect of script choice, selection of cast and crew, rehearsal procedures, performance activity, or anything else that comes to mind.

The final step is one in which students are able to ask questions of each other, with one injunction. They cannot ask questions that blame, attack, or accuse. I have learned the hard way, after much painful and useless misery, that if discussion is not carefully and continually focused, it may degenerate into name calling and blaming, which can leave deep and long-lasting scars. By structuring the discussion to enable students to consider, observe, and describe, even the most dreadful rehearsal or performance experience can be turned into a helpful learning opportunity. Even when a performance is highly regarded I use the same process because it enhances group interaction and collaborative learning.

But what do you do when a student corners you and says, "I know I was bad, why don't you admit it?" or words to that effect? Or, how do you respond when you think the performance was poor and everyone else seems to think it's terrific? Again, I am guided by

Hermes. I speak truthfully, mentioning aspects that work or intrigue or seem good enough. Then, gently and carefully, I raise questions about one or two aspects. If students press me to answer more directly, and I don't want to lie, I say, "I'm a teacher, not a critic. If you want to learn, come to me. If all you want is criticism, find a critic." It's not in my contract to hurt a student just because the student asks me a question.

Some of the most powerful moments in my teaching experience have come from students exploring a text using theatrical techniques. I understand the desire of students and teachers to share these moments with a larger audience. All I ask of teachers is that when they decide to move from the classroom into a larger arena, they help their students to perform in ways that stimulate, encourage, enhance, and increase opportunities for students to grow and develop in a healthy and joyful manner.

Afterword

A colleague asked me, "What would you like your readers to know after reading your book?"

"How to fish."

"I beg your pardon?"

"It's the old Chinese proverb. If people are hungry and you give them fish you feed them once. If people are hungry and you give them equipment and teach them how to fish, they may feed themselves for all their lives."

I hope the ideas suggested in this book inspire teachers to find their own ways to enhance their teaching and their students' learning.

Works Cited

BAUER, YEHUDA. *A History of the Holocaust.* New York: F. Watts, 1982.

BORLAND, HAL. *When the Legends Die.* New York: Bantam Books, 1984.

COLES, ROBERT. *The Call of Stories.* Boston: Houghton Mifflin Company, 1989.

CONWAY, JILL KER. *The Road From Coorain.* New York: Vintage Books, 1990.

FRANK, ANNE. *The Diary of Anne Frank.* New York: Doubleday, 1989.

GHISELIN, BREWSTER. *The Creative Process.* New York: New American Library, 1952.

GILBERT, MARTIN. *Atlas of the Holocaust.* New York: Macmillan, 1982.

GÖNCZ, ÁRPÁD. *Homecoming and Other Stories.* New York and London: Garland Publishing Co.

GOTFRYD, BERNARD. *Anton the Dove Fancier and Other Tales of the Holocaust.* New York: Washington Square Press, 1990.

GUTMAN, ISRAEL (ed.). *Encyclopedia of the Holocaust.* New York: Macmillan, 1990.

HAWTHORNE, NATHANIEL. *The Scarlet Letter.* New York: Bantam Classic Edition, 1986.

HAYSLIP, LE LY, with JAY WERTS. *When Heaven and Earth Changed Places.* New York: Doubleday, 1989.

HEAD, BESSIE. "The Woman from America" in *Tales of Tenderness and Power.* Portsmouth, NH: Heinemann, 1990.

HILBERG, RAUL. *The Destruction of the European Jews.* New York: Holmes and Meir, 1985.

HOFFMAN, EVA. *Lost in Translation.* New York: Penguin Books, 1989.

LESTER, JULIUS. *Lovesong.* New York: Henry Holt and Company, 1988.

MAIRS, NANCY. *Remembering the Bone House.* New York: Harper & Row, 1989.

MALAN, RIAN. *My Traitor's Heart.* New York: Vintage Books, 1991.

MATHABANE, MARK. *Kaffir Boy.* New York: Penguin Books, 1986.

MEED, VLADKA. *On Both Sides of the Wall: Memoirs From the Warsaw Ghetto.* New York: Holocaust Library, 1977.

MILLER, JUDITH. *One, by One, by One: Facing the Holocaust.* New York: Simon and Schuster, 1990.

POSTMAN, NEIL. "Learning by Story," *Atlantic Monthly,* December 1989.

RODRIGUEZ, RICHARD. *Hunger of Memory.* New York: Bantam Books, 1982.

STONE, ELIZABETH. "A Matter of Class," *The New York Times Magazine,* May 6, 1990.

TAN, AMY. *The Joy Luck Club.* New York: G.P. Putnam's Sons, 1989.

VAN DER POST, LAURENS. *Patterns of Renewal.* Wallingford, PA: Pendle Hill Pamphlet #121, 1962.

WALKER, JEANNE MURRAY. *Coming Into History.* Cleveland: Cleveland State Poetry Center, 1990.

Bibliography

The books listed here have been useful in my personal learning, growth, and development.

Mythology

AUSBAND, STEPHEN. *Myth and Meaning, Myth and Order.* Macon, GA: Mercer University Press, 1983.

BACHOFEN, J.J. *Myth, Religion and Mother Right.* Princeton, NJ: Bollingen/Princeton University Press, 1967.

BEANE, WENDELL, and WILLIAM DOTY (eds.). Mircea Eliade Reader, *Myths, Rites Symbols,* Vols. 1 & 2. New York: Harper Colophon, 1976.

BULFINCH, THOMAS. *Bullfinch's Mythology* (originally published as *The Age of Fable*). New York: Collier Books, 1962.

CAMPBELL, JOSEPH. *The Hero With a Thousand Faces.* 2nd ed. Princeton, NJ: Bollingen/Princeton University Press, 1968.

————, *The Masks of God: Creative Mythology.* New York: Penguin Books, 1976.

————, *The Masks of God: Occidental Mythology.* New York: Penguin Books, 1976.

————, *The Masks of God: Oriental Mythology.* New York: Penguin Books, 1976.

————, *The Masks of God: Primitive Mythology.* New York: Penguin Books, 1976.

————, *The Mythic Image.* Princeton, NJ: Princeton University Press, 1974.

————, *Myths to Live By.* New York: Bantam/Viking Press, 1972.

————, *The Power of Myth.* New York: Doubleday, 1988.

CAVENDISH, RICHARD (ed.). *Mythology: An Illustrated Encyclopedia.* London: Orbis Publishing Ltd., 1980.

CHASE, RICHARD. *Quest for the Myth.* New York: Greenwood, 1969.

CHRISTIE, ANTHONY. *Chinese Mythology.* New York: Paul Hamlyn, 1968.

COOK, ELIZABETH. *The Ordinary and the Fabulous.* London and New York: Cambridge University Press, 1976.

COOK, ROGER. *The Tree of Life.* London: Thames and Hudson, 1974.

CRAIGHEAD, MEINROD. *The Sign of the Tree.* London: Artists House, Mitchell Beazley Marketing Ltd., 1979.

DOWNING, CHRISTINE. *The Goddess: Mythological Images of the Feminine.* New York: Crossroad, 1981.

DOTY, WILLIAM G. *Mythography.* Birmingham, AL: University of Alabama Press, 1986.

ELIADE, MIRCEA. *Gods, Goddesses and Myths of Creation* (part 1 Of *From Primitives To Zen*). New York: Harper & Row, 1974.

————, *Myths, Dreams and Mysteries.* New York: Harper Colophon, 1975.

————, *The Myth of the Eternal Return.* Princeton, NJ: Bollingen/Princeton University Press, 1971.

FRAZER, JAMES, and THEODOR H. GASTER (eds.). *The New Golden Bough.* New York: Mentor Books, 1965.

GRAVES, ROBERT. Introduction to *New Larousse Encyclopedia of Mythology.* New York: Hamlyn Publishing Group, 1959.

HAMILTON, EDITH. *Mythology.* New York: Mentor Books/New American Library, 1969.

HARTLAND, E.S. *Mythology and Folktales.* London: David Nutt, 1900.

HOOKE, S.H. *Middle Eastern Mythology.* New York: Penguin Books, 1963.

JUNG, C.G., and C. KERENYI. *Essays on a Science of Mythology.* Princeton, NJ: Bollingen/Princeton University Press, 1979.

KIRK, G.S. *Myth.* London: Cambridge University Press, 1970.

MURRAY, HENRY (ed.). *Myth And Mythmaking.* Boston: Beacon Press, 1968.

OLSON, ALAN M. (ed.). *Myth, Symbol and Reality.* Notre Dame, IN: University of Notre Dame Press, 1980.

WALKER, BARBARA, (ed.). *The Woman's Encyclopedia of Myths and Secrets.* New York: Harper & Row, 1983.

WARNER, REX. Foreword to *Encyclopedia of World Mythology.* New York: Galahad Books, 1975.

Symbols

CIRLOT, J.F. *A Dictionary of Symbols.* New York: Philosophical Library, 1962.

COOPER, J.C. *An Illustrated Encyclopaedia of Traditional Symbols.* London: Thames and Hudson, 1978.

COXHEAD, DAVID, and SUSAN MILLER. *Dreams.* New York: Avon Books, 1976.

FROMM, ERICH. *The Forgotten Language.* New York: Grove Press, 1951.

JUNG, C.G. *Psyche and Symbol.* New York: Doubleday Anchor, 1958.

————, *Man and His Symbols.* New York: Doubleday, 1979.

LUKE, HELEN. *The Inner Story: Myth and Symbol in the Bible and Literature.* New York: Crossroad, 1982.

LUCKERT, KARL. *A Navajo Bringing Home Ceremony.* Flagstaff, AZ: Museum of Northern Arizona Press, 1978.

PURCE, JILL. *The Mystic Spiral.* New York: Avon Publishers, 1974.

ROBERTSON, SEONAID. *Rose Garden and Labyrinth.* London: Routledge and Kegan Paul, 1963.

STEWART, KILTON. *Pygmies and Dream Giants.* New York: Harper Colophon, 1954.

TANSLEY, DAVID L. *Subtle Body.* London: Thames and Hudson, 1977.

VON FRANZ, MARIE-LOUISE. *Time.* London: Thames and Hudson, 1978.

WOSIEN, MARIA-GABRIELE. *Sacred Dance.* New York: Avon Books, 1974.

Religion and Philosophy

BATESON, GREGORY. *Mind and Nature.* New York: Bantam, 1979.

BATESON, GREGORY, and MARY CATHERINE BATESON. *Angels Fear.* New York: Bantam, 1987.

BUBER, MARTIN. *Between Man and Man.* New York: Macmillan, 1965.

CASSIRER, ERNST. *Language and Myth.* New York: Dover Books, 1953.

CHRIST, CAROL P. *Diving Deep and Surfacing.* Boston: Beacon Press, 1980.

DUNNE, JOHN S. *Time and Myth.* South Bend, IN: University of Notre Dame Press, 1975.

ELIADE, MIRCEA. *The Sacred and The Profane.* New York: Harcourt Brace Jovanovich, 1959.

————, *Shamanism.* Princeton, NJ: Bollingen Series, Princeton University Press, 1964.

FRIEDMAN, MAURICE. *The Hidden Human Image.* New York: Delta, 1974.

FROMM, ERICH. *To Have or To Be.* New York: Bantam Books, 1981.

FURNEAUX, RUPERT. *Myth and Mystery.* London: Allan Wingate, 1955.

HENDERSON, JOSEPH. *The Shaman from Elko.* San Francisco: C.G. Jung Institute, 1978.

LANGER, SUSANNE K. *Mind: An Essay on Human Feeling.* (Vols. 1 & 2) Baltimore, MD: Johns Hopkins Press, 1967, 1972.

————, *Philosophy in a New Key*. Cambridge, MA: Harvard University Press, 1942.

LYNCH, WILLIAM F. *Images of Hope*. Notre Dame: University of Notre Dame Press, 1974.

NORTON, DAVID. *Personal Destinies: A Philosophy of Ethical Individualism*. Princeton, NJ: Princeton University Press, 1976.

OLSON, CARL (ed.). *The Book of the Goddess*. New York: Crossroad, 1986.

ROSENBERG, DAVID (ed.). *Congregation: Contemporary Writers Read the Jewish Bible*. New York: Harcourt Brace Jovanovich, 1987.

THOMPSON, WILLIAM IRWIN. *The Time Falling Bodies Take to Light*. New York: St. Martins Press, 1981.

TORMEY, ALAN. *The Concept of Expression*. Princeton, NJ: Princeton University Press, 1971.

WATTS, ALAN. *The Wisdom of Insecurity*. New York: Vintage Books, 1951.

VYGOTSKY, LEV. *Thought and Language*. London and New York: MIT Press and John Wiley & Sons, 1962.

The Arts

BERGER, JOHN. *Ways of Seeing*. New York: Penguin Books, 1977.

BINDMAN, DAVID. *William Blake: His Art and Times*. Boston: The Yale Center for British Art and Art Gallery of Ontario, 1982.

BITTNER, HERBERT. *Kaethe Kollwitz*. New York: Castle Books, 1959.

BRAIN, ROBERT. *The Decorated Body*. London: Hutchinson, 1979.

CSAKY, MICK (ed.). *How Does It Feel? Exploring the World of Your Senses*. New York: Harmony Books, 1979.

COE, RALPH. *Sacred Circles: Two Thousand Years of North American Indian Art*. London: Arts Council of Great Britain, 1976.

DUNCAN, DAVID DOUGLAS. *Magic Worlds of Fantasy*. New York: Harcourt Brace Jovanovich, 1978.

FENG, GIA-FU, and JANE ENGLISH. *Lao Tsu: Tao Te Ching*. New York: Vintage Books, 1972.

GAMWELL, LYNN, and RICHARD WELLS (ed.). *Sigmund Freud and Art: His Personal Collection of Antiquities*. New York and London: State University of New York and Freud Museum, 1989.

GREEN, GERALD. *The Artists of Terezin*. New York: Hawthorn Books, 1969.

HIGHWATER, JAMAKE. *Ritual of the Wind*. Toronto: Methuen Publications, 1984.

KING, NANCY. "From Literature to Drama to Life." In Nellie McCaslin (ed.) *Children and Drama*. 2nd ed. New York: Longman, 1981.

————, *Giving Form to Feeling.* New York: Drama Book Publishers, 1975.

————, *A Movement Approach to Acting.* Englewood Cliffs, NJ: Prentice-Hall, 1981.

————, *Theatre Movement: The Actor and His Space.* New York: Drama Book Publishers, 1971.

LARKIN, OLIVER. *Daumier.* Boston: Beacon Press, 1968.

LAUTER, ESTELLA. *Women as Mythmakers: Poetry and Visual Art by Twentieth Century Women.* Bloomington, IN: Indiana University Press, 1984.

LEEKLEY, JOHN, and SHERYLE LEEKLEY. *Moments: The Pulitzer Prize Photographs.* New York: Crown Publishers, 1978.

MALIN, EDWARD. *A World of Faces: Masks of the Northwest Coast Indians.* Portland, OR: Timber Press, 1978.

McLUHAN, MARSHALL, and HARLEY PARKER. *Through the Vanishing Point: Space in Poetry and Painting.* New York: Harper & Row, 1968.

MILLER, ALICE. *Pictures of a Childhood.* New York: Farrar, Straus & Giroux, 1986.

MORSE, JOHN D. (ed.). *Ben Shahn.* New York: Praeger Publishers, 1972.

NOVITCH, MIRIAM, LUCY DAWIDOWICZ, and TOM FREUDENHEIM. *Spiritual Resistance: Art From Concentration Camps 1940–1945.* New York: Union of American Hebrew Congregations, 1981.

PRATT, DAVIS (ed.). *The Photograhic Eye of Ben Shahn.* Cambridge, MA: Harvard University Press, 1975.

RABINEAU, PHYLLIS. *Feather Arts: Beauty, Wealth and Spirit From Five Continents.* Chicago: Field Museum of Natural History, 1979.

REISER, DOLF. *Art and Science.* London: Studio Vista, 1972.

ROCKEFELLER, DAVID JR. (ed.). *Coming to Our Senses.* New York: McGraw-Hill, 1977.

RUBIN, WILLIAM (ed.). *Primitivism in 20th Century Art: Affinity of the Tribal and the Modern.* (Vols. 1 & 2) New York: The Museum of Modern Art, 1984.

SAMUELS, MIKE, and NANCY SAMUELS. *Seeing with the Mind's Eye.* New York: Random House, 1975.

STRYKER, ROY EMERSON, and NANCY WOOD. *In This Proud Land.* Boston: New York Graphic Society, 1973.

SYLVESTER, DAVID. *Henry Moore.* London: The Arts Council of Great Britain, 1968.

TANAHASHI, KAZUAKI. *Enku.* Boulder, CO: Shambhala, 1982.

THORNDIKE, JOSEPH J. *Discovery of Lost Worlds.* New York: American Heritage Publishing Co., 1979.

WITKIN, ROBERT. *The Intelligence of Feeling.* Oxford: Heinemann Educational Books, 1974.

WOLFF, ROBERT. *On Art and Learning.* New York: Grossman, 1971.

Psychology

BASSOFF, EVELYN. *Mothers and Daughters.* New York: New American Library, 1988.

BETTELHEIM, BRUNO. *The Uses of Enchantment.* New York: Vintage Books, 1977.

BRANDON, DAVID. *Zen in the Art of Helping.* London: Routledge & Kegan Paul, 1976.

COULIANO, IOAN P. *Eros and Magic in the Renaissance.* Chicago: University of Chicago Press, 1987.

DIECKMANN, HANS. *Twice Told Tales: The Psychological Use of Fairy Tales.* Wilmette, IL: Chiron, 1986.

FABRY, JOSEPH B. *The Pursuit of Meaning.* Boston: Beacon Press, 1968.

FREUD, ANNA. *Ego and the Mechanisms of Defense.* New York: International University Press, 1968.

GENDLIN, EUGENE, T. *Focusing.* New York: A Bernard Geis Associates Book, Bantam, 1981.

GOLEMAN, DANIEL. *Vital Lies Simple Truths.* New York: Simon & Schuster, 1985.

GORDON, DAVID. *Therapeutic Metaphors.* Cupertino, CA: META Pub., 1978.

HALL, NOR. *The Moon and the Virgin.* New York: Harper & Row, 1980.

HANNAH, BARBARA. *Encounters With the Soul: Active Imagination as Developed by C. G. Jung.* Boston: Sigo Press, 1981.

HARDING, ESTHER. *Woman's Mysteries, Ancient and Modern.* New York: C.G. Jung Foundation, 1971.

HARNER, MICHAEL. *The Way of the Shaman.* New York: Bantam Books, 1980.

HYNES, ARLEEN McCARTY, and MARY HYNES-BERRY. *Bibliotherapy.* Boulder, CO and London: Westview Press, 1986.

JAFFE, ANIELA. *The Myth of Meaning in the Work of C. G. Jung.* Zurich: Daimon, 1984.

JONES, RICHARD M. *The New Psychology of Dreaming.* New York: Viking Press, 1970.

Journal of Humanistic Psychology, Fall, 1987.

JUNG, C.G. *Four Archetypes: Mother, Rebirth, Spirit, Trickster.* London: Routledge & Kegan Paul, 1972.

JUNG, C.G. (ed. by Joseph Campbell). *The Portable Jung.* New York: Penguin, 1971.

KEYES, MARGARET, *The Inward Journey.* Berkeley, CA: Celestial Arts, 1974.

KOLBENSCHLAG, MADONNA. *Kiss Sleeping Beauty Goodbye.* New York: Bantam Books, 1979.

LARSEN, STEPHEN. *The Shaman's Doorway,* 2nd ed. New York: Station Hill Press, 1988.

LAZARUS, ARNOLD. *In the Mind's Eye.* New York and London: The Guilford Press, 1977.

LESHAN, LAWRENCE. *Alternate Realities.* New York: Ballantine Books, 1976.

LEONARD, LINDA, *On the Way to the Wedding.* Boston: Shambhala, 1987.

———, *The Wounded Woman.* Boulder, CO, and London: Shambhala, 1983.

LUKE, HELEN M. *The Way of Woman.* Three Rivers, MI: Apple Farm, 1982.

LUTHI, MAX. *Once Upon a Time: On the Nature of Fairy Tales.* Bloomington, IN: Indiana University Press, 1970.

MASLOW, ABRAHAM. *Toward a Psychology of Being.* Princeton, NJ: Van Nostrand, 1962.

MAY, ROLLO. *The Courage to Create.* New York: Bantam Books, 1975.

MILLER, ALICE. *Thou Shalt Not Be Aware: Society's Betrayal of the Child.* New York: New American Library, 1986.

MOON, SHEILA. *A Magic Dwells.* Wesleyan, CT: Wesleyan University Press, 1970.

MOUSTAKAS, CLARK (ed.). *The Self: Explorations in Personal Growth.* New York: Harper Colophon, 1956.

NEUMANN, ERICH. *Amor and Psyche.* Princeton, NJ: Bollingen Series, 1956.

———, *The Great Mother.* Princeton, NJ: Bollingen Series, 1972.

———, *The Origins and History of Consciousness.* Princeton, NJ: Bollingen Series, 1954.

ORNSTEIN, ROBERT E. *The Psychology of Consciousness,* 2nd ed. New York: Harcourt Brace Jovanovich, 1977.

OUSPENSKY, P.D. *The Psychology of Man's Possible Evolution.* New York: Vintage Books, 1974.

PECK, M. SCOTT. *People of the Lie: The Hope for Healing Human Evil.* New York: Simon & Schuster, 1983.

QUALLS-CORBETT, NANCY. *The Sacred Prostitute: Eternal Aspects of the Feminine.* Toronto: Inner City Books, 1988.

REYNOLDS, DAVID. *Water Bears No Scars: Japanese Lifeways for Personal Growth.* Quality Paperback Book Club, 1988.

SALE, ROGER. *Fairy Tales and After.* Cambridge, MA: Harvard University Press, 1978.

SCHACHTEL, ERNEST. *Metamorphosis.* New York: Basic Books, 1959.

SCHNEIDERMAN, LEO. *Portraits in Pain and Creativity.* New York: Insight Books, 1988.

SPENCE, DONALD P. *Narrative Truth and Historical Truth.* New York and London: W.W. Norton & Company, 1982.

WATKINS, MARY. *Waking Dreams.* New York: Harper Colophon, 1976.

WHITE, JOHN (ed.). *The Highest State of Consciousness.* Garden City, NY: Doubleday/Anchor, 1972.

ZOLLA, ELEMIRE. *Archetypes.* London: George Allen & Unwin, 1981.

Myths and Tales

ABRAHAMS, ROGER. *African Folktales.* New York: Pantheon, 1983.

ALBERT, MARY. *How the Birds Got Their Colours: An Aboriginal Story.* Sydney: Ashton Scholastic Pub., 1983.

ASBJORNSEN, PETER CHRISTEN, and JORGEN MOE. *Norwegian Folk Tales.* New York: Pantheon, 1960.

AUNG, MAUNG HTIN, and HELEN G. TRAGER. *A Kingdom Lost for a Drop of Honey and Other Burmese Folktales.* New York: Parents Magazine Press, 1968.

AUSUBEL, NATHAN. *A Treasury of Jewish Folklore.* New York: Crown Publishers, 1952.

BENARDETE, SETH (ed.). *Larousse Greek and Roman Mythology.* New York: McGraw-Hill, 1965.

BIEBUYCK, DANIEL, and KAHOMBO C. MATEENE (ed. and trans.). *The Mwindo Epic.* Berkeley and Los Angelos, CA: University of California Press, 1971.

BIERHORST, JOHN. *The Sacred Path: Spells Prayers and Power Songs of the American Indians.* New York: William Morrow and Company, 1983.

BLACK ELK (ed. by Joseph Epes Brown). *The Sacred Pipe.* Baltimore, MD: Penguin, 1953.

BOOSS, CLAIRE, (ed.). *Scandinavian Folk and Fairy Tales: Tales From Norway, Sweden, Denmark, Finland, Iceland.* New York: Avenel Books, Crown Publishers, 1984.

BUBER, MARTIN. *Tales of the Hasidim; The Early Masters.* New York: Schocken Books, 1947.

———. *Tales of the Hasidim: Later Masters.* New York: Schocken Books, 1948.

CALVINO, ITALO. *Italian Folktales.* New York: Pantheon Books, 1956.

CAREY, GEORGE. *Maryland Folk Legends and Folk Songs.* Cambridge, MD: Tidewater Publishers, 1971.

CHALK, GARY. *Tales of Ancient China.* London: Frederick Muller, 1984.

CHANDLER, ROBERT. *The Magic Ring and Other Russian Folktales.* London: Faber & Faber, 1979.

CHAZ, *Tales of Mozambique.* London: Young World Books, 1980.

CHRISTIE, ANTHONY. *Chinese Mythology.* London: Paul Hamlyn, 1968.

COLE, JOANNA (ed.). *Best Loved Folktales of the World.* Garden City, NY: Anchor Press/Doubleday, 1983.

COURLANDER, HAROLD, and GEORGE HERZOG. *The Cow-Tail Switch and Other West African Stories.* New York: Henry Holt & Co., 1947.

CROSSLEY-HOLLAND, KEVIN. *The Norse Myths.* New York: Penguin Books, 1980.

DAVIDSON, H.R. ELLIS. *Scandinavian Mythology.* London: Hamlyn, 1969.

DEGH, LINDA (ed.). *Folktales of Hungary.* Chicago: University of Chicago Press, 1965.

DEPAOLA, TOMIE. *The Legend of the Bluebonnet.* New York: G.P. Putnam's Sons, 1983.

DE VALERA, SINEAD. *Irish Fairy Tales.* London: Picolo, 1973.

———, *More Irish Fairy Tales.* London: Picolo, 1979.

DORSON, RICHARD M. (ed.). *Folktales Told Around the World.* Chicago and London: University of Chicago Press, 1975.

DOWNING, CHARLES. *Russian Tales and Legends.* London: Oxford University Press, 1956.

DRAKE-BROCKMAN, H. (ed.). *Australian Legendary Tales.* Sydney: Angus and Robertson, 1953.

FELDMANN, SUSAN (ed.). *African Myths and Tales.* New York: Dell Publishing Co., 1963.

FISHER, SALLY. *The Shining Princess.* New York: The Metropolitan Museum of Art & A Studio Book, The Viking Press, 1980.

GANTZ, JEFFREY. *Early Irish Myths and Sagas.* New York: Dorset Press, 1981.

GARFIELD, LEON, and EDWARD BLISHEN. *The God Beneath the Sea.* London: Kestrel Books, 1970.

———, *The Golden Shadow.* London: Carousel, 1974.

GARNER, ALAN. *The Guizer: A Book of Fools.* London: Hamish Hamilton, 1975.

GOODRICH, NORMA LORRE. *Ancient Myths.* New York: Mentor Books, 1960.

———, *Medieval Myths.* New York: Mentor Books, 1977.

GRAVES, ROBERT, and RAPHAEL PATAI. *Hebrew Myths: The Book of Genesis.* New York: Greenwich House, 1983.

GRAY, JOHN. *Near Eastern Mythology.* London: Hamlyn, 1969.

GREEN, ROGER LANCELYN. *Tales of Ancient Egypt.* London: Bodley Head, 1967.

GRUNDTVIG, SVEND. *The Emerald Fairy Book.* London: John F. Shaw & Co., 1928.

HAILE, BERARD, O.F.M. *Waterway.* Flagstaff, AZ: The Museum of Northern Arizona Press, 1979.

HAVILAND, VIRGINIA. *Told in India.* Toronto: Little, Brown & Co., 1973.

HIGHWATER, JAMAKE. *Anpao: An American Indian Odyssey.* New York: Harper Torchbook, 1986.

HILLERMAN, TONY, *The Boy Who Made Dragonfly.* New York: Harper & Row, 1972.

HOOKE, S.H. *Middle Eastern Mythology.* London: Pelican, 1963.

HYDE-CHAMBERS, FREDERICK, and AUDREY HYDE-CHAMBERS. *Tibetan Folk Tales.* Boulder, CO and London: Shambhala, 1981.

IN-SOB, ZONG (ed. and trans.). *Folk Tales From Korea.* New York: Grove Press, 1979.

ISAACS, JENNIFER (ed.). *Australian Dreaming: 40,000 Years of Aboriginal History.* Sydney: Lansdowne Press, 1980.

JAMESON, CYNTHIA. *Tales From the Steppes.* New York: Coward, McCann & Geoghegan, 1975.

JEWETT, ELEANORE, M. *Which Was Witch? Tales of Ghosts and Magic From Korea.* New York: Viking Press, 1953.

JONES, GWYN. *Welsh Legends and Folktales.* London: Puffin, 1955.

JORDAN, A.C. *Tales From Southern Africa.* Berkley and Los Angeles: University of California Press, 1973.

KENDALL, CAROL, and YAO-WEN LI. *Sweet and Sour: Tales From China.* London: The Bodley Head, 1978.

KILLIP, KATHLEEN. *Twisting the Rope and Other Folktales From the Isle of Man.* London: Hodder and Stoughton, 1980.

KNAPPERT, JAN. *Malay Myths and Legends.* Hong Kong: Heinemann Educational Books, (Asia), 1980.

———, *Myths and Legends of Indonesia.* Hong Kong: Heinemann Educational Books, (Asia), 1977.

KRAMER, SAMUEL NOAH (ed.). *Mythologies of the Ancient World.* Garden City, NY: Anchor Books, Doubleday & Co., 1961.

LEE, F.H. *Folktales of All Nations.* New York: Coward-McCann, 1932.

LEVIN, MEYER. *Classic Hassidic Tales.* New York: Dorset Press, 1931.

LOPEZ, BARRY HOLSTUN. *Giving Birth to Thunder, Sleeping With His Daughter.* New York: Avon Books, 1977.

MACKENZIE, DONALD. *German Myths and Legends.* New York: Avenel Books, Crown Publishers, 1985.

MACLAGAN, DAVID. *Creation Myths.* London: Thames and Hudson, 1977.

MACMILLAN, CYRUS. *Canadian Wonder Tales.* London: The Bodley Head, 1974.

MANNING-SANDERS, RUTH. *Scottish Folktales.* London: Methuen, 1976.

MARRIOTT, ALICE, and CAROL K. RACHLIN. *American Indian Mythology.* New York: Mentor Books, 1968.

————, *Plains Indian Mythology.* New York: Mentor Books, 1975.

MARSHALL, ALAN. *People of the Dreamtime.* Melbourne: Hyland House, 1952.

MASSOLA, ALDO. *Bunjil's Cave.* Melbourne: Lansdowne Press, 1968.

McALPINE, HELEN, and WILLIAM McALPINE. *Japanese Tales and Legends.* London: Oxford University Press, 1958.

MEGAS, GEORGIOS (ed.). *Folktales of Greece.* Chicago: University of Chicago Press, 1970.

MERCATANTE, ANTHONY S. *Good and Evil: Mythology and Folklore.* New York: Harper & Row, 1978.

MERCER, JOHN. *The Stories of Vanishing Peoples.* London: Allison & Busby, 1982.

MILLER, OLIVE BEAUPRE (ed.). *Tales Told in Holland.* Chicago: The Book House for Children, 1926.

MONAGHAN, PATRICIA. *The Book of Goddesses and Heroines.* New York: E.P. Dutton, 1981.

MULLETT, G.M. *Spider Woman Stories.* Tucson, AZ: The University of Arizona Press, 1980.

NEIHARDT, J. *Black Elk Speaks.* Lincoln, NB: University of Nebraska Press, 1961.

NICHOLSON, IRENE. *Mexican and Central American Mythology.* New York: Paul Hamlyn, 1967.

OPIE, IONA, and PETER OPIE. *The Classic Fairy Tales.* London: Oxford University Press, 1974.

PASCHELES, WOLFF. *Jewish Legends of the Middle Ages.* London: Shapiro Vallentine & Co., no date.

PETROVITCH, WOISLAV. *Hero Tales and Legends of the Serbians.* London: George G. Harrap & Company, 1927.

PINO-SAAVEDRA, YOLANDO. *Folktales of Chile.* London: Routledge & Kegan Paul, 1968.

POLSKY, HOWARD W., and YAELLA WOZNER. *Everyday Miracles: The Healing Wisdom of Hasidic Stories.* London: Jason Aronson, 1989.

POWER, RHODA. *Stories from Everywhere*. London: Dennis Dobson, 1969.

QOYAWAYMA, ELIZABETH. *The Sun Girl*. Flagstaff, AZ: The Museum of Northern Arizona Press, 1928.

RADIN, PAUL. *The Trickster*. New York: Shocken Books, 1972.

RANDOLPH, VANCE. *Pissing in the Snow and Other Ozark Folktales*. New York: A Bard Book, Avon, 1976.

RANSOME, ARTHUR. *Old Peter's Russian Tales*. London: Nelson, 1916.

RIORDAN, JAMES. *The Woman in the Moon*. New York: Dial Press, 1985.

ROBERTS, MOSS. *Chinese Fairy Tales and Fantasies*. New York: Pantheon, 1979.

ROBINSON, GAIL. *Raven the Trickster*. London: Chatto & Windus, 1981.

ROBINSON, GAIL, and DOUGLAS HILL. *Coyote the Trickster*. London: Piccolo, 1975.

SALKEY, ANDREW (ed.). *Caribbean Folk Tales and Legends*. London: Bogle-L'Ouverture Publications, 1980.

SCHWARTZ, HOWARD. *Elijah's Violin and Other Jewish Fairy Tales*. New York: Harper & Row, 1983.

SHAH, IDRIES (ed.). *World Tales*. New York: Harcourt Brace Jovanovich, 1979.

SHERLOCK, PHILIP. *West Indian Folktales*. Oxford: Oxford University Press, 1966.

SIMPSON, JACQUELINE. *Icelandic Folktales and Legends*. Berkeley and Los Angeles: University of California Press, 1972.

SLEIGH, BARBARA. *Winged Magic*. London: Hodder and Stoughton, 1979.

SPENCE, LEWIS. *The Myths of Mexico and Peru*. London: George G. Harrap & Co., 1920.

SPROUL, BARBARA C. *Primal Myths*. London: Rider, 1979.

STEPHENS, JAMES. *Irish Fairy Tales*. New York: Macmillan Co., 1920.

STORM, HYEMEYOHSTS. *Seven Arrows*. New York: Ballantine Books, 1972.

STUCHL, VLADIMIR (ed.). *American Fairy Tales*. London: Octopus Books, 1979.

SUN, RUTH Q. *Land of Seagull and Fox: Folktales of Vietnam*. Rutland, VT: Charles E. Tuttle, 1967.

TEDLOCK, DENNIS (trans.). *Popol Vuh*. New York: Simon & Schuster, 1985.

TOOR, FRANCES. *A Treasury of Mexican Folkways*. New York: Bonanza Books, 1985.

TURNER, FREDERIC (ed.). *The Portable North American Indian Reader*. New York: Penguin Books, 1977.

UCHIDA, YOSHIKO. *The Magic Listening Cap: More Folktales From Japan*. New York: Harcourt, Brace & World, 1955.

UNDERHILL, RUTH M., DONALD M. BAHR, BAPTISTO LOPEZ, JOSE PANCHO, and DAVID LOPEZ. *Rainhouse and Ocean: Speeches for the Papago Year.* Flagstaff, AZ: The Museum of Northern Arizona Press, 1979.

VAN OVER, RAYMOND (ed.). *Sun Songs.* New York: Mentor Books, 1980.

VON FRANZ, MARIE-LOUISE. *Creation Myths.* Zurich: Spring Publications, 1972.

VYAS, CHIMAN. *Folktales Of Zambia.* Lusaka, Zambia: Neczam, 1972.

WALEY, ARTHUR. *Dear Monkey.* Indianapolis/New York: Bobbs-Merrill Co., 1973.

WATERS, FRANK. *Book of the Hopi.* New York: Ballantine Books, 1969.

WENIG, ADOLF. *Beyond the Giant Mountains: Tales from Bohemia.* Boston: Houghton Mifflin Co., 1923.

WILLIAMS-ELLIS, AMABEL. *The Story Spirits: Tales From the Far East, Africa and the Caribbean.* London: Picolo, 1981.

WISTER, A.L. *Enchanted and Enchanting.* Boston: J.B. Lippincott, 1907.

WOLKSTEIN, DIANE, and SAMUEL N. KRAMER. *Inanna.* New York: Harper Colophon Books, 1983.

YAGAWA, SUMIKO. *The Crane Wife.* New York: Mulberry Books, 1979.

YOLEN, JANE (ed.). *Favorite Folktales From Around the World.* New York: Pantheon, 1986.

ZIMMERMAN, J.E. *A Dictionary of Classical Mythology.* New York: Bantam Books, 1974.

Selected Works of Autobiography

ASHTON-WARNER, SYLVIA. *Myself.* New York: Bantam Books, 1968.

BRUNER, JEROME. *In Search Of Mind.* New York: Harper & Row, 1983.

CARY, LORENE. *Black Ice.* New York: Vintage Books, 1992.

CONWAY, JILL KER. *The Road From Coorain.* New York: Vintage Books, 1990.

CHEEVER, SUSAN. *Home Before Dark.* New York: Pocket Books, 1984.

DEMING, BARBARA. *Prison Notes.* New York: Grossman Publishers, 1966.

ELIADE, MIRCEA. *No Souvenirs.* New York: Harper & Row, 1977.

FRASER, SYLVIA. *My Father's House.* Toronto: Ticknor & Fields, 1988.

GOTFRYD, BERNARD. *Anton the Dove Fancier.* New York: Pocket Books, 1990.

HAYSLIP, LE LY, with JAY WURTS. *When Heaven and Earth Changed Places.* New York: Doubleday, 1989.

HOFFMAN, EVA. *Lost in Translation.* New York: Penguin, 1989.

L'ENGLE, M.A. *A Circle of Quiet.* New York: Fawcett, 1975.

LESTER, JULIUS. *Lovesong.* New York: Henry Holt, 1988.

LORDE, AUDREY. *The Cancer Journals.* San Francisco: Spinsters Ink, 1980.

MAIRS, NANCY. *Remembering the Bone House.* New York: Harper & Row, 1989.

MALAN, RIAN. *My Traitor's Heart.* New York: Vintage Books, 1991.

MARKHAM, BERYL. *West With the Night.* San Francisco: North Point Press, 1983.

MATHABANE, MARK. *Kaffir Boy.* New York: Penguin, 1986.

MILLER, ARTHUR. *Timebends: A Life.* New York: Grove Press, 1987.

MORGAN, SALLY. *My Place.* New York: Little, Brown and Company, 1990.

RODRIGUEZ, RICHARD. *Hunger of Memory: The Education of Richard Rodriguez.* New York: Bantam, 1982.

ROGERS, NATALIE. *Emerging Woman.* Point Reyes: Personal Press, 1980.

ROSEN, RUTH (ed.). *The Mamie Papers.* Boston: The Feminist Press, 1977.

SADAT, JEHAN. *A Woman of Egypt.* New York: Pocket Books, 1987.

SARTON, MAY. *I Knew a Phoenix.* New York: W.W. Norton, 1959.

————, *Journal of a Solitude.* New York: W.W. Norton, 1973.

SMEDLEY, AGNES. *China Fights Back.* New York: The Vanguard Press, 1938.

TILLICH, HANNAH. *From Time to Time.* New York: Stein and Day, 1974.

VAN DER POST, LAURENS. *The Heart of the Hunter.* London: Penguin Books, 1965.

————, *The Lost World of the Kalahari.* London: Penguin Books, 1961.

WELTY, EUDORA. *One Writer's Beginnings.* Cambridge: Harvard University Press, 1984.

WHITELEY, OPAL. *The Singing Creek Where the Willows Grow: The Rediscovered Diary of Opal Whiteley.* New York: Warner Books, 1986.

WITTMER, MARGRET. *Floreana.* New York: Moyer Bell Limited, 1990.

WOODS, DONALD. *Asking for Trouble.* New York: Atheneum, 1980.

Selected Works of Nonfiction

BELENKY, MARY FIELD, BLYTHE MCVICKER CLINCHY, NANCY RULE GOLDBERGER, and JILL MATTUCK TARULE. *Women's Ways of Knowing.* New York: Basic Books, 1986.

BOORSTIN, DANIEL J. *The Discoverers.* New York: Random House, 1983.

COLES, ROBERT. *The Call of Stories.* Boston: Houghton-Mifflin Company, 1989.

CREWDSON, JOHN. *By Silence Betrayed: Sexual Abuse of Children in America.* Boston: Little, Brown & Co., 1988.

Bibliography

·· 253

DAWSON, CARL. *Prophets of Past Time.* Baltimore: The Johns Hopkins University Press, 1988.

DOOLING, C.D. *The Spiritual Dimension of Craft.* New York: Parabola Books, 1979.

EISLER, RIANE. *The Chalice and the Blade.* New York: Harper & Row, 1987.

Family Folklore Program. *Family Folklore.* Washington D.C.: Smithsonian Institution, 1976.

FOUCAULT, MICHEL. *The Archaeology of Knowledge.* New York: Pantheon Books, 1972.

JAYNES, JULIAN. *The Origin of Consciousness in the Breakdown of the Bicameral Mind.* Boston: Houghton-Mifflin Co., 1976.

LEE, DOROTHY. *Freedom and Culture.* Englewood-Cliffs, NJ: Spectrum, Prentice-Hall, 1959.

OLNEY, JAMES. *Metaphors of Self.* Princeton, NJ: Princeton University Press, 1972.

OZICK, CYNTHIA. *Metaphor and Memory.* New York: Alfred A. Knopf, 1989.

PALMER, PARKER. *To Know as We Are Known: A Spirituality of Education.* New York: Harper & Row, 1983.

SAWYER, RUTH. *The Way of the Storyteller.* London: Penguin Books, 1942.

VAN DER POST, LAURENS. *Patterns of Renewal.* Wallingford PA: Pamphlet #121, Pendle Hill Publications, 1962.

Creativity and Education

ABBS, PETER (ed.). *Myth and Symbol in Education.* London: Tract/Cockpit Publications, no date.

ASHTON-WARNER, SYLVIA. *Teacher.* New York: Bantam Books, 1964.

BROWN, GEORGE ISAAC. *Human Teaching for Human Learning,* New York: The Viking Press, 1971.

BRUNER, JEROME. *Actual Minds, Possible Worlds.* Cambridge: Harvard University Press, 1986.

———, *Beyond the Information Given.* New York: W.W. Norton & Company, 1973.

———, *On Knowing: Essays for the Left Hand.* Cambridge: Belknap Press of Harvard University Press, 1979.

COX, HARVEY. *The Feast of Fools.* Cambridge, MA: Harvard University Press, 1969.

DEBONO, EDWARD. *Lateral Thinking.* New York: Penguin Books, 1970.

DEWEY, JOHN. *Experience And Education.* New York: Collier Books, 1938.

EDWARDS, BETTY. *Drawing on the Right Side of the Brain.* Los Angeles: J.P. Tarcher, 1979.

FISH, STANLEY. *Is There a Text in This Class?* Cambridge, MA and London: Harvard University Press, 1980.

FRIERE, PAULO. *Education for Critical Consciousness.* New York: Seabury Press, 1973.

GHISELIN, BREWSTER (ed.). *The Creative Process.* New York: Mentor Books, 1955.

GOLDBERG, PHILIP. *The Intuitive Edge.* Los Angeles: J.P. Tarcher, 1983.

GOWAN, J.C., J. KHATENA, and E.P. TORRANCE. *Creativity: Educational Implications.* Dubuque, IA: Kendall/Hunt Pub. Co., 1981.

GRAY, FARNUM, and GEORGE C. MAGER, *Liberating Education.* Berkeley: McCutchan Publishing Corporation, 1973.

GREELEY, ANDREW. *Ecstasy—A Way of Knowing.* Englewood-Cliffs, NJ: Prentice-Hall, 1974.

HOLTZ, BARRY (ed.). *Back to the Sources: Reading Classic Jewish Texts.* New York: Summit Books, 1984.

HOUSTON, JEAN. *The Possible Human.* Los Angeles: J.P. Tarcher, 1982.

HUIZINGA, J. *Homo Ludens.* Boston: Beacon Press, 1950.

KAGAN, JEROME (ed.). *Creativity and Learning.* Boston: Beacon Press, 1967.

KARL, FREDERICK R., and LEO HAMALIAN. *The Existential Imagination.* Greenwich, CT: Fawcett Pub., 1963.

KOESTLER, ARTHUR. *The Act of Creation.* New York: Dell Pub. 1964.

KURFISS, JOANNE G. *Critical Thinking: Theory, Research, Practice and Possibilities.* College Station, TX: Association for the Study of Higher Education, 1988.

JOHN-STEINER, VERA. *Notebooks of the Mind.* New York: Perennial Library, Harper & Row, 1987.

JONES, RICHARD M. *Fantasy and Feeling in Education.* New York: New York University Press, 1968.

LE SHAN, LAWRENCE. *How to Meditate.* New York: Bantam Books, 1975.

PFEIFFER, JOHN. *The Creative Explosion.* New York: Harper & Row, 1982.

RAPHAEL, CHAIM. *The Springs of Jewish Life.* London: Chatto & Windus, The Hogarth Press, 1983.

RICHARDS, M.C. *The Crossing Point.* Middletown, CT: Wesleyan University Press, 1973.

Rothenberg, Albert. *The Emerging Goddess: The Creative Process in Art, Science, and Other Fields.* Chicago and London: University of Chicago Press, 1979.

———— and Carl R. Hausman (eds.). *The Creativity Question.* Durham, NC: Duke University Press, 1976.

Ruitenbeck, Hendrik (ed.). *The Creative Imagination.* Chicago: Quadrangle Books, 1965.

Samples, Bob. *The Metaphoric Mind.* Reading, MA: Addison-Wesley, 1976.

Shor, Ira. *Critical Teaching and Everyday Life.* Boston: South End Press, 1980.

Singer, Jerome. *The Inner World of Daydreaming.* New York: Harper & Row, 1975.

Staude, John-Raphael (ed.). *Consciousness and Creativity.* Berkeley: Ross Books, 1977.

Torrance, E. Paul. *Creativity.* Washington D.C.: National Education Association, 1963.

Vernon, P.E. (ed.). *Creativity.* London: Penguin Books, 1970.

Suzuki, Shunryu. *Zen Mind Beginner's Mind.* New York and Tokyo: Weatherhill, 1970.

Storymaking

Gersie, Alida, and Nancy King. *Storymaking in Education and Therapy.* Stockholm: Stockholm Institute of Education; and London: Jessica Kingsley Press, 1990.

Heilbrun, Carolyn G. *Writing a Woman's Life.* New York: W.W. Norton & Company, 1988.

Keen, Sam, and Anne Valley-Fox. *Telling Your Story.* New York: New American Library, 1974.

King, Nancy. "Myth, Metaphor, Memory: Archeology of the Self." *Journal of Humanistic Psychology.* Vol. 30 No. 2, Spring 1990.

Stone, Elizabeth. *Black Sheep and Kissing Cousins.* New York: Penguin, 1988.

Index of Poem, Story, and Book Titles

Subject Index

Acting: making a moment in, 218–19; teaching dramatic literature through, 139–41. *See also* Dramatic performances

Active learning, 61–64; classroom dynamics and, 65–69; encouraging, 77–79; evaluation and, 74; importance of, 11–15; suggestions for, 64

Active script preparation, 140

Activities: developing, 100, 101–2; structuring, 40–41; task definition, 40–41; varying length of, 68

Advertising slogans, writing, 176

Akido, stepping aside in, 57

Anecdotes, 69, 96

Armbands, paper, creating, 152

Assignments, student responsibility for, 62–63

Assistance: asking for, 101; offering to students, 40; student-to-student, 40–41, 101

Auditory stimulation, 97

Authored stories, 118, 128–39; choosing, 128; cultural influences, 139

Autobiography, 177–93; defined, 178; difficulties of writing, 178–79; emotional issues in, 178–79, 184; self-discovery through, 177–78; as springboard for own writing, 193; student attitudes toward, 177–80, 193; student-written, 178, 184, 191–93; suggestions for exploring, 185–91; truth in, 178–79; value of, 183–84, 193

Awareness, conflict and, 85

Beauty: painting images of, 116–17; sculpting images of, 117; writing about, 116

Beginning, 25–29; beginner's mind, 32; closure and, 96–97; evaluation and, 80–81; how to begin, 28–29; issues in, 37–41; suggestions for, 28–29, 40–41; time limits for, 31; when to begin, 29; working in new ways, 32–37

Beliefs, painting images of, 190–91

Blame, avoiding, 84, 232

Boredom, 61, 64, 69

Borland, Hal, 100, 161, 173

Brainstorming, questions, 78–79

Business, teaching with drama, 66–68

Camus, Albert, 5

Cary, Lorene, 181

Centering, 56–57, 59, 72

Ceremonies, creating, 176

Change, painting images of, 109

Chants, creating, 176

Characters in stories: at precipitating moments, sculpting, 223; interviewing, 19–20; painting images of, 156, 158, 163, 174, 175; sculpting images of, 165, 166–67, 212, 223; writing about thoughts of, 156; writing descriptions of, 163, 174; writing interviews with, 19–20; writing monologues about, 14, 175, 212

Children: painting images of, 185; writing about, 185

Choice, dialogue about, 173

Class planning: choosing a focus, 101; developing activities, 101–2; evoking reflection, 102–3; selecting a text, 100–102; structuring lessons, 41, 44, 65, 100–103; time management, 30–32

Classroom, space arrangements in, 29–32, 55

Clay: benefits of, 97; studying relationships through, 99; types of, 99. *See also* Sculpting images

Closure, 31, 96–97

Clothing, designing, 13–14

Coles, Robert, 179

Collaborative learning, 61–64, 199–202; facilitating, 102; language learning and, 215; value of, 75

Comfort zones, 39–40

Comments, on others' comments, disallowing, 56, 94

Communication: classroom space

arrangement and, 30, 55; importance of, 23–25; nonverbal, 23–26, 30, 141–146, 221

Community: encouraging, 41, 64; establishing, 37–41; information sharing and, 26–28; storytelling and, 1–5, 207

Conflict resolution, 82–86, 94

Context, language learning and, 214

Control: imagination and, 72; physicalization and, 145; spontaneity and, 53

Controversial topics, 96. *See also* Emotional issues

Conway, Jill Ker, 188–90. 192

Crayons, for imagemaking, 98–99

Creativity: discouragement of, 194–95; educational system and, 11–12; empowerment and, 12; grading and, 197–98; nourishing, 17–23; television and, 87; time limits and, 21–23

Crises, responding to, 56–61, 71–73

Critical thinking, 9, 61–64

Criticism, of self, disallowing, 95

Cultural differences: autobiography and, 184–85; exploring, 39; language learning and, 213–14; learning and, 64, 87, 206; writing about, 107

Decision-making, engaging students in, 62–63, 82

Defensiveness, avoiding, 57, 60

Designing: clothing, 13–14; logos, 176; memorials, 7–8, 115, 122, 159; tombstones, 7–8

Dialogue (among students and teachers): facilitating by sharing images, 97–98; grading and, 202–3; importance of, 93, 95

Dialogue (written): about choice, 173; about journeys, 122; about mother-daughter relationship, 168; about relationships, 138; adding to stories, 18–19, 21; in dramatic